D1586597

Communication, Technology and Cultural Change

Communication, Technology and Cultural Change

Gary Krug

SAGE Publications
London • Thousand Oaks • New Delhi

First published 2005

SAGE Publications Ltd
1 Oliver's Yard
55 City Road
London EC1Y 1SP

SAGE Publications Inc.
2455 Teller Road
Thousand Oaks, California 91320

SAGE Publications India Pvt Ltd
B-42, Panchsheel Enclave
Post Box 4109
New Delhi 110 017

British Library Cataloguing in Publication data

A catalogue record for this book is available
from the British Library

ISBN 0 7619 7200 5
ISBN 0 7619 7201 3 (pbk)

Library of Congress Control Number available

Typeset by C&M Digitals (P) Ltd., Chennai, India
Printed in Great Britain by T.J. International, Padstow, Cornwall

Contents

Foreword

Pentimento: 'Something painted
Aimage the painter "repented," or denied
becomes visible again.'

Lives and their experiences are made visible in stories. Lives are like pictures that have been painted over, and when paint is scraped off an old picture appears. A life and the stories about it have the qualities of *pentimento*. Something new is always coming into sight, displacing what was previously certain and seen. There is no truth in the painting of a life, only multiple images of what has been, what could have been, and what now is.

Enter Gary Krug's important new book. His is a brilliant display of pentimento. He shows that there are few certain truths, only multiple tellings, no matter where we start in our histories and stories about the media and technology, something new always comes into sight. This is clearly the case with the social history of the self, the self and its embedded relationships and stories, narratives about language, culture, technology, images, writing, truth, the military-industrial complex, pornographies of the visible and apparatuses of surveillance, cyber-space, cyber-identities, the digital antinomian world. Peel back one layer of paint, one system of discourse, and something new becomes visible.

Of his project, Gary Krug, says, 'The approach taken here necessarily eschews some kinds of linear development, and some connections, particularly across chapters, will not be apparent unless the text is taken as a whole ... this is not so much a university course as it is a series of conversations in a salon.'

I agree, but I prefer the visual imagery of painting and pentimento. Time after time, in each of his bold and innovative chapters, Krug scrapes back the old to reveal something new. His writing has a cinematic, montage-like quality.[1] Montage is like pentimento. Many different things are going on at the same time, images sounds and understandings are blending and blurring, forming a composite, a new creation. An emotional, gestalt effect is produced.

Krug's chapters are infused with the logics of montage and pentimento. The chapters overlap, turn back on one another. They are written, always, out of his history, and of this he is certain. His first sentence, 'This is not the world in which I grew up, although it is the world in which I live, at least a part of me.' His invitation is clear. You and I, dear reader, share this world, if perhaps in different ways. But let us come together, to see if we can make sense of this world we both live in.

He continues, his second sentence defines the project, and locates it within a painterly frame. He is not sure about the firmness of this world. It is in motion. He states, 'the world is constantly remade around us, not only the world of the present, the concrete here and now, but also the remembered world of the past and with it the unrealized world of the future.'

***

When I finish this book I am exhilarated. I have taken a complex journey, moving from the 9–11 event and its memories and representations, through a nuanced discussion of the commodification of language (Chapters 1 and 2), the social histories of photography (Chapter 3), writing and the divided self (Chapters 4 and 5), technologies of truth (Chapter 6), censorship and pornography (Chapter 7), and with Phillip K. Dick, science fiction, and the metaphysics of information (Chapter 8).

***

It is fitting that Gary starts almost immediately with 9–11. This event locates all of us in a complex, fractured, shared present. It started before 9–11 but nowadays, to paraphrase C. Wright Mills (1959: 3) men, women and children everywhere feel that their private lives are a series of traps. They feel a loss of control over what is important, including family, loved ones, sanity itself. The dividing line between private troubles and public issues slips away. People feel caught up in a swirl of world events, from the Middle East to Afghanistan, and Iraq. These events and their histories seem out of control. Life in the private sphere has become a public nightmare.

We live in dark and bitter times. Democratic public life is under siege. A culture of fear has spread around the world In the United States reactionaries and neo-liberals have all but overtaken the languages and politics of daily life, locating Americans in a permanent, open-ended war against faceless, nameless terrorists. We are poised on the brink of yet another war. Preemptive strikes, assassinations, and regime changes have become part of our new Bush-led foreign policy. Patriotism has become the national watchword.

The economy is slumping, unemployment is at a record high. Crony capitalism reigns. Conservative politicians tied to global capitalism advocate free markets defined by the languages of commercialism and commodified social relations. Neo-liberals contend that what is good for the economy is good for democracy. The gap between rich and poor widens. Social injustices extending from 'class oppression to racial violence to the ongoing destruction of public life and the environment' (Giroux 2003: 2) have become commonplace. The ideological relationship between capitalism and neoliberal democracy has never been stronger, and it must be broken.

We live in a new garrison state. Since 9–11 America's public spaces have become increasingly militarized. Armed guards and openly visible security cameras are in now in airports, pedestrian malls, outside hospitals and schools, even on college campuses. The President has authorized war tribunals, and detention camps for suspected terrorists. Civil liberties are disappearing. Racial profiling operates behind the guise of protecting national security. A five-level civil-defense alarm system is in place.

Public education and civic, participatory social science are in jeopardy. Academics and pacifists critical of the war on terrorism are branded traitors. More and more restraints are being applied to qualitative, interpretive research, as conservative federal administrators redefine what is acceptable inquiry (Lincoln and Cannella 2004). Right-wing politicians stifle criticism, while implementing a 'resurgent racism ... [involving] ... punitive attacks on the poor, urban youth, and people of color' (Giroux 2000: 132; also 2001).

***

These are the troubled spaces that Gary Krug's book enters. His closing words give me hope. There is a way out of this mess. Our task is to 'reassert the moral and philosophical necessity to find ourselves in self-reflection and dialogue, to create ourselves in the engagement with texts as if ideas, words, and symbols were still the bridges that consciousness builds to consciousness across the gulf of being.' This mutual recognition of our selves and others through language and conversation is one of our 'first acts as moral and social beings.'

When we do this we remember the problems of the spirit. To rephrase the quote from William Faulkner that starts Chapter One, 'these are the problems that have universal bones, the problems of the heart in conflict with itself.' Gary Krug's book calls us back to these problems of the heart.

Norman K. Denzin
Urbana, Illinois USA

References

Giroux, H. (2003) *The Abandoned Generation: Democracy Beyond the Culture of Fear.* New York: Palgrave.

Giroux, H. (2001) *Public Spaces, Private Lives.* Lanham, Maryland: Roman & Littlefield Publishers, Inc.

Giroux, H. (2000) *Impure Acts: The Practical Politics of Cultural Studies.* New York: Routledge.

Lincoln, Y.S. and Cannella, G.S. (2004) Dangerous Discourses Methodological Conservatism and Governmental Regimes of Truth. *Qualitative Inquiry* 10 (1): 5–14.

Mills, C. Wright (1959) *The Sociological Imagination.* New York: Oxford.

Note

1   Montage, of course, is associated with the work of the Russian filmmaker Sergei Eisenstein, especially his film *The Battleship Potemkin* (1925). In Einstein's films the use of montage allowed him to superimpose several different images onto one another to create a picture moving in several different directions at the same time.

Preface

In his pencil-like embrasure, the look-out and later the gunner realized long
before the easel painter, the photographer or the filmmaker, how necessary is
a preliminary sizing-up. (Paul Virilio 1989: 49)

This is not the world in which I grew up, although it is the world in which
I live, at least a part of me. One can never be sure, for the world is constantly
remade around us, not only the world of the present, the concrete here and
now, but also the remembered world of the past, and with it the unrealized
world of the future. These statements are so commonplace as to border on the
banal, yet the banality illustrates the point. Each of us comes to be within
the language, values, and beliefs of a time and a place. Yet, the process is not
complete at any moment but continues through time. In our memory, though,
we see the moments which still resonate for us as fixed and perfect, finished.
We believe that we were defined in these, created in past moments and dragged
into the present. This a piecemeal view of ourselves, though, and does an injustice to our understanding of the remarkable, transient processes of the creation
of ourselves, though it may be the only way of preserving a sense of continuity. Selective amnesias of all stripes may be required by sanity.

So, this work is an act of anamnesis, a remembering of alternatives through
the reconstruction of certain habits of thought, representation, and action.
Many of the amnesias are made easily possible through contemporary communication technologies and their uses. To discuss the technologies which
have facilitated, created, and transformed human thought one must take
account of the ways in which self, culture, and technology mutually create and
reflect each other. To separate one of these elements out of our thought on this
subject would create an artificial cleavage into what is an organic whole.
Nonetheless, it is the fashion to list the 'communication technologies' in various
taxonomic tables based upon purely conventional and largely unexamined
beliefs: one requires a chapter on economics, one on convergence, another to
examine telecommunications, something on the World Wide Web, and of course
a chapter on computers, etc.

However useful pedagogically in universities that have fought a losing battle
against becoming trade schools since the 1950s, these categorizations are misleading. While the odd chapter on 'social consequences' might appear in texts,
the social and the self are curiously unintegrated into discussions of the
technologies themselves. Such a divorce of self, culture, and technology excludes
the introduction of philosophical and historical dimensions into discussions
of hardware, software, and systems. At best, philosophy in such instances

becomes the question of policy, law, advertising, journalism ethics, or media effects. How we should live, what alternative ways exist of thinking about ourselves and our world, what is the nature of the world into which we become existent: such questions rarely find their ways into communication technology textbooks which are already busily training the next generation of technologists.

My project here is thus not to write a linear historical account of this or that individual technology. Technologies are always systems, and these systems are always linked to other systems. Rather, I seek to explore the relationships between systems of language, technology, and the social institutions and beliefs within which people create themselves. Throughout the book, contemporary problems, descriptions, and issues are raised as terminal points in trajectories to be traced between alternative or older practices and the current moment. I do not, however, propose that the contemporary time is truly an end point or *eschaton* in the elaboration of technologies. Now is simply the most current moment about which we can make observations, and I seek to illustrate that the current times, selves, and techniques are the products of particular lines of development, certain choices, and specific sets of activities. My aim is not to put forward general theories of history, technological change, or society. I seek to elaborate existing narratives and stories, standing histories, and sometimes ignored or neglected relations into a new set of narratives that were not present before. A conversation is formed from the voices present, and in this work, some of the voices are familiar within communication studies and others are still largely strangers.

Chapter 1 explores some of the philosophical background of the problems inherent in studying the relationship of language, the world, and consciousness in historical context. I begin with the present to outline some of the issues to be explored through the book, such as the commodification of language, the modernist imperative to achieve closure of meaning, and the consequences of using technical or scientific language in vernacular domains. This chapter sketches the contemporary scene and references historical, discursive, and philosophical alternatives to some current situations.

One difficulty facing any analysis of the relationship between culture and technology lies in avoiding the deterministic fallacy. Determinism arises primarily from the mistake of viewing culture and technology as somehow independent of the human participants and observers. To put consciousness back into the discussion of technology and society allows for an analysis balanced between the world, language, and mind. The fragmented self of the contemporary world is not caused by technology but emerges with the development of the dominant forms of technology. Similarly, fractured social relations and diminished social participation are not products of technology but are consequentially related to how technology is represented in symbolic forms that are in turn influenced by technology itself.

A central problem of contemporary social life arises from the apparent inability to meaningfully organize people into communities that allow for the existence of politics. The mass media paradoxically create a totalized view of the world in forms and structures that are not amenable to politics. Thus, Chapter 2 takes up the relationship between technology, writing, and the vernacular. Through an exploration of the phenomenology of language, I examine the differences between a vernacular language and a manufactured one. The historical evolution of the split between official language and local ways of talking and making sense of the world traces as well the evolution of technologies of language and their relationship with the social. Philosophy, rhetoric, the liberal arts, and various other technologies of thought and language evolved out of people's engagement with the problems of negotiating meaning and interpretation.

The extent to which communication technologies take on uses and meanings in relationship to other social beliefs is a central theme of Chapter 3. Through an exploration, initially of differing perspectives on the use of images themselves and then in a detailed study of the history of photography, I examine the links between the social uses of images and the meanings that they have in society. The object is neither to document different 'scopic regimes' nor to trace the historical evolution of a modern or 'advanced' way of using images. Rather, the uses of images document diverse ways in which people associate consciousness with other people and with the world. People stand in relationships to both still and moving images, and they assume that what the image means and does is relatively fixed. Although certain theorists and practitioners of modernist and postmodernist philosophy, aesthetics, and art have highlighted the instability of people's relationships with images, the ways in which one formative technology, photography, emerged within discourses of truth reveal the emergence of certain constellations of power.

The modern self emerged within these and other social forms of power. Myths of origin and creation emerged to underpin the legitimacy both of the self and of the institutions and ideas that instantiated it within society and the state. Chapter 4 examines several key moments in the social history of printing and publishing and their uses in society. These historical examples establish the origins of the codes of the later mass media and demonstrate the historical depth of some problems in studying mass communications. For example, the reading practices of real people and the purposes that reading serves for them vary significantly across times and settings. Is the book an object of meditation, a transmitter of ideas, or a study in the meaning and credibility of virtue and truth? Various individuals and groups have sought to define the world both through print and through the printed version of the world, and sometimes these have not been the same thing.

Another major site of contention over the uses of meanings of a communication technology is to be found in letter writing, the history of which is examined in Chapter 5. In both its function and its meaning for the individual writer or reader, the letter was once a major contributor to and marker of the habitus. The same industrial social and institutional forces that created the mail system as an instrument of everyday use were simultaneously creating the need for a self that was divided between two competing forms: a narrative self and a lived self. While each was gendered and reflected existing class structures, the maintenance of multiple selves was necessary as the emerging world of industrial capital created conditions that required one to be simultaneously both present and alienated. The selves that emerged through and which were reflected in the nascent social forms were precursors of the kinds of selves necessary today. Chapter 5 is, then, a study of the ways in which the divided self had historical antecedents in early modernism. In particular, the characteristics of the modern technologically oriented self have their origins in letter writing and related literary practices of the eighteenth and nineteenth centuries. Similarly, many characteristics of contemporary communication systems emerge during this period and have historical roots in the early postal systems.

Some ideological components of modern communication technologies, necessary for their emergence as totalizing social systems, were added in the nineteenth century. First, media began to establish what was information worth knowing and what was not, and second, this information was increasingly bound up with particular religious and industrial beliefs and mythologies. Chapter 6 documents some of the mechanisms by which social truth and mass truth emerged. Mass knowledge and mass 'truth' had their origins in the rise of the newspapers of the nineteenth century. However, this mass truth took a particularly technicistic turn in the twentieth century through the influences of the military-industrial institutions. In particular, Vannevar Bush and his proposed memex are prototypical of many aspects of contemporary thinking about information and its organization.

This manner of organization of information as a self-evident scientific truth has allowed knowledge, training, and information itself to be used since the nineteenth century as forms of social control. Chapter 7 examines the cultural transition to a technological, industrial culture and explores how information came to be seen as something with which to handle the emerging masses. With the triumph of industrially and commercially produced communications over all other forms, a moral and epistemological world was created by corporations and institutions which framed the experience of all who lived within it. A central part of this project was the reduction of 'culture' to quanta of knowledge and information that could be imparted in radio, films, and schools, and that could stand in opposition to the vulgar world of the ordinary person. Key examples are the emergence of film classification and the rise in calls for censorship and control of pornography.

Pornography shares several key characteristics with surveillance, beyond the simple observation that each constructs the subject–object relationship found in voyeurism. Chapter 8 explores the ways in which a military-industrial society conceptualizes and uses information as a 'truth' and as a social control. The logical fallacies inherent in these usages as well as the damage done to people's relations with each other are explored in the contexts of mass media politics, surveillance, and pornography. 'Information' has created a new world that masquerades as the natural. The contemporary understanding and use of information bear several significant similarities to gnosticism and constitute a 'digital antinomianism' in which information itself stands as the self-evident and self-legitimizing 'truth' of the gnostic system.

While these chapters may be read individually as histories of specific activities, later chapters build upon ideas and concepts laid down in earlier ones.

Thus, discussions in later chapters may seem ungrounded if read out of sequence. The approach taken here necessarily eschews some kinds of linear development, and some connections, particularly across chapters, will not be apparent unless the text is taken as a whole.

Finally, because this work crosses many disciplinary boundaries, I inevitably make choices to include some authors and to exclude others. This might trouble some scholars, but I have deliberately sought to avoid too narrow a focus in any given field or area. Rather, my aim has been to bring together diverse threads of discussion into a new conversation. This book is thus not so much a university course as it is a series of conversations in a salon.

Acknowledgements

This book has evolved, as such projects do, in the course of its being written. It was composed on a long peripatetic journey that began in Adelaide Australia and continued through Columbus Ohio, Edinburgh Scotland, Grand Forks North Dakota, Champaign Illinois, Las Vegas Nevada, and Spokane Washington. In each city, I was aided both by friends and colleagues and by various libraries and their staffs. Rather than being limited by the necessity of packing up my notes, moving again, and discovering a new library, I have found that I have evolved through this journey as well. Consequently, neither this book nor I are quite what I thought they would be in 2000 when this project began.

Among the many places where I found helpful friends and assistance, a few must be mentioned by name. The Institute of Communication Research at the University of Illinois has always provided me with a home away from home. Jakob Obie Camp lent me hospitality, assistance, a critical eye, and a sympathetic heart. Jack Donahue of Las Vegas provided a welcoming port during difficult times. John Nerone lent me his historian's perspective on many matters and was instrumental in clarifying my understanding of the process of writing history and several key arguments. John, Ivy Glennon, and Miranda demonstrated as well the true meaning of friendship, extending to me the welcome of their family. Dana Elder offered helpful readings of some chapters in addition to stimulating and enlightening conversations about many of the ideas here. Ben Therrell has been a stalwart friend throughout the writing of this book, showing the greatest patience and humor as I talked out developing ideas. Phil Sellers has always challenged and informed me on numerous aspects of theory and critical thought.

My most special thanks are due to Mimi Marinucci who has managed to combine love and affection with an unswervingly critical eye and ear, and who has saved me on many occasions from my own excesses in writing and thought.

Special thanks are also due to Jamilah Ahmed and the editorial staff at Sage whose patience and encouragement have made this project possible.

ONE

Technology as Culture

Our tragedy today is a general and a universal physical fear so long sustained by now that we can even bear it. There are no longer problems of the spirit. There is only the question: when will I be blown up? Because of this, the young man or woman writing today has forgotten the problems of the heart in conflict with itself ... His griefs grieve on no universal bones, leaving no scars. He writes not of the heart but of the glands. (William Faulkner 1950)

A common truism of the current day is that technology is accelerating at unprecedented speeds. While many refinements and extensions of communication technology into the personal world are indeed occurring with great rapidity, the truism overlooks the more important observation that the greatest changes in communications took place in the nineteenth century, not the twentieth or twenty-first. In that earlier century and for the first time in human history, the message was commonly separated from a messenger, becoming electronic. The speed of a rider on horseback was superseded. The manufacture of books and papers became inexpensive enough to finally permeate the great masses of people in the industrializing world. Most of the basic forms of narrative, the semiotic conventions of images, and the large social relations formed between mass society and mass media appeared over 100 years ago. Yet, despite their origins in earlier times, the contemporary inflections of technology, especially in media, appear with a ubiquity that is simultaneously familiar and strange. Consequentially, the social and personal effects of mediated communications have become more obvious and more celebrated and also more subtle and threatening.

The pace of change remains a factor, however, in the most immediate and generally noticed transformations of the world from something familiar and having historical depth to a place which appears transient and alien even as it becomes the shared world of contemporary life. The speed of change and the acceleration of technological development are major factors in the destabilization of the local and vernacular world. The most cogent of the philosophers of speed, Paul Virilio (1994), has written at length upon the dissolution of the real into vectors of speed and movement. The real, he notes, is being 'accidented' by the virtual: that is, by the creation of the new, the railroad and the airplane create with them the destruction of the old, the derailment and the airplane crash. In just this way, the creation of the virtual world, the electronic world of 'glocalized' presence, destroys the physical presence (Virilio 1997). So, too, the familiar and known disappear into the new products and systems of technology. With a book such as this, for example, the author and reader are guaranteed that specific examples of technology will already be outmoded and superseded before the ink is dried. Books are certainly too slow as a medium to track the changes of communication technologies; monthly magazines barely suffice for the expert. Only electronic communications such as the internet or the television can provide information quickly enough to be even remotely current. As such, the book as a topical source is accidented; it disappears from that position in the social discourses.

This does not mean that the book is finished, though. If reality is too swift, if technology outpaces even science fiction, perhaps the book is more suited to another, more traditional use. The book still excels in its ability to present complex, synthesized ideas and to provide them in a form for contemplation. Such a use changes the subject matter and the focus of the book, but it is a deliberately slow medium of communication and is uniquely suited to this end. Further, the act of reading the book, as opposed to being online, links us back in time to other ways of perceiving the world. It establishes a linkage to the physical and psychical processes of earlier times.

Much of this book is concerned with describing the differences between communication technologies of the present and those of the past. I do not seek merely to document the physical and social forms of these technologies, however. Communication as a human activity has, for most of its history, existed as activities taking place between the minds of people. The book and the paper were dumb and deaf without living voices and minds to give them existence in the shared human world. Only the electronically mediated world can appear to have existence and indeed a life separate from the human. Thus, the relationships between physical communication technologies, the social settings in which they appear, the cultural meanings that people construct around them, and the selves and beliefs of human beings, are integral to understanding this history.

The 9–11 Event

Like many people around the world, I watched the burning buildings at the World Trade Center collapse on television. This event took place in 'real time', that is to say, 'live'. Excluding the insignificant delay of some fractions of a second in transmission between the cameras and my television, I saw the events as they happened. Or did I? What in fact did I witness? Linked into a global network of observers, I participated with others in two activities. First, I observed passively, watching the barely edited stream of images and listening to the commentary of newscasters. Second, I tried to make sense of the emerging events. In the second task, I was guided by the comments, hypotheses, and statements of the newscasters. How was such an event to be framed either as experience or as meaning?

Regarding the experience of the event, I was struck by the disbelief that people in TV interviews and in real life expressed about what they had seen. This was the immediate state which came from the event, and only after innumerable special reports and mini-documentaries and special newspaper segments has this story been woven into a form. The recurring statement of witnesses was: it was like a movie. Our only experience of this order of event is in movies, and even the coverage on TV of the planes striking the towers quickly employed the editing techniques of film: the slow-motion shot, the multiple angles of the same event, etc. Time was frozen, dissected, rearranged, and presented for us as 'that which happened'. Signifiers of attack and disaster drawn from times long past were invoked and their images commingled with these new ones: 1941, Pearl Harbor, the explosion of the battleship *Arizona* – all this in a year that had seen the release of a new film about Pearl Harbor.

During the 9–11 event, the entire technology of advanced electronic media and the institutions of journalism were fulfilling one of their primary social functions: the creation of memory and meaning in ways that can be taken for granted. Luhman writes that 'memory consists in being able to take certain assumptions about reality as given and known about in every communication, without having to introduce them specially into the communication and justify them' (2000: 65). The World Trade Center attacks, now commonly known and referred to in the US simply as '9–11', had to be written and rewritten into the memory of the media, bound to signifiers from the past, framed as a 'terrorist attack', and so on. What had appeared to everyone watching that morning as the unfolding of more and more strange images, as more and more shocking revelations (other planes, all air traffic grounded), and as apprehension (which is the purpose of this sort of 'spot terrorism'), became meaningful. In so doing, the meaning of the event in the media solidified in several senses.

Obviously the idea of attack would be solidified as the stimulus for an American counter-attack, a plateau of political discourse upon which policy could be constructed. However, the silences of that morning, poignant amongst the incessant chatter, rumors, and misinformation, revealed the incapacity of the media in the face of an event that was ongoing. The unfolding event that flooded initially in unedited and uninterpreted streams throughout the world could not be made to stand still. It resisted the objectification necessary for modern communications, the modern social, and the modern self. The world cannot simply be, it must be some thing. The 9–11 event is what happens when events visibly outstrip the ability of media to position the world as object.

Captured now and held forever as a few moments of digitally encoded patterns of light and sound, the 9–11 event is no longer a part of a historical process of material events driving the perception and understanding of the world. Rather, it has become a moment upon which we can gaze, indeed are compelled to gaze back upon, but it is not the event we see. The media, the government, and the endless entourage of talking heads and experts have paralyzed and frozen the meaning. The 9–11 event has ceased to be a part of the present and exists as a past moment understood from the vantage point of the present.

Yet it is the silence amongst the public chatter, the lacunae in speech and discourse, which most eloquently revealed the process of consciousness confronting the emergence of historical reality. This process is precisely what the media subsequently effaced, encapsulating the event forever in a few repeating seconds of image and sound, all safely bundled into the 'ideas', 'opinions', and 'responses' which followed. Instead of seeing the event as one of those moments when events shatter our ability to contain them, we now reflect upon *what it meant*; and for a brief moment, what the world meant was not determined by technological systems because they had not yet framed the events which were so unexpected and inconceivable as to appear truly new.

That the event was symbolic is a banal observation already captured in the compression of thousands of moments into the single word 'event'. Certainly those responsible planned their actions as a kind of theater on the global stage, and the world was already positioned in the drama that Baudrillard called *terrorismo dell'arte* (1990: 45). Newspapers in the US and UK devoted the whole of their front pages to full color photographs of exploding towers. The event was especially shocking and incomprehensible to the West for there was no sense of either the history or the reality of the terrorists in political or popular rhetoric. As Robert Fiske (2001) observed, 'we will be told about "mindless terrorism", the "mindless" bit being essential if we are not to realize how hated America has become in the land of the birth of three great religions'. Despite such attempts to historicize and so make meaningful the 9–11 event, the logic of contemporary politics and representation demanded a causality equally removed from history: terrorism as an abstract politics rather than as a means to an end.

Ensconced in the Western fetish with the fixity of meaning, we find that only shocking events have the power to make us ponder the oblivion so created. From Duchamp's playful ennui, through the manifestos of Marinetti and the Futurists, through numerous artistic attempts to find another way to shock and so awaken the sleeping consciousness, meaning has proven the consistent modernist enemy of aesthetics and perception. But this is not quite accurate. 'Meaning' becomes limiting only to the extent that it minimizes our relationship both to the world and to our historically grounded understanding of being in the world. 'Meaning' becomes limiting if it is construed to be the socially accepted positioning of a subject within some dominant system of signification and the orientation of that position to the exclusion of other possible positions and relationships of signs. Meaning in the modern, capitalist, patriarchal sense is always an exclusion, a terminus of the processes of consciousness writing histories of itself through language.

These processes stop with the assumption of 'meaning' and one particular point of view emerges, one that always faces away both from the event and from the historical project of consciousness. What remains is consciousness gazing at the frozen moment which now stands in place of the world. The 9–11 event now stands in the social domain as an event justifying a 'war on terror' that can have no end. Once the meaning had coalesced into a form, both the history and the future could be written in terms of this form. Despite numerous unanswered questions, inconsistencies of narrative and chronology, and unexplained improbable events, the 9–11 event has settled into public discourse and discussion in an official form.[1] It means something.

As persons possessing this 'meaning', we need neither examine the world circumscribed by this meaning nor extend consciousness into new forms of language to link this meaning to existing beliefs. Rather, the world is already given and its meaning is already bound to the prevailing and dominant beliefs and myths. The outcome of 'meaning' severs people from the praxis of their own historical projects and from relationships to others. Kovel notes that 'a person is correctly seen as a member of a faceless mass because of a lack of concrete relatedness to others in a historical project' (1981: 223). Paradoxically, the more that people find themselves isolated from meaningful histories, the more appealing become the myths and meanings of the social in an eternal procession of moments in present time. The events in the world, defined for us as 'the way things are' and proclaimed by a thousand media heralds, are parroted again and again in everyday interaction, ensuring that even the personal is reinscribed into this overdetermined history.

A Brief History of Objectification

Eric Voegelin (1987) pointed out that noetic philosophy emerges out of a tripartite formula involving consciousness, the world, and language. To change any one of these three components is to alter the others as well. None of these three is independent of the other, and each arises in a particular way from its relationship with the other two. The technologies of communication, especially as these develop as systems, directly transform both our language and what stands for us as the world. In addition to our vision of the immediate world as what stands before us, we have also a shared common world, already replete with meaning, that is not known by us directly. This common world constitutes the shared social of news, of nations, and of the often anonymous powers that affect us in a thousand ways every day. The mediated world has the force of law, government, and social approval. It is ubiquitous and nearly omnipresent. As a consequence, our consciousness is increasingly our awareness of and participation in this created world through languages and symbolic systems that are themselves already structured by technology. Any philosophy of mind or self in the contemporary world must account for this relationship.

The inability to account for all the elements of mind, language, and world is one of the major failings of philosophies and histories that embrace a technological determinist perspective. When McLuhan (1964) wrote of the extension of the human senses and nervous system into the world through the electronic media, he was guilty of the homunculus fallacy, a finally atomistic belief that the mind, the self, and consciousness exist as independent and autonomous entities that use media, technology, and language rather than being created through their implication in the same social processes as those which produced technology and media and the forms of language. Even if one accepts McLuhan's words as a kind of trope or metaphor, his idea lacks a verisimilitude with the world necessary to be believable. McLuhan begins with the contemporary perspective that sees language already as a tool. In famously writing 'the medium is the message', he adopts the modern understanding in which 'message' and 'medium' have already replaced 'speech' and 'presence of the other'.

Similar liberal presuppositions influenced the thought and writing of many scholars in their evaluation of the uses of media in such tasks as national development. Daniel Lerner (1958), Wilbur Schramm (1964), and others saw a role for the technology of mass media in extending the virtues of modern society into those areas of the world apparently most in need of industrialization, that is, improvement. It is not enough to say that the theories, and often policies, that developed out of these writers elide questions of power and of the ethics of its use. Rather, their understanding of technology as a kind of amplifier of power together with their understanding of media as a conduit for the transmission of ideas make any possibilities of dialogue superfluous. Framed as essentially linear models of human communication, such formulations do lead us to examine those processes in which consciousness and the self are implicated.

The self becomes aware of itself in the mediated world as a part of it. As this world has moved toward a consolidation of itself in language, in representation, and in its development of ever more self-referential forms, the process of the formation of the self becomes linked to this consolidation. The development of the self, the individuation of consciousness as a sense of itself in the mediated world, shares the same vector as the social itself. The emerging sense of a self-directed, self-aware person takes place within the context of symbolic systems that are increasingly only internally referential. Awareness is not of the world but of the systems of mediated representation. An increase in personal knowledge about the world equates with the extension of mind ever deeper into the mediated systems of representation and meaning. Individual choice and personal freedom thus become based on the ability to discriminate between a limited number of elements presented and represented in the mediated world, whether shampoo or political candidates. Consciousness and desire, as markers of individuation, exist more and more in the already constituted and finished social forms. Notions such as personal freedom emerge from the consolidating system and ultimately refer back to it. As there is no other world that matters, freedom is the freedom to choose from among existing forms.

If we perceive the world primarily through mediated systems of representation, the world becomes largely another aspect of technology, and this changes both consciousness and language. We do not then perceive a world emerging through our engagement with it, a process that Heidegger called *aletheia*, that is, unhiddenness or revealing. For the ancient Greeks, the apparent or seeming reality of the world, *doxa*, was incomplete. The true world, the world as it is, had to be revealed through an engagement with it. We perceive instead a world whose purpose and meaning are already given. Heidegger notes a shift in meaning with the Latin philosophers: 'The Romans translated this [*aletheia*] with *veritas*. We say "truth" and usually understand it as the correctness of an idea' (1977: 12). The correctness of an idea, of course, has little to do with the notion of *aletheia*. Western societies commonly rely upon either science or religion for answers to questions of truth, but this is only because the responsibility for producing the unhiddenness of the world, for bringing the world into existence in perception and thought, has been largely replaced with a duty to consume information properly combined with the ability to reproduce the currently fashionable truths of the world. The mediated world appears as a world, yet all attempts to produce the *aletheia* or truth of this world finally return to our *doxa*, to the way that our world appears, that is, as various statements that ultimately can be neither legitimated nor dismissed. The contrast between the two meanings is easily seen in the contemporary triumph of opinion over knowledge.

I am not saying that we no longer see the world or that our perception is wholly of television and movies and online entertainment. Certainly the wind blows in my face, the sun warms my skin, the ground resists the press of my foot. All of these things I feel. Yet, what they mean to me, how they feel, how I speak of these to others, are to a large extent already set up for me. I am encouraged to frame my experiences into the shop-worn clichés of a language that drones perpetually through the airwaves and over the broadband connections. The habits of thought and the values and attitudes reflecting my beliefs about the world I encounter develop in ways that privilege the mediated world while denigrating the immediate world. This fact was made stunningly clear to me when a student approached me after a lecture and said, 'What you said last week was true: I saw it on TV.' One could argue that this is only a case of one domain of language, the spoken word, contesting with another, the television, for dominance. However, the 'truth' of my statements was only another assertion like all others until it was integrated into the system of consolidated meaning. I may stand by my words in a literal way, but so what? If I were any good, would I not be on TV? If my words were true in the contemporary sense, that is, in close accord with the popular and official discourses, would not my lectures be supported by the evidence of their constant vindication and elaboration on CNN and *Entertainment Tonight*?

The emergence of perception and history

The basic problems of perception and of being remain perennial regardless of whether the world which stands before consciousness is the polysemic play of infinitely referential discourses or a field of rocks. In describing the difference between the perception and the apprehension of the world as object, Husserl differentiates what he called 'primordial' experience, that is 'becoming aware' or 'perceiving', from apprehension (1962 [1931]: 45–6). The latter emerges when the thing perceived, the *eidos*, is transformed into another kind of experience either through memory or through anticipation: 'The other man, and his psychical life, is indeed apprehended as there in person ... but unlike the body, it is not given to our consciousness as primordial' (1962 [1931]: 46). The perception of individual moments and things presents one with a world in which the characteristics of each moment are 'accidental'. The shape, sound, taste, and feel of each moment could as easily be other than it is. The human experience of this is the direct apprehension of the world as one thing and as it is. This need not sound mystical or fantastic, for it is precisely the state spoken of by Zen monks, by martial artists, by marksmen, and by others who require a degree of concentration that silences the self and so effaces the boundaries between self and the world. To achieve such a state from everyday consciousness only requires an act of meditation or concentration acquired through practice. Dewey observed that 'in well-formed, smooth-running functions of any sort ... there is no consciousness of separation of the method of the person and the subject matter' (1985a [1916]: 173). One's distancing from the world through language and thought makes the world abstractly knowable as something separate, but this process simultaneously removes one from participating directly in the historical moment of the world (see Ricoeur 1981: 131ff).

The experience of individual moments of time, being manifested as particular things having particular characteristics and qualities, requires their being linked together in some associational manner. There is an ordering of the world into some contingent universals and relationships (Husserl 1962 [1931]: 47). This ordering manifests itself as empirical knowledge emerging from perception within the complex of being and language. Language, and particularly the more durable forms of it such as writing and printing, are technologies which greatly extend the potential of the idea to fix experience and to locate oneself in relationship to the world and to others. This requires first the positioning of the self in the world and, second, the subsequent projection outward of an idea of the self that is encountered and reflected back upon consciousness (Denzin 1989).

So, how are people in the world; what are the characteristics and what are the processes of their being? It is perhaps indicative of the times that the discussion of being appears in what are arguably the two least read bodies of literature in the Western world, philosophy and poetry. The materialist acceptance of the world as it appears in language is so deeply enshrined in the discourses of power and their internalization as everyday consciousness that a perspective of the world as something *becoming* is extremely difficult to present in simple terms. A study of the conversion of the world into things, already fixed in meaning and experience, formed much of the early work of the poet Rilke, in: his *Ding Gedichte* (*Thing Poems*). Only after a lengthy hiatus did he clarify a sense of what had failed for him in the perspective he had inherited from Western culture. What emerged was a perception which is hard to call anything but spiritual. At any rate, that about which Rilke wrote in the *Duino Elegies* emerged from a different order of being, and much of his problem as a poet is to forge a relationship between his own consciousness and the emergence of this other order of existence. In the eighth of the *Duino Elegies*, Rilke (1977: 123–5) describes in detail the experience of directly facing into *alethia*, of confronting the emergence of being as an ongoing process of experience, and he describes as well its absence or loss in the common experience of reality:

> With all eyes the creature sees the open
> but our eyes are as though turned around
> and placed around them as snares
> circles the freedom of departure.
>
> [Mit alle Augen sieht die Kreature
> das Offene. Nur unsere Augen sind
> wie umgekehrt und ganz um sie gestellt
> als Fallen, rings um ihren freien Ausgang.]

He continues, writing of the process of education into the shared perspective of the world as completed which takes place in the early years of life:

> Already, with a young child,
> we turn him around so that he
> sees the state of things backwards, not the openness
> that is so deep in the face of an animal.
>
> [Denn schon das frühe Kind
> Wenden wir um und zwingens, daß es ruckwärts
> Gestaltung sehe, nicht das Offne, das
> Im Tiergesicht so tief ist.]

Throughout the poem, Rilke draws out both the primordial experience of the world and the human necessity to lose this experience, to replace it with knowledge and anticipation. His portrayal of the human world is one of spectators incapable of seeing out of the depth of their own being. The consequence of this attitude toward being and toward becoming is the loss of both the world and the self, as Rilke makes clear later in the poem:

> It fills us to overflowing. We order it. It falls apart.
> We order it again and fall apart ourselves.
>
> [Uns uberfullts. Wir ordnens. Es zerfallt.
> Wir ordnens wieder und zerfallen selbst.]

Linked finally to our linear progression of sense-making, bound to that which is meaningful, we learn the longing for that which cannot be. Near the end of the poem, he asks the rhetorical question, 'Who has turned us around like this? [Wer hat uns also umgedreht…?]'. Rilke does not answer the question, but Eric Voegelin does.

The inextricable relationship between self and the world, mediated through language, arises in the writings of Eric Voegelin as a fundamental paradox of consciousness. He writes that 'consciousness has a structural dimension by which it belongs, not to man [sic] in his bodily existence, but to the reality in which man, the other partners to the community of being, and the participating relations among them occur' (1987: 16). In other words, language, which constitutes one part of our knowing of the world, is shared. Voegelin refers to this process as 'metaxy' to denote the 'between-status' of consciousness. Consciousness is always a consciousness of some thing or some state, and it emerges and develops within relations with the world which are ordered by language.

Through the mediation of language, experience is already within the domain of the shared, of the human and social; and so consciousness, in holding some analogy of its relation to the world in the present, some model or construct, which for that time is the world, holds it already as a *techne*. Meanwhile, the world flows past, becoming more distant the longer one holds onto the construct. The moments of perception and the ideas that arise through the mediation of language constitute the elaboration of personal histories as well as those we elaborate in deliberate cooperation with other people.

We must remember, though, that our structurings of experience transform how we will understand subsequent experiences. We fit new events into our already existing relationships and analogies. In this sense, Merleau-Ponty (1962: 30) writes that 'history is not only an object in front of us, far from us, beyond our reach, it is also our awakening as subjects'. Our historical use of language positions us toward the world of experience. At the same time, our experience of the now positions us toward the past.

Walter Benjamin reminds us that 'history is the subject of a structure whose site is not homogeneous, empty time, but time filled by the presence of the now [Jetztzeit]' (1969: 261). Each moment constitutes itself and our awareness of it in real, concrete relationships. Thus, without a cognizance of the elaboration of history as a series of interactions between consciousness and the world, we will devise ourselves and our ideas, such as history, from our current subjectivity and time; we will perceive the world from where we are. Each moment constitutes itself and our consciousness of it in real, concrete relationships. Our current subjectivity, our existence in concrete, dialectic relationship with the world, structures our sense of what has come before. It is this thesis which presents his most famous allegory and insight.

> A Klee painting named 'Angelus Novus' shows an angel looking as though he is about to move away from something he is fixedly contemplating. His eyes are staring, his mouth is open, his wings are spread. This is how one pictures the angel of history. His face is turned toward the past. Where we perceive a chain of events, he sees one single catastrophe which keeps piling wreckage upon wreckage and hurls it in front of his feet. The angel would like to stay, awaken the dead, and make whole what has been smashed. But a storm is blowing from Paradise; it has got caught in his wings with such violence that the angel can no longer close them. This storm irresistibly propels him into the future to which his back is turned, while the pile of debris before him grows skyward. This storm is what we call progress. (1969: 257–8)

Progress in the Western, additive sense drives the angel of history always away from what has been. The question remains as to the nature of progress; and for the contemporary Western world, progress is technological elaboration and growth. The world that emerges from such progress and in which we come to consciousness and find ourselves implicated is that technological world.

The Framing of Technology

The language that frames our experience of the world and with which we write our histories has changed dramatically over the last few centuries. Not only have words and meanings altered, but the entire domain of language has altered. Rather than arising out of local, human experience elaborated through conversations with other people, language now comes prepackaged and reflects not the needs of human beings but the values of capital, the machine, and the technological system. To put it simply, our world increasingly consists of words, pictures, and the social frameworks of signification which bind these together as interlocked discourses of meaning. Our consciousness moves not in the world-as-other but through the already constituted experiences of mediated words, sounds, and pictures. It is not that the mediated world is less real, but that the meanings of things within it are already given, and these meanings are what is culturally valuable. Only those things already framed as important within the contemporary social world exist. The mediated world is no less real than the obdurate, local world, but from the standpoint of the former, the latter does not truly exist.

Thus, the values inherent in the language, as well as the proportions between things that appear as the *logos*, have altered. As a consequence more people can identify 25 pop groups than 25 species of tree; more people can name 10 brands of toothpaste than can identify 10 constellations. The problem is that, as Korzybski (1980 [1933]: 58) noted, we tend to confuse the map with the territory. Studying only the map, we lose sight of the world and see only consciousness and language. Our constructs stand between us and the world, not as a simulation of the world, but as substitution for it (Virilio 1994). We have in a sense confused the Platonic mimesis with the world itself. The process of substituting representation for the real strips thought of an ontological grounding in the physical world. This loss of connection with the real brings about numerous consequences, a major one being that the processes by which consciousness encounters the mediated world differ significantly from the processes by which consciousness encounters the obdurate real world. It is not simply that what is important for us to know has changed; our way of knowing has altered as well.

How did we get to living in a 'computerized, mass-media-dominated world where information technologies define what is real' (Denzin 1991: 25)? Perhaps more importantly, how have people changed as a consequence of inhabiting the mass mediated world? Clearly it is not the same as what went before, and neither should we assume that the people who come to consciousness in this new world, whose selves are the products of the implication in this mediated world, are the same as those people who went before. What is different, and what remains the same? We must be clear about the processes that relate consciousness, the world, and language in historical and material processes.

Logos

All communication technologies contribute to the objectification of experience. This is in part an extension of their role as the facilitators in the exchanges of language that take place through words, symbols, and pictures, but this objectification is also an intrinsic characteristic of modern technology itself. Right at the beginning we must be cognizant of several related words: *logos, techne, poiesis*. Each suggests something being made, something created by humans as they struggle with the unfolding of being. While we are accustomed to the word *techne* in many of its forms, we are not so familiar with *poiesis* or *logos*. Technology originally meant something like the field of things that people made, artifacts. Now, however, it has taken on a life of its own. Technology, especially in communications, has undergone an anthropomorphosis: it has become something alive, something almost supernatural. In many contemporary formulations it wants, it develops, it has autonomy. If, for some people, information has become sentient and our world animated, it is because people have lost the distinction between the world and the representational processes in which they are implicated. We have even reached the point where the dream of artificial intelligence seems to some almost within reach.

Similarly, the closest word we have to *logos* is something like knowledge or perhaps logic; but knowledge, now divorced from a relationship to the physical world, has in turn lost some key similarities to *logos*. *Logos*, in many uses, arose out of an engaged perception of the world. Knowledge has undergone a kind of objectification and has been devalued into being a concept, often confused with the concept 'information'. Further, the concept of information has historically grown more and more extrinsic to human perception, becoming more of a thing and less of a process or state of being. The 'accessing' of information may allow one to 'possess' knowledge. To see the current state of knowledge, one need only note the extent to which classrooms have become magic lantern shows with dot point condensations of ideas presented on overhead transparencies, meticulously copied verbatim and regurgitated on tests. Or if one is more technologically sophisticated, the overheads may be supplanted by a multimedia demonstration wherein all subtleties of thought are compressed into gaily lit and easily digestible 'factoids' and multimedia slide shows.

For many centuries, knowledge was considered not as a thing but as a process of engagement with the world. One of the early meanings of *logos* was an accounting or telling of things. The word was also used to indicate a proportionality between things. Heraclitus, in some of the few fragments which remain of his work, explored the issue of proportionality between things in the world as the source of *logos*. One fragment of his writing states: 'Having heard not me, but the logos, it is wise to concur that all is one' (fr. 50, quoted in Hussey 1972: 39). In this statement, he suggests that the *logos* lies outside himself and his words, but he does not mean *logos* exists as a thing. What, then, is the *logos* for Heraclitus? Hussey suggests that the commonly understood meaning of *logos* as 'meaning' emerges in the first half of the fifth century. The sense in which Heraclitus uses the word is more in keeping with the idea of proportion: Hussey writes that 'his thought is that logos expresses a proportion or analogy in the universe and therefore, that the logos is reasonable and the law it expresses, in virtue of this proportion' (1972: 41). For Heraclitus, the understanding of the world, that is, the perception and understanding of the proportions and relations between things, derives from the nature of the world itself, though not all persons perceive this. Thus, human thought emerges from analogy with the perceived world.

Proportion exists in the comparative sense, between things in the world. We draw relations between moments of time, events, things that appear before us, and these relations are always contingent upon the sorts of relationships that we ascribe to the world through the use of language. From the appearance of 'nature' to the appearance of self as something thrown ahead of us into the world (Denzin 1989), our relationship to everything that we are not is contingent upon the symbolic orderings and relations which we may impart to or find within the perceived universe. The universe may exist without our perceptions, continuing its obdurate existence independently of our observations (though quantum physics suggests otherwise), but our observations fix our relationship to the universe, narrowing an infinite number of possibilities into a finite number of empirical realities.

Technology vastly limits the number of possible meanings that the world may have by limiting the ways in which the world is brought forth, becoming unhidden. Originally technology was a kind of *poiesis*, a making or performance of an action toward an end that brought about a revealing or bringing forth (Heidegger 1977: 10–11). *Techne* was thus an action toward an end, a relationship which consciousness had with the world through which the world was revealed to consciousness, through which it achieved a state of unhiddenness. This kind of knowledge was linked closely to another which was conveyed with the word *episteme*, and which Plato argued was the absolute certainty derived from the world of forms (see Havelock 1963: 29–30, 34). Modern technology, however, does not function in a poietic way. Modern technology 'challenges' and 'enframes' the world (Heidegger 1977: 14–19). We encounter not the revealing of the world but only the possibilities of transforming it or of using it. Applied to communications, modern technology necessarily displaces the revealing of the world with the characteristics of technology: the world is challenged to mean something, to appear in a particular way, to exist within particular framings, or uses, or gratifications.

Similarly, the structure of society itself was for the Greeks linked to their understanding of the cosmos. As everything social depends upon some consensual ordering of the objects of perception, some structure must be given to the world before it becomes comprehensible as opposed to merely perceived, and it is this process that creates the social. From very early in Greek thought, the ordering of the human social world was linked to the divine ordering of the universe (Meier 1990: 91–2). The world of civilized people could thus instantiate some characteristics derived from the divine, notably, *dike* (justice) and *aidos* (reverence for the judgments of others). The *nomoi* (laws or conventions) around which the *polis* was organized were themselves gifts from the gods (see Manville 1990: 49). As such, participation in citizenship was closely linked with moral improvement and with life lived in accordance with the truth of the world understood as divine dictates.

In contrast, the mass mediated world of contemporary telecommunications posits a world based neither on a perceived, primordial experience of the world nor on a philosophically derived understanding. There are implicit orderings in the world, but these come neither from nature nor from the divine, nor from the good and true, but from engineering, system architecture, and marketing. The order that may be found in this world exists not for the moral improvement of the human but for the further extension of the system itself. Thus alternative interpretations, alternative meanings and orderings that might be creatively arrived at as an act of *poiesis*, are actively discouraged. The world is given as immediate in forms already meaningful, and these forms are largely complete in themselves. They exist as modern myths (Barthes 1972 [1958]), and as such they occupy much the same position as those ancient myths that Plato sought to supersede with critical thought.

Technique

The characteristics of the created, mediated world have evolved historically from the cultural practices out of which modern technology emerged. Lewis Mumford (1963 [1934]) blamed much of the enframing character of modern technology on habits and values acquired early in the human experiments with industrial technologies, particularly the mining of coal and iron which built and powered the industrial revolution from the 1760s on. Because mining is most cost-effective in the beginning when the resource is plentiful and easiest to reach, it leads to an attitude of impermanency and 'is the worst possible base for a permanent civilization' (1963 [1934]: 157). He continues, 'the animus of mining affected the entire economic and social organism; this dominant mode of exploitation became the pattern for subordinate forms of industry' (1963 [1934]: 158). From the mines grew the steam engines and railroads which in their applications exemplified the same disregard for both human beings and the environment. The Scotsman Patrick Geddes (1968 [1915]), observed that technologies evolved through stages, and he christened the era of steam and iron 'the paleotechnic', in contrast to the 'neotechnic' age of electricity and alloys which was emerging when he wrote.

We tend to think about technology as an independent force in the world, but the major characteristic of modern technology, as distinct from previous techniques, is the extent to which it binds together as many areas of the social as possible, creating a complex arrangement of social forces which overdetermines action and meaning. Modern technology appears to locate ever larger degrees of autonomy and control in these forces, diminishing the amount of control held by the individual person. Jacques Ellul (1966: 111) defined this major feature of modern technology as a 'necessary linking together' of different technologies, which produced a kind of autonomous technological system. Ellul (1966: 79–111) noted that modern technologies also exhibit a growing automatism of technical choice, a tendency to self-augmentation, and an autonomy with respect to economies and politics. The conclusion within his analysis is the increasing elimination of everything not technological (1966: 84). Mechanized agribusiness replaces farming; increasingly complex networks of public transport displace walking or cycling. Within such a totality of technology the individual person is trapped. Ellul wrote:

> the individual is in a dilemma: either he decides to safeguard his freedom of choice, chooses to use traditional, personal, moral or empirical means, thereby entering into competition with a power against which there is no efficacious defence and before which he must suffer defeat; or he decides to accept technical necessity, in which case he will himself be the victor, but only by submitting irreparably to technical slavery. In effect, he has no freedom of choice. (1966: 84)

The absent freedom of choice which Ellul notes had been the one possibility of freedom from technology in the writings of Mumford and earlier Geddes. In describing a world whose vanishing point is its complete reorganization to the principles of efficiency and mechanical automatism, Ellul (1980: 101) reveals that the individual instances of technology had advanced their hold on the organic, traditional world, becoming now a *technological system*.

Technology is the form that *techne* and power take when a certain level of complexity is reached. It appears to have its own logic, its own autonomy, and its appetite for growth and extension into other areas of life is apparently boundless. Geddes, like Mumford in his earlier writings, did not see the totalitarian structure of technology, in part because it had not elaborated to the degree of complexity or extended itself into the world to the degree that Ellul observed. Now, simple acts of personal, meaningful, that is non-trivial, decision-making in *techne* are seldom possible, for regulation, surveillance and control ensure that the power of the technological system is supreme. For example, in the industrialized nations one can no longer practice medicine as a *techne*, as an art, because of the interlocking controls of state surveillance, licensing, and the institutional needs for uniformity in diagnosis and treatment. Paradoxically, as social control of activities becomes near complete, alternatives arise, as we see in the growing popularity of alternative medicines and therapies, acupuncture, etc., but these too are swiftly regulated and standardized so that any variation from approved practice results in expulsion from the field. For example, chiropractic treatment has only since the 1980s gained a grudging admission to respectable medical practice, and now is a mainstream health profession.

The internet and world wide web were celebrated in their beginnings precisely because they allowed highly complex technological systems to be used individually, as acts of *techne* or art. This apparent freedom quickly became confused with issues of privacy, government control of information, surveillance, and individual rights. However, perhaps realizing on some level that, as Winner (1985: 36) wrote, 'the greatest latitude of choice exists the very first time a particular instrument, system, or technique is introduced', some sought to arrest the inevitable development of the system and its solidifying into more efficient and lucrative forms. Manifestos and calls to maintain the free status of the internet are naïve, for the very amount of data and the geometrical growth in the number of sites challenge the social powers, much as radio challenged government and capital half a century earlier. The development of AOL and the early, abortive blueprints for MSN heralded the restructuring of the internet into more orderly cooperative domains that will surely emerge.

Much is already appearing in social discussion about the limiting and controlling effect that the Microsoft Paladin system will introduce through extensive use of certificates in connections and in software. But we need not wait for software to seal the cracks of the internet. Already, e-books, e-zines, and especially advertising with its ubiquitous pop-up and banner ads, are teaching a whole new generation that knowledge, news, and all other social communication, even e-mail, come with ads. Most importantly, those who think the internet sets people or information free miss the point: this 'freedom' only exists within the domains of technology and is creating, at the same time, entirely new ways of thinking, writing, plagiarizing, playing, interacting and reading which are completely suffused with the characteristics and limitations of technology.

The technological lifeworld

Within the technological system people exist in spaces that are already constructed, and they have adapted themselves to this world as simply the way things are. Even nature is manufactured in the forms of parks and green spaces, at best engineered by civil planners to provide a simulation of nature in technology's conception of it: the optimal number of the most desirable trees, the proper amount and kind of grass, etc. In these places 'play' or 'recreation' are allowed to occur. Those activities, which Geddes (1968 [1915]) called 'instruments of vital self-education', increasingly have no place in the city or suburb. Rather, children 'are jealously watched, as potential savages, who on the least symptom of their natural activities of wig-wam building, cave-digging, stream-damming, and so on must instantly be chevied away and are lucky if not handed over to the police' (1968 [1915]: 97).

Urban planning or 'urban renewal' destroys the architectural memory of the city and of the people who lived there. Hillman (1989: 185) quite rightly characterizes this as terrorism and links it to the displacement of a symbolic system that can contain and express the experiences which have traditionally defined the human. Illich notes that in the ancient world the ritual space of the city had to be undone as a social creation, but now 'architects can only condemn it and bury it under cement. And, as the world is cemented over, dwelling space is extinguished' (1985: 19). Being no longer a social creation but the product of technology, the city is made and unmade through the application of techniques, with no recognition of the human except as people's 'needs' have been quantified.

Just as public spaces are transformed, private spaces, too, are reworked into the form of the technological. The space of the home is made over in new rational ways. Giedion observes that:

> the satisfaction and delight that were medieval comfort have their source in the configuration of space. Comfort is the atmosphere with which man surrounds himself and in which he lives. Like the medieval Kingdom of God, it is something that eludes the grasp of hands. Medieval comfort is the comfort of space. (1970 [1948]: 301)

Space, however, cannot be manufactured, it can only be occupied and its containers engineered. The products of design, mass production, and desire recreated the home and the individual spaces within it: hearth became kitchen became food preparation area. Whereas once the place in which meals were prepared was a social, and gendered, center of the house, it has become increasingly the place to locate the machines and 'resources' for food where individual objects of consumption are taken from the freezer to the microwave.

The technological world is a world of constant change but always change in one direction: towards control exercised by the extension of sight and electronic connectedness through space, that is, through action at a distance. This extension is acquired not only through the ever more ubiquitous CCTV cameras, which extend the centralized control of the police for the purpose of providing more 'security'. Rather, every aspect of telecommunications tends to draw one away from the local and concrete and into participation with a social world which cannot be physically present and which is desirable because it is more immediate, more changeable, more ephemeral, and finally more entertaining than the real. The duration of the physical world gives way to the instantaneous transmission of the new. The immediacy of electronics brings what Virilio (1986b; 1997) called the vector of speed into the world and hence accelerated the disappearance of the physical world; what appears on the screen is more real and important than the physical space or inhabited place. He writes that 'teletechnologies of real time are ... killing "present" time by isolating it from its here and now in favor of a commutative elsewhere' (1997: 10–11).

Applied to consumer communications, the technological system outlined by Ellul took two forms. On the one hand, those domains of human communication that could be converted into the new forms were increasingly translated but with changes to their aesthetic form and social function which were derived from the media of technology itself. The social story which might once have been told around a dinner table or the hearth was first syndicated in newspapers, then shown at the nickelodeon, later broadcast on the radio, more recently projected on the television, and now watched as videotape or DVD. As newer technologies of communication emerge, they extend into new niches of human life and so transform them. The presence of a television, video games, and a VCR/DVD in an automobile for the amusement of children would have been an excess only a few years ago, but now is becoming common, as is the necessity of having not only a television for each individual in the family but also strategically placed sets throughout the home.

The current wave of communication technologies carries the extension of internet connections into every home, office, shop, and school, which of course guarantees the education of almost every person into using the new systems, allowing the old ways of doing things face-to-face, in libraries, in offices, to be increasingly phased out in the interests of corporate efficiency. Banks can then close branches, government offices can reduce staff and public hours; all questions and concerns can be speedily addressed online. Unless, of course, one has a question which is not locatable among the menus and submenus of the website or which does not appear among the options on the automatic telephone switching system. Then the consumer realizes that it is not that the query is poorly formed or the question wrong, but rather that one's reality simply is not recognized by the system. Rephrase your question into something recognized by the system, or give up in frustration and go away.

The new technologies and media have become an indispensable part of everyday life. The evolution of telephonic communication provides a clear example of how human activity and people themselves are brought within the technological system, and it reveals as well the convergences of technologies taking place with the telephone. The contemporary telephone incorporates digital technologies which are useful not only because of clarity and the reduction in needed band-width, but because digitizing the telephone system paves the way for incorporating other digital technologies. Caller ID, voicemail, text messaging, automatic call-back: the range of telephonic options not only complicates verbal communication by systematizing it, it also 'modernizes poverty' (see Illich 1973) by essentially requiring more and more money to be spent on systems and features which come to be seen as essential to life. The current 3G or third generation of cellular telephones incorporate digital imaging, internet, and games into the telephone, and tout the coming technologies of real-time music and video over cellular phones – effectively merging radios and television, which were cheap to buy and cheap or free to use, with cellular phones, which require contracts, equipment upgrades, and (with the new features) new subscription services.

The expansion and merger of communication technologies continue the consolidation of the social as a whole. For an example, the new E911 (extended emergency services) now introduced in the US cellular phone system provides the location of the caller's phone, and already some manufacturers are incorporating global positioning system devices into the phone just as they have been incorporated into cars. The idea, of course, is that the phone is there for one's convenience, safety, etc. Here the virtues of technology sneak in: one is always capable of contacting others, but therefore one is always contactable; one need never be alone, for isolation and loneliness are too reminiscent of the alienation and scarcity of meaningful social contact in everyday life for many people. So, one purchases ever more advanced communications to be more efficient, more contactable, more wired into the system.

The characteristics of technology in its contemporary form do not derive solely from technology itself. Rather, the attributes of technology are bound to other social systems of ideology, thought, and representation. For example, the E911 service is useful for locating persons who might be unable to give their location to emergency services, but it also eliminates the invisibility of location which had pleased those seeking privacy and troubled authorities. The OnStar automobile system links cars with the manufacturer, allowing the car to be traced if stolen, opened if accidentally locked, etc., but also allowing insurance companies and intelligence agencies to track individual cars' routes and locations, plot the speed of travel, surreptitiously monitor conversations in the car, and so on. Each piece of technology, together with technology as a system, works with the other beliefs toward creating a unified totality that does not admit for variance.

Technological language

As technology alters the world in which people live, so also it changes their perception, their thoughts, and hence the viability of their previous symbolic orderings of their world. This is not simple technological determinism. Rather, a dialectical relationship exists between the structures of meaning and the concrete expressions of technology. The world that we create becomes the world that we inhabit and upon which our subsequent thoughts and actions are, at least in part, contingent. Changes in the symbolic ordering of the world, although they may occur rapidly, are not instantaneous, and technology outruns the capacity of law, regulation, and other 'brakes' to slow it down. Thus, significant gaps continue to develop between the existing social world and technology. These gaps are quickly bridged by the transfer of technical terms and concepts into the social world, so bringing about an adaptation of the social to the needs of technology. Manfred Stanley refers to the technological ordering of language as technicism, which he defines as:

> a state of mind that rests on an act of conceptual misuses, reflected in myriad linguistic ways, of scientific and technological modes of reasoning. This misuse results in the illegitimate extension of scientific and technological reasoning to the point of imperial dominance over all other interpretations of human experience. (1978: 12)

Technology dramatically alters our understanding of the world both by becoming the object of the world and through assimilating language into its goals and values. At the beginning of the electronic age, we have turned to seeing information as something having a being in the world, an essence. However, it would be more precise to say that mediated information stands in place of the world. It is easy to become confused: we believe that we are speaking about the world, but we are speaking about a world which technology has already structured, and this changes the functioning of symbolic language in important ways.

Ellul observes that 'the technological system is a real universe, which constitutes *itself* as a symbolic system' (1980: 177). Thus, the world is already constituted in regular forms according to the *telos* of the technological system. The world appears to us as already symbolic. There is no real world behind the symbols, only the simulation of a real world, as Baudrillard (1983) has argued. The elaboration of symbolic meanings about the world is replaced with a circulation of signifiers which no longer refer to real world beyond themselves but instead obscure the fact that the real is no longer present in language or in consciousness.

Encompassed within the technological, we will write new stories about the stories; metacommentaries and exegeses will flourish. We will make pictures of pictures. We already do, and the pastiche, parody, and irony inherent in a world already filled with images has been one of the central aesthetic themes of modernist art and aesthetics from the first decades of the twentieth century. Marcel Duchamp, observing an industrial art show, is reported to have said, 'Painting is finished. Who can do any better than this propeller? Can you?'. The displacement of the object of a language, in this case art, changed the practice of art. The only way to escape from technology was to break out of it: 'When railing against the dominance of instrumental reason, the aesthetic consciousness of modernity always admitted its allegiance to "another state of being", i.e., to the explosive break or rupture with the continual inertia of linear social development' (Scherpe 1987: 98).

Technological systems introduce developments from outside a given local society which intrude in such ways as to be uncontainable in meaning; these developments are senseless and no language can contain and bind them meaningfully to the reality of ordinary people. Historically, when new technological systems have appeared, there was initially an attempt to grasp the meaning of the new in time-honored, culture-hallowed symbolic forms which inevitably prove inadequate to the task. The paradoxes raised by the emergence of modern technology proved finally insoluble in any coherent and consistent way. An intolerable tension arises between two symbolic systems, one coming from the rationality of technology, the other from the disorderly domain of human existence and its lengthy history of religious, aesthetic, and philosophical thought. The tension between these two spawns new myths which work to prevent resolution. As the twentieth century began, Henry Adams

> proclaimed that in the last synthesis, order and anarchy were one, but that the unity was chaos. As anarchist, conservative and Christian, he had no motive or duty but to attain the end; and, to hasten it, he was bound to accelerate progress; to concentrate energy; to accumulate power; to multiply and intensify forces; to reduce friction, increase velocity and magnify momentum, partly because this was the mechanical law of the universe as science explained it; but partly also in order to get done with the present which artists and some others complained of; and finally – and chiefly – because a rigorous philosophy required it, in order to penetrate the beyond, and satisfy man's destiny by reaching the largest synthesis in its ultimate contradiction. (1961 [1918]: 406)

Adams neatly captured the conflict that a world view of instrumental rationality created for human beings. He explicitly recognized that within the framework of the dominant philosophy of technique, resistance is inherently irrational.

If resistance to the current situation results in defeat or stalemate, another response to the totalizing effect of technology might be another form of escape. This is another aspect of the problem which appeared to von Schlieffen as the *Einkreisung* (encirclement) that he sought to break through, the stasis that the Futurists sought to outrun, the tyranny of meaning that the Dadaists sought to shred and the Surrealists to outflank (see Kern 1983).

With technology, once the inadequacy of traditional, normative language is established, one has no alternative but to chase after technology, seeking to experience through it. We find the technological gaze on the television, the periscope, the microscope, the CAT scan; and increasingly the image defines what we are. Our age 'knows itself from the reflections that flow from the camera's eye' (Denzin 1991: 155). This condition arises because:

> language must itself be integrated into the system in order to play its role. Hence, the structuralist studies of language, which are precisely characteristic of that technicization; hence, likewise, the trend toward viewing the text as an entity in itself, an object. And the orientation toward focusing on *how* one says something rather than on *what* one says, in order to demonstrate technologically. (Ellul 1980: 116)

Extreme technicism, that is, the subordination of language to technology, not only appears in representational language but comes to infuse other traditional modes of organizing the world as well. Technique dominates the aesthetics of the popular in every domain. After Warhol the magazine becomes a parody of its own immolation in an exclusive concentration on style, technique, and the immediate. House, trance and techno music reiterate the rhythms of the machine, while the contrary examples of punk, grunge, and so on are, in their beginnings at least, reactions to the constraints of the system and, after that, simply more, commodified, prepackaged forms of expression.

The Social and the Self

Technology has transformed the world and the language with which we understand and symbolically manipulate it. As a consequence, social relations and institutions are changed as well, and the subjectivity of people existing within these relations and positioned by these discourses is similarly altered. Such changes have profound implications for how the social, the individual, and the ethics of engagement between them should be formulated. Partly in reaction to the technologizing of those disciplines such as sociology and psychology and their growing focus on human reality as quantifiable phenomena, other branches of knowledge have split off. Cultural studies, symbolic interactionism, social psychology, social anthropology, media studies, and a range of other interpretive approaches to culture have arisen in attempts to explain the technological changes to the social world and to theorize how questions of freedom, gender, race, class, and identity might now be articulated and studied, but few outside the academic world take them very seriously. And in truth, such disciplines are not much use for the main business of contemporary education: vocational education for technical employment.

Still the old cultural institutions stumble on through the new world, translating the mythic ideas and social beliefs of eras into the contemporary articulations of power, but all of the old institutions are in crisis. Schools, universities, churches, law courts, congresses and parliaments, police forces and prisons: all the institutions formed and developed prior to the emergence of the technological system are struggling to reinvent themselves. This recreating of the old forms of power is more than churches erecting websites or lawmakers trying to legislate new policies about intellectual property. Whatever cannot be translated into the new technical rationalistic language will necessarily be marginalized, excluded from serious social notice and comment, and threatened with extinction. Some of the older institutions translate fairly well into the new forms: law enforcement and incarceration industries are perfectly adaptable to the new technologies. Supermax prisons incorporate the latest in automated systems for controlling every aspect of the inmate's life, and in Columbus, Ohio, police used helicopters with FLIR (forward looking infra-red) imaging systems to beam real-time images of rioting students to mobile C3 (command, control, communication) vans which in turn coordinate deployment of ground troops – Desert Storm in domestic miniature. However, other institutions, such as churches, are socially useful to the technological system only to the extent that they can lend moral mythologizing to the contemporary forms of power and so contribute to the orderliness of the social.

The face-to-faceness which formed the basis of 2000 years of thought about the nature of the social, the form and function of the *polis*, and the role of government has been disappearing since the beginnings of the great social migrations of the 1820s, and little has emerged to replace the 'affection and attachment' (see Dewey 1985b [1927]) upon which social life and the subjectivity of the individual were traditionally formed. Although new technologies of communication create communities organized around shared thoughts and feelings, in the end these are communities that can disappear with the flick of a switch, feelings that need never be tested in the world, and thoughts that have no ontological grounding outside mass mediated language. Indeed, people are arguably more isolated, more depressed, and more alienated in direct proportion to the amount of their life that they shift from spending with real people to spending with television, the internet, the radio.

To be plain, the world in which people once elaborated themselves no longer exists. The self that Mead (1962 [1934]), Blumer (1969) and others studied and theorized through the high modernist era was a product of its involvement in ongoing social activities, acts of social symbolizing, exchanges of symbolic recognition. Yet as shown above, the conditions for creating that kind of self no longer exist. New selves emerge, but these lack the institutional frameworks that would give them stability, the social history that would give them a political praxis, and the grounding in a language that is more than the consumption of self-referential signs. The new selves articulate themselves in part by taking up the languages and rationalities of technology, spawning wholly new possibilities of being in the world while at the same time inscribing their relationships to eternally renewing technologies.

Thus, we find that we coexist between two worlds: the world of lived experience of the real, grounded for a short time longer in the experiences of the body, already proclaimed technologically changed by some (see Haraway 1991); and the world of representation, simulation (Baudrillard 1983), and substitution (Virilio 1994). Yet as the social increasingly becomes representational and is transformed into an aesthetic experience, so the body and the domain of experience are transformed as well. For a while they will continue to function as the 'real' before becoming merely the half remembered mythic experience underlying the new real, obscuring the fact that the realm of the body will no longer exist.

Fixed within the eternal *nunc stans* of the represented world and the social discourses which have been elaborated from it, consciousness has no historical natural past to which it may return. Neither is there an organic body still visible from our perspective; we have only the body without organs. Sex itself disappears into virtuality (Virilio 1997). Caught like flies in amber, we find that a common solution is to quit being flies, to dissolve the self or at least to accept that the self is not the consistent, centered whole which was promised by the popular mythologies. Deleuze and Guattari write that 'no longer are there acts to explain, dreams and phantasies to interpret ... words to make signify; instead, there are colors and sounds, becomings and intensities. There is no longer a Self [*Moi*] that feels, acts and recalls' (1987: 162).

The writer Philip K. Dick developed this theme of the loss of the self in artificial constructs in several fictional works, and of these developments in the world he wrote:

> Perhaps, really, what we are seeing is a gradual merging of the general nature of human activity and function into the activity and function of what we humans have built and surround[ed] ourselves with ... But now we find ourselves immersed in a world of our own making so intricate, so mysterious, that as Stanislaw Lem the eminent Polish science fiction writer theorizes, the time may come when, for example, a man may have to be restrained from attempting to rape a sewing machine. (1995: 184)

In Dick's account, everything from the contemporary world is present: substitution, desire, mechanization. The fictional account of a man trying to rape a sewing machine is not substantively different from a man having sex with an image on the computer screen. The screen, the image, and the desire emerge together into the mediated world. The implications of this confusion are explored in more detail through the following chapters, but I should note here that unless we recognize the role of technology in transforming both the means of seeing and the world that is seen, we risk an endless confusion of means and ends.

If our interactions with the world are no longer straightforward, neither are our relationships with other people or even with ourselves. Technology, and particularly the technologies of communication, has so mediated and transformed both our subjectivity and the objects of our perception that some writers, such as Haraway (1991), have argued that a new metaphor is required to replace the now obsolete metaphor of humanity: the cyborg, a half-human, half-machine entity. 'Cyborgs are post-organic creatures in our unchosen "high-technological" guise as information systems, texts, and ergonomically controlled labouring, desiring, and reproducing systems' (1991: 1). Cyborgs arise in relationship to a similarly technological world. Haraway continues: 'The second essential ingredient in cyborgs is machines in their guise, also, as communications system, texts, and self-acting, ergonomically designed apparatuses' (1991: 1). Only such a creature could inhabit the new world which is itself machine masquerading as nature, and for Haraway, only such a creature has the potential to create new freedoms out of the patriarchal, militaristic, dominating oppressions of the social.

Numerous analysts have discussed in detail the fragmentation of the social sphere and of the narratives and selves of people within it (for example, Denzin 1991: 24–8; Haraway 1991; Turner 1990: 71–7). The failure of dominant discourses within the social to be able to define the world with the power that they once had creates absences that are filled with new processes. Whereas people previously were positioned by the discursive formations primarily located within institutions that could define social reality, now the responsibility for positioning the self in discourse is shifting increasingly to the individual. Gilles Deleuze (1992) writes of the 'corporatism' which has come to augment the governmentality and confinements documented in the writings of Michel Foucault. The contemporary self is fragmented in part through the multiple processes in which the self can come into being, the multiple domains into which consciousness can project itself in language and representation. As I shall show later, this multiplicity of selves creates real conflicts in people's lives. Selves created within the representational realities of electronic media, for example, may have fundamentally different values and beliefs from selves elaborated in the company of other people.

Yet other strategies exist for living within and perhaps resisting the technologizing of the world, the social and the self. New communities are theorized and constituted in the physical world as well as online (Rheingold 1993). New personal strategies continue to emerge in resistance to the commodification of language and the social (for example, Fiske 1989). Still, the compelling theoretical problems facing any study of communication technologies remain the extent to which virtuality and the other epiphenomena of technology constitute a new social domain, as opposed to merely an extension of old epistemologies (Levy 1998), and the extent to which these significantly alter the world of personal experience, power, and social action.

We define ourselves in the systems of aesthetics, fashion, wealth, desire, and sex as these are structured for us in advertising, entertainment, and mass production. Certainly, people have the ability to make choices from within these systems; we are not 'cultural dupes' or powerless automatons (see Denzin 1992). While there may be numerous ways in which people transform, resist, and create local cultures out of elements of modern, capitalist, global commodity production, the limits of these choices, the parameters within which they may be made, are well policed by both the people around us and the various institutions responsible for maintaining order and 'normalcy', such as law enforcement, psychology and psychiatry, and education. We may choose what we like from the range of commodified desires, meanings, and identities, but the limits of permissible freedom are defined in consumption of commodities (Baudrillard 1981; 1990). Real choice is limited by what is already approved and permitted; the modern self is largely *prêt-à-porter* and what we perceive as choice is little more than accessorizing the wardrobe or wearing it in unusual ways. The contemporary self is manufactured; the advertising of it is our education into the social and into public languages; and the purchasing of it drives the economies of late capitalism.

TWO

Technologies of Language: Writing, Reading, and the Text

In the realm of poverty of imagination where people die of spiritual famine without feeling spiritual hunger, where pens are dipped in blood and swords in ink, that which is not thought must be done, but that which is only thought is unutterable. (Kraus 1984: 71)

The New Age of Orality

If there is so much regularity and uniformity of media, why is there no coherent social formed with and within it? The dream of an informed democratic polity seems as distant today as it ever did. In a slightly different form the same question was asked by John Dewey in 1927 in his response to Walter Lippmann's *Public Opinion*. Dewey sought the reason why the 'great community' had not come into being despite movies, radio, trains, and the other early mass technologies. As these technologies certainly organized people socially, and as they facilitated the transmission of both ideas and people, one might well assume they would help to create a well-organized and informed people.

We have everywhere, we are told, the tools and technologies to create a world in which the electronic town meeting, to use Ross Perot's malapropism, is both desirable and possible. Yet the great mass constellations of belief and social action have taken place not in the organization of an informed and active political public but in the creation of armies, as seen in two world wars, and great masses of generally uniformed consumers. There are as well other, more subtle organizations of the social – not around narratives and politics but around aesthetics and feeling states. One sees the popularity of Samuel Barber's *Adagio for Strings* and the 'O, Fortuna' from Orff's *Carmina Burana* appearing in film and television commercials. These latter are not known as high art, and are rarely seen in terms of the contexts of ideas and aesthetic in which they emerged. Rather, they appear as cultural tropes of affect and shared pathos in the service of advertising or as background to movies such as *Platoon*.

The fate of the public is similar to the fate of the physical world in the era of digital communications. One is asked in the Microsoft advertisement, 'Where do you want to go today?', and one is exhorted by AT&T to 'Reach out and touch someone' on the telephone. Such statements are not just hyperbole; they are also strangely revealing in promising precisely what the particular technologies cannot deliver. The obvious action one cannot perform on a phone is touch someone, and the missing potential of the internet is the mobility to take one somewhere. In this deliberate irony such technologies reveal not a liberating potential but their circulation in the economy of signs. Just as TV dinners cannot create domestic harmony but point to one of the key sites in the loss of domesticity, so communication technologies cannot create communities but only point toward their impending extinction through the duplicitous promise of creating them.

Literacy

In the same manner, the constant reinvention of literacy in various areas of culture points toward the loss of a prior kind of literacy. Numeracy, computer literacy, video literacy, cultural literacy: the metaphor runs out of control. The education business proposes to deliver various forms of literacies for the new needs of technology, but it only succeeds in demonstrating the disappearance of another form of literacy. The missing literacy is not the ability to read but the mental competence to internalize cultural stories, images, and narratives as ideas and to examine them in a critical way. This would involve not educating people about how to make or 'read' films and TV but creating a social world in which reality is not primarily a manufactured commodity to be dispensed and consumed. Further, such a competence would require a vernacular language, a language grounded in one's lived experience within which to form the critiques in ways that were personally meaningful. This critical faculty requires the ability to differentiate one's sense of self from his or her participation in and identification with commodity culture.

The proliferations of literacies do little to remedy the underlying problem: that technical and social complexities of everyday life demand extreme degrees of expertise to achieve the smallest competencies. Rather than uniting people into societies and communities, the expertise itself establishes new values and displaces older ones. Speed, efficiency, and modernity itself undermine the possibilities of meaning and attachments between people and their world. As Nye notes, people 'quickly come to see new technologies, such as electric lights, space shuttles, computers, or satellites, as "natural". At the same time, the lifeworlds constructed with older objects ... begin to slide toward incomprehensibility, as those who created that landscape pass away' (1996: 180). The mediation of technological communication renders gratuitous the obligations and mutual respect of people as a feeling rather than as a pragmatic necessity. One does not 'flame' others with e-mail, not because one feels a sense of respect for others but because to do so would demonstrate poor 'netiquette' and so mark one as a 'newbie', a dilettante, and a non-expert. Membership in the technological social is predicated on technical performance, and virtue is evaluated in related terms.

A meaningful social and political world would require that each person was involved in some way with the totality of that world. Politics limited to a minor corner of the world is by definition parochial and narrow, as it was when Mill wrote, 'the world, to each individual, means the part of it with which he comes into contact: his sect, his church, his class of society' (1987 [1859]: 77). Individual people cannot be concerned with the common good but only with their self-interests, or at best with the immediately local. Such localism of thought and values is different from the isolation of the preindustrial hamlet or village, for in such settings there is often a necessity for communal politics. We, however, cannot share in even a small fraction of the totality of our society, and as such we are driven to individualism. Within a society that seeks to organize itself in narrowly rational ways, the purpose of individualism – and this is true since the introduction of the word in 1760 – is 'social refusal and self-indulgence' (Saul 1992: 473). The individual as a whole person has no place in a highly specialized society. The only choices are to surrender whole-heartedly to the social or to resist by refusing to participate, by refusing to be efficient, by resisting providing information. One wonders if the sudden rise of privacy as a personal and legal issue, quite apart from the minor matter of economic fraud, arises now because it removes the last great tactic of individual resistance to the social: the refusal to provide accurate and complete information.

The rise of specialisms of all kinds fragments the social world into narrow and unconnected domains of expertise and interests, and the knowledges required to exercise specialisms in activities such as consuming and using things are different from the knowledges required to make things. At the same time, the social refusal of the individual to participate in a shared world, the obstinate clinging to opinions in the face of social facts, produces isolated pockets of mutually negotiated self-interest. Two factors, then, mitigate against the formation of a viable sense of community and commonweal in modern society: structural fragmentation and the concomitant formation of localized and largely unconnected social worlds. Thus Dewey could write, 'There is too much public, a public too diffused and scattered and too intricate in composition' (1985b [1927]: 137).

This narrowing of the social and isolation of people from one another reduce the diversities of human life to simple encapsulations which provide the form but seldom the substance of an idea. For example, in teaching it is difficult to get students to examine complex arguments that they then understand and can use outside the context of the exam or term paper. Rather, many favor 'dot point' condensations of books and articles for which they must 'be responsible' (as if they were baby sitting or taking care of someone's dog) in examination and feel cheated when one does not provide this for them. On the one hand, there is nothing especially new about this; many of the early 'books' of ancient Greece, the *biblos*, were not books at all but fragments and statements used as guides and supplements to oral teachings (Havelock 1976: 69). What differs, however, is that the contemporary student has the books, and the oral lecture is extension, elucidation, and exegesis. Rather than the oral being a guide through the written, a condensed, epigrammatic form of the written is again demanded as a guide through the oral. In a strange sense, we are creating an epistemological and interactional topography that is similar to classical Athens but differs in some profound and puzzling ways.

Manufactured Social Language and the Hyper-real

As Giddens notes, 'modernity opens up the project of the self, but under conditions strongly influenced by standardizing effects of commodity capitalism' (1991: 196). Culture is, by and large, a product financed by detergents, automobile manufacturers, and pharmaceutical companies, and supported by the increasingly privatized education and information industries. By virtue of making it onto television screens, the radio, the lifestyle pages (increasingly simply called 'style'), cultural artifacts become worth knowing and worth knowing about. Whatever falls below the culture industry radar is counter-cultural, overly specialized, or simply not worth knowing as it fails to be entertaining. As Neil Postman observed, mass media have made entertainment itself 'the natural format for the presentation of experience.' (1987: 87). This shared social experience of entertainment transmits and reiterates all the important messages of the culture, and, in so doing, helps to create people who expect life to be entertaining, to be a spectacle (Debord 1990), and who will tolerate any illogic to continue the show. Entertainment becomes the hyper-real (Baudrillard 1983).

The most stunning illogic concerns the reality of the show itself and the extent to which cultural productions are taken as models of the real. The 'cinematic society' (Denzin 1995) defines itself and the audience in ideologically determined structures of visual representation. What can be seen is important, but all that is produced is the representation, the image of the thing, never the thing itself. Our experience of what is important about the world is thus constructed representationally through a fraudulent mimesis (1995: 199). Yet this imitation appears more real than real and so competes directly with other forms of reality. As a consequence of the 'cinematization of American society', Denzin explains, 'reality, as it was visually experienced, became a staged social production. Real, everyday experiences, soon came to be judged against their staged, cinematic, video-counterpart' (1995: 32). He continues, 'the metaphor of the dramaturgical society or "life as Theater" ceased to be just a metaphor. It became an interactional reality. Life and art became mirror images of one another' (1995: 32). Yet the text is the authority; it is that which is worth remembering, worth repeating, and worth paying for.

The purpose of texts within the cinematic society is to provide templates for thought and action. We live in a world of mimesis; imitation functions as a social and psychological norm despite the fact that everyone 'knows' that the representations are not real. Still, these imitations of people, of situations, and of the world stand as substitutes for the physical world and structure our perceptions, understandings, and expectations. As Blumer (1933) documented and as the writers of 1930s film magazines demonstrated, people compare their lives to what they see on the screen, and they model this behavior in their own lives. In part through this mimesis and in part through the substitution of a learned language for a vernacular, the subjectivity of the represented other becomes the subjectivity of the viewer (See Denzin 1995: 199). In this way, an identification takes place which is similar to the mimetic identification which characterizes oral cultures, as I will show later in this chapter. The end of this imitation is the replacement of older subjectivities with new ones finally better suited to living with the constantly changing, Cartesian 'evil deceiver' of the simulacrum.

The derealization of the world

The spectacular, cinematic, virtual world brings about a 'derealization' of the world. The representational world is organized not around the everyday experiences of people, but around the distilled, formalized expressions of power in culture, and as people orient themselves to these structures, those prior structurings of thought and experience are devalued and lost. Externalized language becomes the template for thought (Olson 1994). From the standpoint of what had been, this new creation looks like a kind of destruction. Thus, Paul Virilio (1994) explains this process as a 'wounding of the real' which subsequently wounds everyone who takes part:

> This phenomenon is similar to madness. The mad person is wounded by his or her distorted relationship to the real. Imagine that all of a sudden I am convinced that I am Napoleon: I am no longer Virilio, but Napoleon. My reality is wounded. Virtual reality leads to a similar de-realization. However, it no longer works only at the scale of individuals, as in madness, but at the scale of the world. (1994)

The issue of scale is crucial, for the sheer amount of words and statements which one receives every day in a modern industrial society largely guarantees that almost nothing encountered in the world comes without its own, ready-made meanings and a preferred relationship toward us. These implicate both the individual person and the thing so encountered within already established social relations. As a consequence, the ability quickly to determine the form of this relationship is a major social skill and the key to successful shopping.

Words and images, already ordered and structured into easily recognizable forms, displace content. What matters is the surface, and there is no time to look further as a new construction, complete in its merging of sound, image, and text, is already present, displacing and updating the previous one. A variety of devices are used to construct the 'preferred' understanding. Genre, author, source, medium, format (see Barthes 1972 [1958]; Foucault 1984) all limit the range of possible meanings and guide one to the 'intended' relationship with the word. This occurs largely without the need for conscious thought, for the grammars of video, music, text – that is, the grammars required for mentally inhabiting the spectacular society – are second nature before one starts school.

The dominant, visual media of cinema and television operate primarily through the retelling of national and cultural myths and narratives (Ray 1985). As the studios created cinema and video, they also created the subjects who would expect and take pleasure from these forms. The illocutionary function of music, films, and public language overwhelms all other functions. Oriented toward the visual, the major media must be optically tasty, giving rise to phrases like 'eye candy' to refer to women's bodies used gratuitously to please male viewers. Even those films and videos which do not rely on overstated technical effects for audience appeal still rely on their ability to please visually and thematically. The first pleasure of the cinematic text must be visual before any other identification can take place between the viewer and the screen. The viewer's identification is predicated on the deliberate acceptance of what is on the screen as directly experienced, that is as an *interior* and personal experience that is at the same moment shared by his or her participation in the constructed event. The experience of the viewer is already situated within meaning. One is shown what he or she enjoys through the structuring of that pleasure in a particular narrative and visual form.

There is not a widespread personal examination and introspection about the cinematic experience. Indeed to have a truly personal interpretation is to withdraw from the shared experience of the media event, to be outside the social. Rather, one relates his or her life to the cinematic experience which is already a shared social domain. One has already been told what to feel and think about it, that is, how to consume the event. This is, indeed, the primary function of popular criticism and reviews: to give the dominant or preferred reading (see Denzin 1991). The cultural logic of the cinematic world is to encourage the extension of the experience and lessons of the film into the lived world, to emulate the relationships, feelings, and values of the narratives. This translation of the cultural narrative into the personal world is never a direct, 'hypodermic' effect. Rather, people work the thematic elements into their lives and personal relationships through interpretive acts which remake these into forms with more local and personal meanings (Hebdige 1979; Fiske 1989).

The restructuring of cultural forms and the experience of living through them become the primary way for people to be in the world. The constant interpretation of the cinematic consumer world and the concomitant reconfiguration of the self to fit the latest images and stories induce a detachment from the world. Louis Sass (1992) discovers in contemporary experiences of culture 'a loose sort of unity'. He identifies:

not a single underlying presence but at least a common thread or two. These have to do with the presence of intensified forms of self-consciousness and various kinds of alienation. Instead of a spontaneous and naïve involvement – an unquestioning acceptance of the external world, the aesthetic tradition, other human beings and one's own feelings – both modernism and postmodernism are imbued with hesitation and detachment, a division or doubling in which the ego disengages from normal forms of involvement with nature and society, often taking itself, or its experiences, as its own object. (1992: 37)

It is as if people living in the modern world are trapped between a cultural logic that demands the presence of the 'real' in the world and the simultaneous location of that real in one's own desire and experience. The identification of self through the signs of commodity culture encompasses the entire world in a solipsism that can never be completed.

Contemporary orality

The level of dramatic identification in archaic cultures is similar to what one finds in the spectacular or cinematic culture. One finds a tendency toward an almost pathological identification with the narratives, stories, characters, and situations of contemporary media which rivals the psychic participation in the narratives of archaic cultures. Yet we are not an oral or archaic culture in this sense. Our sense of ourselves derives from widely shared social symbols, but we encounter these primarily in highly mediated forms while the personal and local domain forms the sites at which we practice and perform these selves. We have fairly high levels of literacy in all the modern nations of the world, but we have lost faith in the power of the written word and of social signification to deliver the presence of reality, to stop once and for all the endless train of signification (Barthes 1970: 48). Whereas once a consensual social reality, told in myth and story, connected the transcendent to the everyday, no transcendent ordering lies behind language and society, and without such a notion of truth, opinion and propaganda are as good as fact.

No longer existent in the social realm, truth is now located in the illusion of a socially isolated self. Entire industries for shaping, motivating, educating, and maintaining the modern self have emerged from the fields of advertising, psychology, cosmetics, and pharmacology. These and other institutions devoted to the self force consciousness inward in an unending examination and in attempts at improvement to produce the presence of the real. Various forms of sex and sexuality are especially well suited for this convoluted inversion, for they provide the commodified social forms of consumption (clothes, fragrance, activities, prostitutes, cyber sex) as well as the possibilities of various intensities of experience which, in their momentary dissolution of self, can masquerade as genuine, natural, unstructured experience (see Deleuze and Guattari 1987: 162). J.G. Ballard writes that 'many people ... use sex as a calculated means of exploring uncertainties in their make-up, exploiting the imaginative possibilities that sex provides' (1990: 54). One finds that 'dimestore De Sades stalk the bedrooms of suburbia, reenacting the traumas of weaning and potty training'.

Part of the problem of creating a self in the contemporary, hyper-real world arises from the way in which language and symbols are experienced. Not only are the narratives mimetic, but experience itself is mimetic, for the experienced world exists not in a direct way but as a substitution and simulation based on ideological constructions. This condition did not come into being overnight but evolved slowly as technologies of reading, writing, and thinking evolved in particular cultural contexts. These do not exist separate from consciousness but are interwoven with it. A word must be heard, a book read, an idea shared. Human beings meet each other on the field of perception, but the rules of engagement are framed by language, and this language has grown more remote from the human and more external to experience with each new technology applied to it. While the benefits of a generalized, shared language are indubitable, the principles upon which that language is organized and promulgated, together with the exclusion of other forms of language from the decision-making processes of the shared social world and from the speech of ordinary people, limit thought, perception, and the self to a relatively few forms (see, for example, Weiner 1954).

Harold Innis (1950; 1951) elaborated the importance of alternative languages of social expression in terms of achieving a balance between time-binding and space-binding media. Time-binding media are those best suited to preserving ideas across time, to providing a duration, and they tend to dominate in conservative, religious, hierarchical societies. Space-binding media are better suited to the transmission of ideas through space and are essential for the construction and maintenance of empires. In Innis' view, in order for a culture to grow and thrive in a stable way, there must be a balance between those media that preserve ideas and resist change and those that democratize, transform, and spread ideas. In other words, there must be some 'dynamic harmony between technology and culture' (Kroker 1984: 104). The industrial West, in Innis' analysis, was highly biased toward the spatial media which gave them monopolies of communication in time; newspapers divided the world into days, the television and radio fragment it into minutes and seconds, and, extending Innis' argument, the computer grants control of micro and nano time, creating finally a 'real time' as a new domain. Meanwhile, those institutions which preserve and repair reality across time (Carey 1989) grow increasingly marginalized: the courts, the church, and face-to-face communication.

Innis identified and updated an uncertainty about the meeting of otherness and interiority which has resonated through Western thought since at least the time of Socrates. The contemporary world has, however, become more complicated since Innis' day. Technology has become the experience of nature both in what we see and in the templates of understanding that we bring to it. As such, language itself becomes another thing, and the bringers of language are 'transmitters' of information which is often only data about the world. As late as the mid seventeenth century, Milton could write that 'books are not absolutely dead things'. The experience of language was still the experience of something ontologically similar to another person, albeit mediated in the text. Now, the traditions, institutions, and even the language that sustained and expressed the self in a counterpoise to extrinsic forms of knowledge are eroding. Those techniques which articulated a self balanced between the inwardness of eternal self-examination and the extensiveness and loss of ego boundaries in the world now lack the power to function as intermediators between the two domains. Thus, one is faced with a simple choice of trust or law, psychology or moral conviction, a hypertrophied ego from introspection or an over-extended ego from excessive projection and introjection (see Sass 1992: 222, 230).

We may call this process exteriorization: the transfer of what had been the self-regulations of psyche, ordered by learned social rules, into processes and ideas acquired from second-order systems and expressed in artificial, already structured social events. Exteriorization gives rise to increasing alienation from one's own world and one's own thoughts, feelings, and expectations. In short, a vernacular language and world have been replaced with a constructed world, and this warrants further investigation.

The acquisition of vernacular language

The institutions and discourses of every age posit the conditions within which consciousness confronts the self reflected back to it through culture. However, they also provide the processes and substance from which the reactions of consciousness to the world emerge. Consciousness thus exists in the shared social world of culture, language and symbols, but it has as well its own intentions, desires, and experiences quite independently of culture. The tension between culture and self grows proportionally to the degree of divergence between the socially constrained self and the intentions of consciousness. In oral cultures most of language would be articulated within the local, shared social life and as such would be grounded in and expressive of people's experiences. While certain structural conditions of life were certainly outside control (fate, wars, famines, etc.), the everyday expressions of how to be in the world and with other people were, if not homemade, at least locally made. Even ideas which might be imposed from outside the local, for example, Roman Catholicism or occupation by other invaders, did not necessarily profoundly or suddenly transform the everyday social negotiation of experience. Rather, social and epistemological structures coming from the outside were negotiated and translated into the local.[2]

Reading and writing, in their early development in European culture, followed this same pattern of negotiation. While contemporary writing and reading are personal, silent tasks, undertaken in some degree of privacy, the separation of these activities from the shared social domain took place only slowly and over centuries. Language as something independent of the physical presence of other people, as something which could exist as text or disembodied words, had to be slowly differentiated through a series of technologies which would separate the internal, psychological processes of language from the social settings of language. As language acquired this personal form, the self constituted within language could acquire a similar kind of independence from the social. The self could become, from the standpoint of consciousness, its own perception of the social, the starting point of all proof of existence, as in Descartes' *cogito, ergo sum*. Descartes' formulation, however, posits the field of perception as already within the shared world of language, as Merleau-Ponty (1962) has shown.

The contemporary possibilities for language and the self are fairly recent phenomena. In earlier times, language was not so transformed by mediating technologies. Speech and hearing are not, in themselves, technologies but rather ways that people are with each other in the world. We do not encounter meaning ready-made in words and gestures. Rather, the word's meaning is 'first and foremost the aspect taken on by the object in human experience' (1962: 403). Words must be situated within a learned social history of convention before they become meaningful, and this occurs through a process of imitation. We learn our tongue, the vernacular language of everyday existence and immediate expression, without formal training (see Illich 1992: 119–42). There is no art, nothing artificial or made, involved in the initial learning of language. Language is acquired in the interactions with those people around one.

As a consequence of learning language within a group which already shares a range of everyday interests, values, beliefs, and expectations, the speaker of a vernacular is integrated into the group as a vital member and participant. Classically, this language was referred to as the *patrius sermo*, 'the speech of the male head of the household' (1992: 133). The society defines itself in its words as much as in its actions, and sharing those words marks one not only as a member but as a creator and preserver of the group. Words and actions are inseparable in an oral culture, for language exists only in the context of people speaking to each other: one stands literally by his or her words.

One's world is circumscribed through the vernacular language which marks the limits of immediately shared understanding. Further, those who do not share the same language are not members of the same local community, whether that community is defined as the *domus* (the household) or as the village or town. The world in which a vernacular is spoken, precisely through the fact that it is immediately shared and negotiated in the day to day, is deeply inlaid with memories, experiences, and meanings which one shares with others and which imbue the world with depths of cultural textures. It is 'a permanent field or dimension of experience' (Merleau-Ponty 1962: 361) and so helps to shape the forms of the self in the terms of that shared understanding and history. Events resonate through time, touching people and places for generations. The interactions of people engender the meanings of their words and actions, and in so doing, create 'a certain hold upon the world' (1962: 354) in which one's self is perceived.

Whatever language might be spoken over the next mountain peak or around the next bend of the river was not the language which one learned at the family table. But still, one would likely have a knowledge of the other tongues. Illich notes that:

> communities in which monolingual people prevail are rare except in three kinds of settings: in tribal communities that have not really experienced the late neolithic period, in communities that have experienced certain intense forms of discrimination, and among the citizens of nation-states that for several generations have enjoyed the benefits of compulsory schooling. (1992: 123)

These foreign languages would also share some characteristics of the vernacular, for they would have been acquired, less fluently perhaps, in just the same ways that the mother tongue was learned: trial and error in everyday situations with other persons. One learns language without reference to formal grammars or schemata.

Vernacular language is distinguished not only by how it is learned but also by the kinds of relationships within which it develops. Vernacular language emerges between beings who recognize the necessity of mutual coexistence and who exist as equally real for each other. While there may be differentials of power between people in the social dimension, in the dimension of percep-tion all people sharing the same field of experience are familiar, and they share as well the ability to organize the reality of that world, its emergence into meaning. Merleau-Ponty writes that:

> Once the other is posited, once the other's gaze fixed upon me has, by inserting me into his field, stripped me of part of my being ... I can recover it only by establish-ing relations with him, by bringing about his clear recognition of me. (1962: 357)

The establishment of relations occurs through the use of language, and the *poiesis* so experienced is the mutual human creation of selves in the shared social world.

When one encounters another in the world, one sees the world around that person differently precisely because the other has the power to act on the world, to organize and arrange it in ways which are independent of one's self.

> No sooner has my gaze fallen upon a living body in the process of acting than objects surrounding it immediately take on a fresh layer of significance: they are no longer simply what I myself could make of them, they are what this other pattern of behavior is about to make of them. (1962: 353)

The actions of other people have the potential to be surprising, unexpected, unpredictable. Moreover, the mere fact of their existence in the world guaran-tees that the world as well will be imbued with the possibilities of their actions. In meeting others, we enter one another's worlds, each stripping the other of part of that person's being, and the only possibility of recovering that lost being is through engaging the other in mutual recognition. Such recognition is established mainly in language, in speaking.

Shared Understandings: Politics and Language

The tensions between vernacular and taught languages reveal but one example of the many social formations of language in competition with one another, and they reveal only one dimension of psychic and social differences associated with differing origins and uses of various types of language. A taught language, a 'mother tongue', could not emerge independently of the institutions of linguistic scholarship, centralized political organization, the standardization made possible by printing, and so on. In turn, these institutions were created in response to specific natural and social conditions. Some writers have, perhaps, been too quick to generalize sweeping abstractions about the psychic and social effects following from technological changes in language. The rise of writing, in particular, made possible some significant changes in the uses to which language was put and to the structural forms in which it appeared. However, writing arose in various ways in so many widely varied social contexts that generalizations about its impact as a singular event are not very revealing. Further, to attribute to writing alone the many grand changes in, for example, early Greek philosophy and politics, risks overlooking other factors which, taken as a whole, show a much more complex history.

Writing did not change history so much as it was carried along on a flood of sweeping historical changes and in turn contributed to them, becoming useful as a technology of language in the context of new ways of thinking, speaking, and organizing society. Neither were the changes assisted by writing either sudden or dramatic. For example, even after the introduction of writing, the great epics and lesser poems of Greece were told in oral form for hundreds of years. These stories, as the living cultural memory of Athens, had become by the mid fifth century BCE so well established that 'Plato could deal with poetry as though it were a kind of reference library or as a vast tractate in ethics, politics and warfare' (Havelock 1963: 43). The metaphor may be a bit of a stretch, but it illustrates that 'poets were in an important sense the preservers and transmitters of their cultural heritage' (Thomas 1992: 116). A part of the important knowledge of the Athenians was commemorated in Hesiod's *Theogeny* where he acknowledges 'the *nomoi* and *ēthea* of all', which Havelock translates as 'the custom-laws and careful/carefully kept folkways of all' (1986: 56). In turn, Xenophanes, Heraclitus, and Herodotus each cited both Homer and Hesiod as didactic partners in the education of the Greece of his day (Havelock 1982: 123).

In the cultures of early classical Greece, the story was not told for entertainment but rather acted as a 'performative utterance' of a 'verbal archetype' which supplied the group with a 'linguistic statement or paradigm, telling us what we are and how we should behave' (Havelock 1963: 41–2). Eliade explains the role of such statements, writing that in archaic cultures 'reality is acquired solely through repetition or participation; everything which lacks an exemplary model is "meaningless", i.e. it lacks reality' (1954: 34). The learning of these stories combined with their retelling in regular public and private performances ensured that the values and beliefs which they enshrined became the patterns of thought and expression that would guide the actions of the hearers. The ancient Greeks, however, elaborated social forms that to some extent superseded the necessity of repetition in favor of performance within the domain of the *polis*.

Not merely the language provided meaning and reality; for the Greeks, the context in which language was used was an inseparable component of meaning. The concrete forms of the rhetoric and discussion taking place among the members of the *polis* constituted another social center around which wholly new templates for thought, behavior, and social relations could be formed. Meier writes that:

> The Greeks enjoyed not only a civic (or, in their terms, political) *presence*, but also a civic (or political) *present*, which went hand in hand with political identity: a civic *presence* inasmuch as the citizens were able to assert their will by being present and participating in political affairs; a civic *present*, inasmuch as they had a special mode of experiencing present time. The present for them was not the 'moving point of dust where past and future meet', but a broad and richly charged band of immediate experience. (1990: 22)

Thus, there was for the Greeks another social domain for the formation of meaningful existence. It was not found in the stories themselves, but in the emergence of a particular form of social existence which solidified into the *polis*.

Havelock (1976: 5) observes that this participation grew from the specific social system of the *polis*, which preceded the city-state, and Meier (1990) locates the origins of the *polis* within a series of social crises arising simultaneously with the extension of Greek colonies into the wider Mediterranean region (see also Manville 1990). Certainly, around the ninth century BCE a very ancient social organization began to transform, and with it the manner in which people conceived of their relationship to each other changed as well. In practical terms, *oikoi*, or families, began to recognize and define larger social units. In Athens, the hierarchical organization of the social extended from groups tracing a common descent (genos) to groups organized around a common ancestor (*phratria*) and finally to the widest group, the *polis* (Benveniste 1973: 258). Each successive step widened the sphere to which the individual person was obligated in reciprocal relations and respect, that is, there was a progressive elaboration and negotiating about who was included among those with whom one shared a sense of *aidos* (see Benveniste 1973: 278, 281).

The Athenian *polis* required first the elaboration of the idea of a shared social space extending beyond family and household and governed by shared rules. It had its roots in the emergence of the *isonomia* that preceded it. The people of Athens agreed to exist under unified, common *nomoi*, that is, the 'norms and relations that a people accept as valid and binding' (Manville 1990: 198; see also Starr 1990: 36–7). The need to negotiate these norms, as well as the criteria of membership and participation within the *polis*, created the social conditions in which persuasive language could emerge. Wilkerson writes that 'rhetoric, as the art of persuasion and compromise, was tailored to fit this new social milieu' (1994: 22). In order for a whole society to understand how another's interest can become a shared interest for all, 'a new political role has to appear, not just a new player to take over an old role. This calls for social reasoning of a quite different and more abstract kind' (Meier 1990: 29). Meier observes that the political order of the *polis* was split off from the existing social order and set over against it (1990: 20). The *polis* necessitated and created a standpoint of self and thought that was separate from the immediate identification with feeling. The abstraction of an artificial social world required new rules for thinking, speaking, and living within it, and the pressures to develop these new skills contributed to the development of critical thought. The transition from the felt, active world of Homer's Achilles to the dialogic, intellectual world of Plato thus had its roots in the reorganization of Greek society that took place 300 to 400 years earlier. Writing appeared in Greece somewhere within this period, perhaps 1000 to 750 BCE, and many of the changes attributed to the advent of literacy are more social than technological in origin.

Even within the embryonic *polis,* communal and externalized personalities would find their identity not in the personal and isolated *cogito* but in the belief of the group and its values, as these are presented in the traditional tales of Homer and Hesiod as well as in the everyday life and action of ordinary people who sought to create a new kind of social sphere. Even after the advent of writing and reading, language almost always occurred in a social setting with people whom one knew, who were physically close, who participated in the same experience of the narrative drama and in the same dramas of everyday life. These activities constitute the field in which vernacular language emerges, that speech which 'was drawn from the cultural environment through the encounter with people, each of whom one could smell and touch, love and hate' (Illich 1992: 122). In such a setting, one is not what he or she thinks but what he or she does. One existed only to the extent that others wove him or her into their shared social narratives. Only the external manifestation of thought in action would impinge on others and so allow the people around one to comment, to write one into the social reality, and this action was already heavily determined by identification with the group.

Thus, two languages existed even in preliterate Greece: a language of the vernacular, quotidian speech used in everyday settings and the formalized language of the cultural story stock of poems and epics. No conflict existed between these two, though, for they were clearly separated in use, and while the poetic would inform ordinary habits of thought and action, people still spoke to one another in prosaic forms. The separation of a formal language from a vernacular relies on several social structures that would only appear millennia later. The formal, mythic language lent meaning and temporality to life: 'The rest of his life is passed in profane time, which is without meaning: in the state of "becoming"' (Eliade 1954: 35). Similarly, the function of this mythic structure was being transferred to new forms of the social. Still, it was onto these two forms of language that writing was appended. And at roughly the same time, a new rhetoric, political sphere, and politics were emerging as well. None of these can be teased out of the others as cause or effect, for each constituted a part of the great cultural transitions sweeping Greece between roughly the first millennium and the fifth century BCE.

Writing

The phenomenological experience of early writing follows closely from the experience of speech. The habits of thought in relation to language which had developed over tens of thousands of years did not easily change. Different forms of writing developed, transformed, and were taken up in different ways in various places and times so that generalizations about the reception of writing are dangerous. Further, our own understanding of literacy, writing, and representation as a whole strongly influences our attempt to appreciate what the emergence of writing meant to people. Deeply embedded within literate cultures that are on the verge perhaps of becoming postliterate, our perception of literacy is fashioned by our uses of it. Only a few records exist that document the emergence of this technology within Greek society, and these tend to focus more upon its effects, the worries which it caused, or the magic of it, than upon the experience of early writing.

The reception and use of writing were initially not as an encoding of speech or thought but as an aid to memory by repeating externally, in concrete form, an act of mental visualization which had already taken place. Carruthers (1990: 11) notes that she could find no single instance where the act of writing was regarded as a supplanter of memory, not even Plato's *Phaedrus*. From its origins in Greece through the middle ages, alphabetic writing was superimposed upon forms of language and memory already present even down to the metaphors used to describe the process of memory. Socrates uses the image of a seal impression on wax to describe memory in *Theaetetus*, and the metaphor of writing or inscription as memory appears in Cicero, Quintillian, and Augustine, each noting the importance of marking things as a sort of mental image to improve memory (1990: 22). Havelock writes that 'the use of vision directed to the recall of what had been spoken (Homer) was replaced by its use to invent a textual discourse (Thucydides, Plato) which seemed to make orality obsolete. The singing muse translates herself into a writer: she who had required men to listen now invites them to read' (1986: 62).

In a sense, then, writing had been imagined before it existed. While Thomas (1992), Carruthers (1990) and others have demonstrated that the visualization of inscription as well as orality itself continued to be significant into medieval times, if one tempers Havelock's enthusiasm a bit, it is possible to say that orality was not made obsolete by textual discourses but rather provided a model for them. It is not until 1500 years have elapsed that writing becomes divorced from speech and is used independently of speech.

Early uses of writing

If the *polis* was essential for the formation of classical, literate, Greece, the appearance of that particular social form may well have contributed to the need for increasingly common and important examples of writing. Writing would not have become widely accepted in Athens and other cities unless there were compelling reasons for taking it up, and these reasons were not immediately recognized by the Greeks. Havelock observes that the first 300 years of writing and reading in Greece were a sort of 'craft literacy' which 'made little practical difference to the educational system or to the intellectual life of adults' (1963: 39–40). Neither was there a driving rationale for most people's learning to read or write. Harris (1989: 30–5) notes that several factors may have mitigated against the widespread adoption of literacy, including the availability of mediators in the forms of public scribes or readers either for hire or who might render some written work out of kindness. Certainly, there is little evidence that writing was confined to scribes as it appeared as decoration on vases, in graffiti, in dedications, as well as in public inscriptions (Thomas 1992: 57). Indeed, the elite of Athens were orators and performers, while those who initially used the alphabet may well have been of lower social standing such as stonecutters or potters (Havelock 1986: 89).

The audience and purposes of writing remained restricted at least until the fifth century. Early alphabetic writing for the Greeks had, however, many purposes, being used to identify the owners of vases, to inscribe tombs, as religious decorations, and even as nonsense decorations on black-figure vases (Harris 1989: 46; Thomas 1992: 57). Some evidence exists in the form of 'curse tablets' that writing was thought to strengthen the power of the spoken word and thus was linked to magic. In short, depending upon who was the recipient of a written thing and what their pre-existing beliefs and needs were, writing was taken up variously. Standardized uses of writing could only emerge out of repeated social usage such as might produce consensus, and there was not the body of literature present to create a community of literate people until Plato or later. While public, official inscriptions indicate some evidence of growing expectation of the presence of literate people in the community, these would still have been a small number. 'There must have been an audience of hundreds in most cultivated cities, such as Athens, Corinth, and Miletus, and a nucleus of dozens of literate men in many Greek cities [in the sixth century]' (Harris 1989: 49). Even as late as the middle of the fourth century, Aristotle could write in *Politics* of the four uses of literacy as: money-making, household management, instruction (*mathesis*), and civic activities (1989: 26).

Until around the middle of the fifth century BCE, if a man (and most literate people were male) learned to read or write, it was in a limited way and was not generally acquired until adolescence, that is, after one already had a proficiency in language and a grounding in the narrative literature of the time. Plato notes in Book II of the *Republic*:

> You know, I said, that we begin by telling children stories which, though not wholly destitute of truth, are in the main fictitious; and these stories are told them when they are not of an age for gymnastics. (377)

Writing was introduced slowly into existing social and educational systems and these, being exclusive, did little to spread its reception among people outside the elite classes. However, the growing prestige of literacy emerged from its linkage with power: the legal system, in the setting forth of laws in written form and in the demand for legal contracts, contributed to the social stature of literacy and strengthened its relationship to the state (Harris 1989: 69). Literacy came to be seen as more important in the bringing of legal cases and was even a prerequisite for one's participation in government.

The acceptance of writing was thus slow, and the changes to consciousness which Havelock and others attributed to writing were likely less spectacular and sudden than they suggested. However, writing does affect thought and language. A totemic consciousness exists only in cultures that are deeply steeped in orality, and the name of the thing has power over it, prompting both euphemistic names and various types of magic. To separate the word from the thing, some sort of distancing of language is needed, and writing provides just the right sort of structure to achieve this. Olson has argued that 'writing is not the transcription of speech but rather provides a conceptual model for that speech' (1994: 89). Olson explains that writing 'spells the death of "word" magic or more precisely, "name" magic. Words are no longer emblems; words are now distinguished from both things and names of things; words as linguistic entities come into consciousness' (1994: 75). As such, the word no longer represents some property of the thing, but now stands in place of the thing. The word can now be examined in relationship to other words and concepts and can become an abstract idea for reflection.

Actions and attributes in oral Greece appearing in the deeds of heroes and gods become in classical Greece philosophical concepts (1994: 76). Creating the word from the flow of sound, writing created the idea of the word and established it as a thing in the world. Havelock (1963: 206) theorized that writing freed the mind from 'long patterns of habitual and mental responses' to set pieces of narrative, thus helping to create the conditions in which rational philosophy and critical dialectics could develop. Writing, in its slow development within the context of spoken language, established a syntax which could then be turned around upon a spoken language and applied to it. Dialectical questioning forced the restatement of things known in the old poetic forms into prosaic forms, disrupting their unquestioned acceptance. 'To ask what [the traditional poem] was saying amounted to a demand that it be said differently, non-poetically, non-rhythmically, and non-imagistically' (1963: 209).

It is impossible to identify with precision the moments these changes began to appear. Possibly some of the changes in attitude toward classical narratives were already taking place in the time of Hesiod (eighth century) and even Homer (eighth or ninth century) (Havelock 1982: 209). Certainly, there are limits to the kinds of complexity of thought an oral culture can preserve, and these limitations may have begun to be felt and addressed around the time of the advent of writing. New social forms of organization appeared around the same times as noted above. For whatever reasons, although the Greeks had taken up a modified Phoenician writing system as an alphabet as early as 750 BCE, the use of this system in any consistent and proficient way did not develop until the middle of the fifth century, and it was at this point that the influences of the new technology were beginning to make themselves known. What we now understand of this period derives from a handful of writings which have survived the intervening millennia, and among the most important of these are the writings of Plato.

Plato

Plato's words on writing contain a complex set of discussions about orality and literacy. There is some evidence that elements of literate thought had already begun to appear in Greek culture as early as the eighth century, but the oral traditions of oratory, drama, and poetry were still strong. Literacy, though present, was not yet widespread. As such, Plato's own understanding of literacy in the setting of his philosophical project reflects an ambiguity toward the new technologies of reading and writing. In the *Republic* he is apparently critical of the characteristics of his oral culture, and in the *Phaedrus* he is critical of writing.

Being literate himself, Plato undoubtedly understood the advantage of literacy in creating a distance between the knower and the known. Havelock regarded those of Plato's dialogues that assail writing and poetry, particularly the *Republic* and the *Phaedrus*, as attacks upon and attempts to separate his language and thought from the pre-existing orality of Athenian culture. This approach explains some of the philosopher's seemingly paradoxical statements about writing and knowledge. Plato's project has been characterized as being, in part, the destruction of 'the immemorial habit of self-identification with the oral tradition' (Havelock 1963: 201). Plato's approach to rationality, as proposed in his academy as well as in his vision of the utopian republic, privileged mathematics, geometry, and analytic thought applied to both the natural world and the human domain. This is not to suggest that the preliterate Greeks were incapable of logic or rational thought but rather demonstrates that a new kind of analytic thought, based upon the analysis of words and concepts as things in themselves, was emerging for a variety of reasons.

Many of the elements of critical thought were already present in Greece before Socrates and Plato and hence before the widespread acceptance of literacy. These had developed through the lyric poets, through pre-Socratic 'adventures in thought', and through the influence of political classes and the rule of law (Wilkerson 1994: 34). Certainly, the continuing evolution of the *polis* and the need to redefine people's relations to one another in an ongoing way also contributed to the elaboration of abstract and critical thinking. As the *polis* was isometric with the cosmos, this social project led to profound reconsideration of all aspects of life. Meier writes that 'for a long time, and especially since the days of Solon, men had seen a mutual correspondence between the order of the *polis* and the order of the universe. Changing notions of the one generated fresh perceptions of the other' (1990: 91–2). He continues, 'Such shattering events called for a profound rethinking of everything, including the relations among the gods' (1990: 92).

Plato's thought and writing thus must be set within the general social context of rethinking the whole of heaven and earth and of developing the rational critical tools for so doing. The ability rationally to assess the world was paramount to Plato's thought. In the *Republic* he writes:

> And the arts of measuring and numbering and weighing come to the rescue of the human understanding – there is the beauty of them – with the result that the apparent greater or less, or more or heavier, no longer have mastery over us, but give way before the power of calculation and measuring and weighing. (602)

The abstract arts of determining the attributes of the physical world assist human understanding, giving people power over the being of the world. This is a knowledge which is present in the Homeric epics, but the Homeric Greeks had no compelling reason to develop such skills as critical thought and rhetoric. 'The primary condition for the development of the art of rhetoric – belief in the efficacy of human decision – missing in Homer, was not fully present in ancient Greece until the fifth century' (Wilkerson 1994: 34).

Not only the physical world but also the human world of stories must be examined and abstracted. In the *Republic* Plato discusses as well the need to evaluate the poetry which provided so much social identity of the time. Plato's issue with the poetic forms is that mimesis, dramatic imitation and impersonation, returned one to the identification with the representation of the thing in contrast to the *episteme* of the academy (Havelock 1963: 31). Rationality depends upon critical thought, and this critical faculty requires that separate examples in a narrative can be 'torn out of context, correlated, systematized, unified and harmonized to provide a formula' (1963: 217). Plato seeks to lift events out of the contexts of the poetic and epic forms and analyze, for example, justice itself rather than the acts of just or unjust people. Such an analysis, if not requiring writing, certainly benefits from writing and from the mental techniques that emerge from literacy, that is, from finding moments on the page that do not fade with the speaker's words and that can be compared, contrasted and analyzed.

The narrative or idea that is thus taken out of the oral context enters a new condition of existence: 'the absolute isolated identity is not only a "one", it is also a "being"' (1963: 219). Created outside the streaming world of time yet referring to it, 'the abstracted object of knowledge has to lose not only plurality of action in time but also color and visibility. It becomes "the unseen"' (1963: 219). In other words, the rational process of technology creates something which, for Plato, corresponds with the world of the true, of the form, but this new creation does not appear in the world but only in the mind. The form or the idea can then serve as a model for things that one can make in the world and that have a recognizable and visible being. On this ground Plato may attack not only poetry in general, but Homer specifically:

> Friend Homer, then we say to him, if you are only in the second remove from truth in what you say of virtue, and not in the third – not a image maker, that is, by our definition, an imitator – and if you are able to discern what pursuits make men better or worse in private or public life, tell us what State was ever better governed by your help? (*Republic* 599)

Plato charges that Homer's poetic observations are not true in the sense that they are a received, third-order representation of the world rather than meditation on the world as it is. He does not dispense with Homer, but locates him within the classification of literature.

The Platonic self

The psychological changes attending the rise of the *polis* and the advent of literacy had begun to appear but had not yet taken hold sufficiently to displace the old psychology of orality, and the greatest proponent of orality was, for Plato, poetry. 'Poetry is not so much non-functional as antifunctional. It totally lacks the precise aims and goals which guide the skilled educator in the training of his intellect' (Havelock 1963: 25). The needs of the new settings in which the thinker and speaker found himself demanded an ability to differentiate, classify, and abstract all manner of things as well as the relations between them. The mimesis or imitation was the process through which the template of oral narrative was taken up, but it was this imitation that caused the problem. He writes in Book X of the *Republic* that 'the imitator is a long way off the truth, and can reproduce all things because he lightly touches on a small part of them, and that part an image' (598). He elaborates that the imitation is both what the poet labors under and what the audience sees as well:

> Painting or drawing, and imitation in general, are engaged upon productions which are far removed from truth, and are also the companions and friends and associates of a principle within us which is equally removed from reason, and that they have no true or healthy aim. (*Republic* 603)

Note that Plato locates this imitation not only in art itself, but also within people as a kind of deception or confusion, and it is from this fog of illusion that rationality will free people. People have internalized a false sense of the world based on artistic mimesis, and they must now internalize a true sense of the world.

The way to make a consciousness based on truth rather than upon received wisdom lay not in abandoning the traditional folk wisdom of the epics and poems but in evaluating them critically. Plato does not recommend the destruction or elimination of the old wisdom but rather supports its careful use in society. He recognizes that some narratives might prove unsuitable for children, for the unprepared and unschooled, and might lead them into confusion, and some tales might prove especially damaging. Even these, though, are not rejected completely. Plato recommends of these that:

> if there is an absolute need for their mention, a chosen few might hear them in a mystery, and they should sacrifice not a common pig, but some huge and unprocurable victim, so that the number of hearers may be very few indeed. (378)

Rather than use the forms of things as known through poetic imitation, through mimesis, the Platonic science would use 'the unique and exact Forms as models' (Havelock 1963: 30).

Socrates and Plato did not invent this new consciousness; it had been growing in the minds of many people, and it certainly depended not just upon writing, but upon a range of social factors which are difficult to identify. Undeniably, however, literacy was central in creating new social habits of reading, writing, discussing and understanding language. As noted above, the emergence of this community of literate people depended as well upon a supply of readers and texts. However, in the 400 or so years between Homer and Socrates, changes were emerging in the minds of the Greeks which are of importance to understanding the historical evolution of the self.

The Homeric folk psychology 'lacked a vocabulary and its corresponding concepts for thinking about the mind' (Olson 1994: 240), and especially for thinking about the individual, the subject. Havelock describes Homer's Achilles as an example of a person 'to whom it has not occurred and cannot occur that he has a personality apart from the pattern of his acts' (1963: 197). The person in archaic society exists meaningfully only to the extent that he or she is implicated in the dramas described in the narrative forms, and as such has no self-regulating identity. Such a person 'sees himself as real, i.e. as truly himself only, and precisely insofar as he ceases to be so' (Eliade 1954: 34). There were simply no models for self-directing, self-conscious people in the old poetic forms. Responsibility, motivation, and action arise for the Homeric Greek from the shared social, from gods or causes which are not located within the person or in the mind. In order to shift the location of these to the person, a new language is called for, and numerous terms undergo changes in meaning and usage, not least among them the use of the terms related to mind and cognition.

The creation of a separate domain for concepts is necessary for exploring the characteristics of them. The Homeric Greeks had no words for religion, or psychology, or soul. The meaning of the word *psyche* changed from 'signifying a man's ghost or wraith or a man's breath or his life blood' and came to mean something like '"the ghost who thinks", that is, is capable both of moral decision and scientific cognition and is the seat of moral responsibility' (Havelock 1963: 197). The ancient language located mind in the experience of feelings or sensations, caused by outside forces or entities. Thus, '*thumus* is the experience of stress which moves one to action', while '*Phrenes*, lungs, provide a place for retaining words, fears, and even wine, which beclouds *thumus*', and *noos*, derived from 'to see', resides in the chest (Olson 1994: 239). By the middle of the fifth century, these had been refigured into attributes and intentionalities located in the head.

These ways of thinking about the mind were not just descriptions but also prescriptions, mental templates for a new kind of 'common-sense' understanding of what the human being is and of people's awareness of themselves as self-conscious entities who can now be the objects of their own examination and contemplation. In the mental act of creating language as a thing outside the person that could be studied, examined, and theorized, ideas become independent of the spoken word. They change from being 'the winged word that always rushes by before it has been fully grasped' (Illich and Sanders 1988: 7) to apparently fixed forms, timeless ideas, and meanings. The distinction arises between what is said and what it means, that is, between the spoken sound and what is thought about it. Applied internally to one's own ideas and words, a critical consciousness of self is made possible; and articulated socially, a responsibility for self becomes necessary.

Plato saw a timeless set of forms and truths which must have seemed to be absolutely real for him in his moment of radical vision. He was envisioning the next step that his culture was in the process of taking, and so he saw both the present, in his view mistaken, moment and the future possible world of forms and rational philosophy. What Plato did not envision was that this change was a movement along a continuum from one kind of consciousness to another rather than a progression toward truth as an additive advance in human consciousness.

Plato could make his philosophical move not only because he had writing at his disposal, but also because he had a vernacular language which was separate from the formal language of the poets, separate from the language of the rhetor, and which was newly viable as a means of argument, expression, and debate.

Dialogues of orality and literacy

If writing imposed a new structure onto speech and thought, it also created the possibility that some kinds of information exist outside the mind. The Platonic forms which lay behind all appearance were one kind of external idea, and the histories, philosophies, truth, wisdom, and knowledge were still acquired in the philosophical way, through meditation, but new techniques for manipulating language following the patterns of reading grew to a new importance.

An apparent paradox in Plato's thought concerns his ideas about writing. Writing is a tool, an aid, and not to be overly relied upon. Writing is described in *Phaedrus* as a *pharmakon*, both a medicine and a poison depending on its use. Plato says that 'this facility will make the souls forgetful because they will no longer school themselves to meditate. They will rely on letters. Things will be recollected from outside by means of alien symbols, they will not remember on their own.' The written word can only remind one of what he or she already knows; writing is the semblance of wisdom. 'The danger in it was that men might begin to rely upon writing instead of truly learning things by imprinting them first in their memories' (Carruthers 1990: 31). Thus for Plato, neither the old oral narratives nor the new skills of letters could truly introduce knowledge about the world into the mind. Rather, such knowledge could only be acquired through argument, dialogue, and meditation. This was in part possible because participation in the *polis* had come to provide the social identification for people that had been provided by the poetic forms. Further, the knowledge of which Plato wrote was internalized knowledge acquired through thought and meditation, and such a model of knowledge presages a relation that the physical body would have to book learning through the middle ages (see Illich and Sanders 1988: 24–8).

As literacy developed in Athens and other parts of Greece, diverse ways of reading different sorts of written material developed. Lists, public laws, *ostraka*, and graffiti would not have been read in the same ways, and philosophical writings or the epics of Homer would have been read differently still, yet all of these are subsumed under the idea of literacy, blurring the differences. Kaster notes that 'the slow writers, and persons who could painstakingly sign legal documents but were otherwise illiterate, or the man who could only read block letters, would all have called themselves, literate; they were clearly "not without letters"' (1988: 43). However, the specific modalities of reading as they developed would have become formalized in social structures and institutions which in turn would reinforce their linkages to lines of social power as well as guarantee their continuation through the practices of students. As language became another thing in the world which could be studied and theorized, so it could also be operated upon using empirical and logical thinking to transform it into a tool. Particularly, schools would formalize the new techniques derived from literacy into teachings about reading and about language.

The liberal arts

The project of privileging critical thought was influential on the shape of education and the organization of knowledge through late antiquity and into the medieval period. Music, which had once been a central pillar of education, became less important. Rhetoric, dialectics, and grammar, that is, those disciplines devoted to language and literature, served practically in the presenting of one's self in formal social settings and so were essential to having a professional and political life. These skills developed a new importance in the Classical period and later. While oratory had always been esteemed in Greece, the art of rhetoric was specifically a technology for enhancing speech and argument oriented toward specific ends, identified by Aristotle as forensic, deliberative, or epideictic, and it separated speakers who meant what they said from those who spoke for an effect. This fact did not go unnoticed, for upon the receipt of this Greek art for manipulating language, many in Rome were skeptical of the effect it would have on debate and public speech. In 161 BCE the Roman senate approved of the expulsion of rhetoricians and philosophers, suspecting that they perverted truth and might invert the common belief, framed by Cato: *rem tene, verba sequentor* (hold to the matter, the words will follow) (see Clarke 1971: 30). The problem with rhetoric is that sometimes the truth will fall before a well-turned argument.

These subjects were not ends in themselves but were preparatory. Seneca argued that the liberal arts prepared the mind for virtue but did not themselves impart it, and centuries earlier Plato, in *Phaedrus* (269), had held the *enkuklia* as subordinate to philosophy (see Clarke 1971: 3–4). Grammar taught literature, essential for knowing the myths and stories and the structure of the language in which they were told. Dialectic or logic, however, in its early form, forced the restatement of the poetic truths in prosaic forms, demanding an abstraction of content and principles from the rhythms and images (Havelock 1963: 208–9). The most important of the arts after the archaic period, though, was rhetoric, for in both Greece and Rome it led to a political and public career.[3] Aristotle writes in the *Nicomachean Ethics* that the highest science is politics, and this was still a politics which sought, at least in theory, to model the cosmic structure in the structure of human relations.

Such applications of deliberate thought for the manipulation of language are not primary functions of language; they are not essential to the learning or practice of language in everyday life, and in fact grammar and rhetoric were taught in Greece only after one had already learned to read and write. Yet such skills are essential to a public life, for in the social field of adults, the world is not self-evidently the same for each. The ends, desires, and skills of one or other persons may, then, provide the motive and abilities to sway others to accept one particular view. Yet, however skilled a Greek or Roman orator might be, however subtle or even misleading his reasoning, in rhetoric one must recognize and engage the other person or persons. They could not be objects to be ignored or organized without their consent within the context of the *agora*.[4]

Medieval writing and the internalization of the word

The emergence of writing created an uneasiness and a tension between the domain of orality and that of literacy, a division that would grow especially as literacy came to be implicated not only with class and prestige but with tradition and thus cultured thought. As early as the fifth century AD the Bishop of Clermont, Sidonius, would write that 'the educated are as far superior to the uncultured as human beings are to beasts' (Kaster 1988: 91). Writing, perhaps as early as the sixth century BCE, began to be accepted as a way of storing information separate from speech (Thomas 1992: 64), but the technologies of texts and the mental habits for using them which emerged around the twelfth century increased the independence of the text from spoken word. Certainly something significantly new was introduced to human thought with writing and reading.

The development of a complex epistemology for the written word which was at the same time independent of speech relied on exposure to much writing as well as upon a social consensus about how writing was to be understood. Social institutions such as law courts also were slow to adopt widespread use of writing, and where it was adopted, it always coexisted with oral forms. Thus, a limited number of texts as well as limited exposure to reading in general hampered writing's taking on of an independent existence and limited literary practices to the courts and monastic settings of medieval Europe. In social function, the early written text served as a supplement and record of events which were still grounded in human interactions.

Its very physicality bound the book to a concrete existence in the medium of writing even though an oral dimension was required to liberate the knowledge of the book. Even before the great illuminations of medieval texts, the letters themselves, their color and size and design, were used as mnemonic devices for finding passages of texts. These would be seen not only by the reader but by the audience as well. Illustrations within a text would provide visual metaphors for the written words, further helping the internalization of the text. However the technologies of writing and reading remained separate. Reading by no means guaranteed the ability to write. Clanchy notes that 'writing was considered a special skill in the Middle Ages which was not automatically coupled with the ability to read' (1979: 88). In the new universities of the eleventh and twelfth centuries, reading remained the key skill: 'In lecture, students studied from books open before them, but it is significant, I think, that the manuscript illuminations typically show them without pens' (Carruthers 1990: 159).

Rather than being displaced, orality continued in new forms, operating in tandem with reading into early modern times, and it is the form which this orality took that reveals much about the relationship between reading and speaking. New prose forms of composition and story-telling emerged which coexisted with and influenced the oral forms. Alphabetic writing had appeared in a culture with highly developed social forms of speech and disputation, and when writing was subsequently taken up by people in Sicily and on the Italian peninsula it did not immediately bring the writings of the Greeks but was used in the contexts of the various languages and narrative traditions within which it appeared. The new writing did not yet exist separate from the spoken, and neither did the words within it have real value until internalized within the speaking, the body, the mind, and the soul of the reader.

Certainly technological changes were being made to writing which both improved its permanence and added to its ease of use, particularly as a reference. While the Greeks preferred papyrus which was imported from Africa for their writing surface, the Romans greatly expanded the use of parchment as a permanent writing surface. Parchment is much more durable than papyrus and survives the wet, cold weather of the European climate better. The second technology was the widespread use of the codex, the book form, in preference to scrolls. The codex form enables one to turn to a sought-after page or passage without unwinding a scroll from the end and searching through it, and from late Roman times the codex became the dominant form for storing writing. Those works which were sufficiently popular or which were deemed to be of enough importance were copied into this new form. 'Books that made the transition [to codex form] successfully had a reasonable chance of surviving and being read in the centuries to come, while books that did not were likely to be orphaned' (O'Donnell 1998: 52).

The principal medium of the middle ages continued to be parchment, though paper was introduced into Europe at least as early as the twelfth century by Arabic traders traveling from China. Initially suspicious of the new material and uncertain of its long-term durability, people were reluctant to use paper and in some cases were even forbidden to do so by law. Within 200 years, however, the use of paper was greatly extended and it had begun to be manufactured in Europe (Febvre and Martin 1976: 20). By the end of the thirteenth century, paper had largely supplanted parchment as the medium for the book.

If spoken language took place in social settings, so too did book reading, and in many cases book writing. The amanuensis who took dictation from a speaker continued in one form or another into the modern era, supplemented by various technologies ranging from the wax tablet and the use of minuscule writing as a kind of shorthand (Clanchy 1979: 89) to, much later, stenographic recording equipment. Throughout the ancient world and the middle ages, books were read aloud and often to others. The orality of the word produced from the written page linked speech to writing from Quintillian through to Hugh of St Vincent. In such practices, 'reading is to be digested, to be ruminated, like a cow' (Carruthers 1990: 164). By the same token, composition was also a *ruminatio*, a regurgitation of what had been taken in, digested, and produced again. Illich cites several medieval references which describe monastic reading in terms of food and oral pleasures. The scriptures are 'sweeter than honey in the honeycomb', and St Bernard, referring to reading, says, 'Enjoying their sweetness, I chew them over and over' (Illich 1993: 54–6).

Writing and reading were heard, and while some people could read in silence, the usual manner of reading was aloud in the presence of others. This social context ensured that reading remained an experience similar to meeting people. One did not simply see the text; one heard it with the same attention that would be given to a speaking person. The book is heard as another person, or as the voices of many people, who has or have a presence in the world of being which, while not quite equivalent with the human, is still not within the world of things. The book has the potential to change the reader's thinking and to reorder the world. In precisely this sense, the author emerges as a textual figure whose importance is assured through his influence on others and his survival in their minds and memories. He does not exist as a person with intentions separate from the text but is found in the text, *ad res* (Carruthers 1990: 190–1).

This physical internalizing of the text ensured as well that meditation, which from the time of Socrates was the only source of true wisdom, kept a place in reading. And as meditation was preserved, so also was memory. Carruther's study reveals that 'medieval culture remained profoundly memorial in nature, despite the increased use and availability of books', and she identifies the primary factor for memory's retention as 'the identification of memory with the formation of moral virtues' (1990: 156).

Such a determined method for testing knowledge within the body through meditation was a significant advance from the studies of Athens where, as Kaster notes, 'far from understanding his culture, the man emerging from the schools of grammar and rhetoric would have no overall view of history, only a memory of disjointed but edifying vignettes; no systematic knowledge of philosophy or of any philosophic school, but a collection of ethical commonplaces' (1988: 12).

The integration of the old oral skills into the new forms demanded by an approach to a body of literature aided in the development of techniques for balancing orality and literacy to a degree that had not existed before and has not existed since.

Interpretation

The framework of theology, and particularly of the patristic writings, undoubtedly contributed to a solidifying of the practices of both education and literacy. Medieval religious scholars accomplished what the Greeks had never done, that is, to establish a canon of literature under the control of a priesthood, and so to centralize and standardize aspects of reading and scholasticism throughout Europe. Carruthers explains that:

> All exegesis emphasized that understanding was grounded in a thorough knowledge of the *littera*, and for this one had to know grammar, rhetoric, history, and all the other disciplines that give information, the work of *lectio*. But one takes all of that and builds upon it during meditation; this phase of reading is ethical in its nature, or 'tropological' (turning the text onto and into one's self) as Hugh defines it. (1990: 165)

To hold and organize everything within the self required memory skills that could only be developed slowly and with practice. This oral linkage kept writing tied to familiar kinds of memory as well. The epistemological function of theology linked the internal memory with an external guide, providing a shared structure to the internal experiences of reading and meditation; theology provided an interpretive dimension.

This interpretive function is required in reading. Olson (1994) has demonstrated that writing lacks the ability to convey directly the illocutionary power of language; writing gives very limited detail about the mental state or immediate intention of the author. The written word is not real in the same way as the spoken word; it cannot present the other speaker as immediately present, and so there is no mutual recognition between people in the literate situation. Reading enabled one to imagine that recognition and identification with the author as with another person were still possible, but the only way in which both the reader and the writer could appear within the sphere of a shared existence would be through the reader's internalizing of the author. As the author's intent through much of the middle ages appeared only on the page, the loss of this internalizing process demanded another way of understanding the author. Without this process, the reader must rely on interpretation to understand intent, and this interpretation relies upon social strategies of reading and exegesis which begin to develop in earnest at about the same time.

Other technologies emerged from changing social conditions, including the rise of bureaucracies and universities, and the need to manage the growing libraries, chanceries, and correspondence. Certainly increasing numbers of books and papers required more efficient management systems, but also they led to physical systems for linking related parts of different texts to one another. Concordances, indices, and library inventories transferred the connections made in one's mind into the book itself or other writings (Illich 1993: 104). The use of bibliographies was in part St Jerome's fourth century answer to pagan authors (as well as threatened Christians) that Christianity could muster significant numbers of scholars and philosophers (Rouse and Rouse 1986: 133). This is much the same process as bringing witnesses to a court or a hearing, but the witnesses were assembled in the written text. The bibliography begins to appear frequently in the late twelfth and early thirteenth centuries, but its use was changing. Now the bibliography as well as indices were used as methods of cross-reference both to scripture and to other works as an early form of 'non-linear access' (O'Donnell 1998: 56). The writing down of fully-formed complex glosses of works suggests that these were already largely complete and held in memory to be written down later in response to the demand from the universities (Carruthers 1990: 159). No longer would memory or discussion be the sole ways of drawing connections between works; the connections could appear on the page.

However, not everyone would have read in the meditative fashion of monastic tradition, and all written matter did not serve the same function. Both within and without the centers of monastic reading, works written not to enlighten or edify but to document and certify grew increasingly important through the twelfth century. Clanchy (1979: 120) notes that 'for monks, the primary purpose of writing was to inform, or misinform, posterity', as for example in the veneration of a saint or stewardship of his relics. Clanchy continues:

> Thus the monastic approach to records was ambivalent: documents were created and carefully conserved so that posterity might know about the past, but they were not necessarily allowed to accumulate by natural accretion over time nor to speak for themselves, because the truth was too important to leave to chance. (1979: 120)

As the status of writing and reading changed, and as the phenomenological experience of them also altered, new ways of thinking which were modeled on the new forms of language took a turn as well. Writers such as Erasmus and Montaigne questioned whether memory and knowledge were coincidental or separable (Rossi 2000). Writing became a solitary practice which no longer afforded readers the encounter with others but rather enabled the encounter with their ideas. Illich writes that:

> only after Hugh's death, sounding lines on the page fade and the page becomes a screen for the order willed by the mind. Rather than a means to revive a *narratio*, the theological and philosophical book becomes the exteriorization of a *cogitatio*, of a thought structure. (1993: 105)

Physical technologies such as page layout and an increasingly uniform script contributed to the visual form of this change in thinking. In its development as an abstraction, the book changed from 'a pointer to *nature* to a pointer to *mind*' (1993: 119), and once freed from the constraint of a human presence, reading became a metaphor for understanding both the 'signs' of a text and the 'signs' of nature.

After Printing

It was not that monastic reading changed or failed. While monastic scholars adopted the new linguistic technologies and applied these to scholarship and teaching, new forms of writing and reading were becoming widespread in other areas of society. The link between the Catholic Church and literacy, always firm, was altered and weakened by a growing number of secular clerks, registrars, secretaries, and accountants (McKitterick 1989; Pryce 1998) and an increasing use of documentation in royal courts (Clanchy 1979). Increasing demand for writing and reading contributed to a growing social pressure for inexpensive reproduction that emerged in Mainz around 1430 and rapidly developed throughout Europe (Febvre and Martin 1976; Eisenstein 1979).

As with writing itself, many of the changes brought by print took place only slowly over centuries while others were much more immediate. Linguistic boundaries were fixed as books began to be published in local languages rather than Latin (Febvre and Martin 1976: 309, 323–4; Eisenstein 1984: 82). Instead of the idiolects of individual Latin writers or the styles of schools (such as were set in the Carolingian court), language became more uniform in spelling, dialect, and grammar within larger groups of people, and this contributed to the emergence of particular dialects and the marginalization of others. Official, national languages begin only after printing.

Other aspects of life were even slower to change, particularly where they reflected people's use of language in traditional or everyday settings. Into the eighteenth century, the printed word continued to have for some a sort of magical quality, as one found in early literacy in Greece. For example, the Bible continued as a sort of icon or talisman, and even waving the pages in the face of a sick person could effect a cure (Houston 1988: 225). Similarly land transfers, although registered centrally in Scotland from 1617 (one of the first countries to so do), continued in the old fashion. 'The written "instrument of sasine" was recorded in official volumes, but the actual transfer usually took place on the land itself, and involved the handing over of a clod of earth to the seller before witnesses' (1988: 224). Eisenstein observes that most rural villages remained a hearing public until probably the nineteenth century, even though they had been transformed: the local story-teller being 'replaced by the exceptional literate villager who read out loud from a stack of cheap books and ballad sheets' (1984: 93). In the United States, such public readings, especially of newspapers, took place in post offices well into the nineteenth century (John 1995).

Among the most immediate changes was the acceleration of messages in writing through society and the sheer amount of written material available. Pamphlets and broadsheets were produced in such speed and abundance that propaganda wars erupted in the fifteenth and early sixteenth centuries. In pre-Norman England no library lists over 100 works in its collection (Thomson 1986: 28), while after the advent of printing both monastic and personal libraries commonly exceed 500 holdings (Febvre and Martin 1976: 263–4). The effect of this increase in books, pamphlets, broadsheets and such was not, however, a general increase in universal knowledge, and in much early printing an amplification and reinforcement of existing ideas resulted from the 'ever more frequent repetition of identical chapters and verses, anecdotes and aphorisms, drawn from very limited scribal sources' (Eisenstein 1984: 89). This both increased the spread of mistakes and ensured an often conservative impulse to the emerging literacy. Febvre and Martin write that:

> Although printing certainly helped scholars in some fields, on the whole it could not be said to have hastened the acceptance of new ideas or knowledge. In fact, by popularizing long cherished beliefs, strengthening traditional prejudices and giving authority to seductive fallacies, it could even be said to have represented an obstacle to the acceptance of many new views. Even after new discoveries were made they tended to be ignored and reliance continued to be placed in conventional authorities. (1976: 278)

Especially following the development of printing, the author and the text have a status of being which, as it subsequently wanes in the experience of reading, emerges in the philosophical ideas of the Renaissance. One such belief held that there was an occult knowledge in writing which lay behind that which was revealed in the alphabet. In the fifteenth and sixteenth centuries hieroglyphs were believed to express ancient secrets not captured in alphabetic writing, and some persons theorized the existence of lost languages, the languages of Enoch or Adam, for example, which revealed the true nature and hidden secrets of the universe. By the seventeenth century, 'language was envisioned as an aggregate of discrete sounds, each denoting a mental image, which in turn mirrored a natural world of separate physical objects' (Hudson 1994: 43). From around 1600 on, writing had an ambiguous status in the world, operating now as a corrupter of natural goodness and now as a liberator from ignorance (Hudson 1994; Foucault 1970). The uncertainty about the relationship between writing and orality reflected an uncertainty about the status of the sign and the signifier to guarantee the real.

It is only on the basis of a shared set of beliefs about particular practices and truth that language can be believed to represent what is. Dumouchel notes that:

> truth as adequation between what is in the mind and what is in the world is an illusion, the illusion *par excellence* of the Occident, the illusion of a pure presence, God, Nature, Man, that founds and guarantees the system of signs, the illusion of an origin that transcends, orders and guards the domain of signification. (1992: 84)

The Pure Signifier and Lost Presence

Writing and the Platonic *eidos* suppose a truth, a pure signifier that does not refer to anything else except itself (see Derrida 1972). As Dumouchel writes, 'this object would be the object of a perfectly singular experience, in order to be communicable, to gain a signification, it must become an ideal object, an eidos … a repeatable entity that can be associated with the signifier every time it is used' (1992: 83). Initially residing in the group's participation in oral narratives and stories, the truth was simply what was and this was exemplified in the acceptance of a psychic and social template of thought and behavior. A presence maintained with narrative established both the group structure and personal identity within the group. All behavior which was structured within the group had meaning; it took place within a framework which was meaningful because it was impersonal, because it belonged to the group. This presence is not yet differentiated into ideas which might exist within the mind, and so Heraclitus can locate the *logos* – which is still not yet words – as originating outside himself. With the evolution of writing and books, this truth ends up being successively displaced.

Writing produces the signifier as a visible thing, a marker which clearly stands between consciousness and the world and which raises the undeniable awareness that language is now not treating a real world itself, but only a marker for it, its trace (Derrida 1972; 1976). While other social forces undoubtedly contributed to the emergence of the idea as separate from the poetic and epic narratives, reading was the crucial technology required for the elaboration of a signifier which was finally differentiated from the presence of the thing; the old 'word magic' began to break down as the independent word took form. For centuries the truth, the reality of the written word as an instrument for transmitting ideas (rather than as a marker or listing of things), had to be translated into a personal and direct physical experience of the world. This was accomplished through the internalization of words which could be woven into one's own primary perceptual experience of the world. The written words of others were woven as well into the fabric of memory and consciousness in visual metaphors with other visual assistance from the page. As such the 'presence' was still not externalized but existed as a lived experience of thought flavored by reading.

In the late twelfth century, particular technologies of language transformed the scholastic reading into a scanning, an amassing, an accounting and reckoning of ideas which no longer located the presence of god in the *experience* of the word beheld in meditation but in the *idea* of the word. God and truth were no longer present in the word which was now confined to the page but, like Prester John's kingdom, were progressively moved further and further away until their absence in the cultural reality of early modern thinking became unavoidably obvious. The *eidos* became the idea, and this was now becoming simply information.

The presence was apparently missed and longed for. The displaced presence was sought for elsewhere in language: in lost tongues, in occult secrets, and in the sciences themselves which proposed to replace the lost presence of god with the new presence of a revealed physical world. Leibniz, Descartes and others sought to find a universal system for representing ideas as graphic characters, and Bacon favored an ideolectic system of writing similar to Chinese (Hudson 1994: 44). This language of science combined with the techniques of bourgeois literacy in the service of business, and from them emerged a new language which was true not because it revealed god but because it was efficient, didactic, teachable and, above all, finally necessary to people who were increasingly able to define themselves in groups with which they had only tenuous and literate connections.

The original presence carried in speech was a recognition of the presence of the other which invokes and validates the existence of the self. Reading enabled one to engage the other initially by a psychomotor act of eating and chewing, literally consuming the other, taking the other within to be part of oneself. Interpretive strategies, however, allowed the reader to hold the other in mind as an idea, and in so doing, interpretive strategies shift the focus of attention from the transitive experience to the substantive (see Sass 1992: 220ff). Rather than the experience of the other as presence, interpretation requires the signifier as the present marker of the other, as that which can be interpreted. The place where one would find the illocutionary parts of language shifts to the ideational and epistemological, and as this model of language is imposed on thought (Olson 1994: 89), self begins to be defined in the ideational realm. One's emotional self and experience of the emotive are then the experience not of the other but of the increasingly culturally elaborated *idea of the other*. The self begins to exist within the signs and signifiers alone which can never present the presence that precedes language: the pure gaze of the other.

The illusions which resided in the written word and its discourses of science and power in the end failed to produce the presence of the world, but dramatic changes to the social organization of society, people's constant movement, the diminishing importance of enduring social attachments and affections – all factors that Dewey mentioned in 1927 – have contributed to the absence of a counter-language in which the truth could reside. Hence one sees the rise of religious fundamentalisms of all forms which promise a way of balancing the temporal duration of timeless truth with the spatially biased book. The importance which these movements will have in the future should not be underestimated, for there are few other candidates left who can propose to produce the truth, and very few people seem prepared to inhabit a consciousness of poststructural indeterminacy.

If the other has defined us *a priori* and already has a preconceived view of how *all* people so encountered are to be understood, he or she would be unable to engage in recognizing us as centers of our own subjectivity. Everyone whom such a person met would be already set not only into pregiven social relationships but into a more primordial form as an object. A second possibility is that the available language itself might eliminate the possibility of the other person as capable of determining some significant part of reality. This is the case wherein, for example, technical language determines that a given other person is a set of reflex arcs, or an object for experimentation, or a consumer. This is also an argument raised by Plato against the book, and may well be applicable to the experience of watching television.

The television presents language as if it were a person, but we encounter it not as either a thing or a person but as a strange hybrid. Contemporary media technologies present us with language in many forms, but we cannot respond to this language or engage it in dialogue. It orders our world but without a reciprocal relationship that would enable us to order its world. We cannot establish relations with it. In a similar way, the absence of a vernacular language and its replacement with a taught, official language offers few alternatives for meaningful expression. It is, as Dupuy (1980) says, a hellish world, devoid of grace and of the unexpected.

The contemporary world is a place where popular knowledge consists largely of trivia, detached factoids about sports, celebrities, 'personalities', and other ephemera of contemporary life. These are not knowledge or even information; they are tropes, the literary devices of a new kind of orality. Just as a person living in fifth century Athens would be judged by his ability to recall phrases from the *Iliad* and to use examples from this work in everyday speech, so the contemporary speaker is deemed witty by his ability to use lines from pop songs or commercial jingles. As such, 'a growing percentage of personal utterances has become predictable, not only in content, but also in style' (Illich 1992: 127). The recall of these bits and their use in speech and writing do not constitute literacy – despite the misuse of the word in phrases such as 'cultural literacy' and 'video literacy' – but rather present the material of an externalized language. This language is not, however, rigidly preserved as it would be in an oral culture. Rather, the language itself is constantly remade, its metaphors reworked, the elements of its expression forever unlinked from any stable shared social world.

THREE

The Trajectory of the Image

Well! Like other branches of art, photography already possesses two distinct schools: one above all occupied with the ensemble, the other attached to the minute representation of details; the school of the fantasists and that of the realists. (Charles Bauchal (1852), in Jammes and Janis 1983: xii)

One of the most curious and at the same time distressing truths we know is, that a man may be miserable and not be conscious that he is so. He need not be insensate; but what we understand by the term misery does not distress him, it does not engage his mind, it tells upon him simply as an animal. Such man is more contented and more gross than the beasts with which we find him associated. (George Bell 1849)

The Beginning and End of the Image

The history of the image traces a trajectory that begins and ends with the disappearance of the image itself. In its beginnings, the image was that which could not endure as a record; it existed to invoke, to provide a point of identity in the physical world for something not yet physical. In the millennia that followed, the image became, slowly, a surface which fixed a point of view in time, freezing the relationship between the viewer and the represented object in an idealized relationship of permanence and stability. This fixity is achieved initially through the holding of a moment in time in the image. For a brief while, the myth of the photograph promised a 'true' representation of the world and even lent its name to such ideas as 'photographic memory', which connoted the completely accurate recall of the experience of a moment. Such a notion supported the ideas of perceptions which were completely reliable and consequently of a self which was completely trustworthy in its relationships to the world. Possessing finally a recording method which, as a product of the new sciences of chemistry and physics, could document the world as it was, as object, people found in photography what all prior recording methods had lacked: a way of verifying and of proving the experience of consciousness. If the moment of perception could be preserved, the experience of perception could be replicated, studied, and shared.

One's relationship to the other, to something in the world, could be stabilized, and so consciousness could hold the perception of itself as an object, as something in the world for examination, contemplation, and manipulation.

Even the moving picture, and later the video, derives from this idealization of a stable relationship between the viewer and the image, and both rely on the ephemeral property of the contemporary image, its lack of duration. Mass production, combined with the media in which the image appears, today produce an image that cannot endure. Massive reproduction of every conceivable image, and especially of the great works of art, ensures an inflation in the frequency and number of images that one perceives such that the value of any particular image is lessened. The great majority of images that one encounters do not endure, nor are they meant to. They appear for a moment on a billboard, in a magazine, in a newspaper, or even more fleetingly they flash for a moment as scan lines or pixels on a screen surface. The motion picture depends upon this disappearance; one sees not movement but the rapid juxtaposition of still images taken through time which blur together on the retinas of our eyes. One image must disappear to be replaced by the next to create the illusion of motion.

As we encounter an image, it is already positioned for us within aesthetic and semiotic systems that tell us how to read it. The language locates the image within the world of things, and it locates us toward its system of meanings. The image marks our position within the systems of meaning-making, the semiotics, and the beliefs which produce and deliver it to us, and for this reason, the effect of the image is found not in the content or the meaning but in the systems that create and structure one's relationship with the image. These aesthetics position us in relation to the image so that the meaning we find in the image and its effect on us seem a natural cause and effect. It is as part of the taken-for-granted world that the image 'conveys' meaning or feeling independently of a system of meaning. The image draws consciousness out of its relation to the world and into a relation with systems of representation. The relationship that we have to the image is not fixed but evolves, guided by various cultural logics that influence the form and operation of media.

Borrowing from other conventions, the contexts or genres of images for a while imparted a stability to the relationship between the image and the viewer, granting both a position of relative stability within the social. The identity of the viewer was vouchsafed by the discourses and aesthetics employed: art connoisseur, consumer, citizen, audience member. In the same manner, the meaning of the image was likewise stabilized: work of art, advertisement, news, entertainment. These conventions emerged slowly and only seriously began to coalesce into their modern forms in the eighteenth century when the institutions and philosophies emerged that could give form and permanence to the discourses that underpinned them. Art as we know it could not exist without museums and art critics. Advertising as something more than mere announcements of the availability of goods and their prices requires mass societies fed by mass media pandering to mass appetites.

If the image today does not endure, it is because the locus for the production of meaning has shifted from discourses and aesthetics which would stabilize our relationship with the image to those structurings of meanings that deliberately destabilize that relationship and so also destabilize consciousness and the self. Rather than integrating experience with a range of knowledges and understandings, the contemporary aesthetics fragment the totality of experience, for they do not orient the perception of the image with one's personal history or with those narratives of explanation and understanding. Rather, the image exists to evoke momentary desire, emotion, or identification with impersonal, mass-produced, ideas and beliefs. The dominant aesthetic in contemporary culture does not lead to slow contemplation and integration but is geared instead toward the immediate grasp of what is simply the next in a seemingly endless barrage of images and demands upon consciousness to be in a particular way. Our primary aesthetic addresses the immediate problem of simply orienting oneself among the flashing lights and blowing pages of an intensely image oriented culture, but it does not and cannot assist us in the task of locating these images into the totality of our personal history and experience. The aesthetics which we commonly have at hand simply do not orient us toward the image in that way.

An aesthetic, just as any other discourse or other tool for organizing knowledge and experience, emerges from and must fit with the other major organizing forces within a society and a culture. They must share common values and principles, and people are educated to these as they become the conditions of their everyday existence. However, it should no longer be a point of debate that the conditions of existence in the Western, capitalistic, technological, mass society are such that the principles of most existing narratives and discourses are oriented toward the spatial and away from the temporal, toward the collective and away from the individual, toward the social and away from the personal.

In the contemporary world, the purpose of the image has become its function as a product of mechanized production and financial exchange, especially as these are personalized in desires. The purpose of the advertising image is not to bring the absent object present, but to structure emotional reactions that are related to our consuming the product. The commercialization of the image is not limited merely to advertising, however. Even works of 'great art', the culturally hallowed masterpieces which adorn museums and the boardrooms of the corporate headquarters of multinational firms, have been stripped of their function as art and transformed into markers of wealth and power. As Robert Hughes has remarked, the extremely high prices paid for art 'have already done incalculable damage to the idea of art as a socially shared medium freely accessible to thought and judgment' (1991: 410). The viewer's relationship to the work in this case is constrained by the 'truth' of the work established as a function of value; a work of art is important because it is expensive. The price also excludes any consideration of the merits of the piece independently of the value. Capital, like technology, displaces all other values so that the discourses which position the social meanings of art no longer function. Aesthetic interpretation is still possible but socially meaningless, and one who seeks to establish understandings through a completely capitalized system of values finds only lessons about the value of one's own labor in the world.

Thus advertising has become both the most pervasive social discourse in the industrialized world and the model for other forms of communication. Desire, affection, even time are translated into commodities. A recent advertisement for the Discovery Channel exhorted, 'If you have to miss a moment in time, don't let it be this one.' The logic of commodification and exchange becomes the primary organizing principle of the social in the 'form and operation' of the media (Baudrillard 1981: 169). What is crucial to observe and know becomes indistinguishable from what is picayune. Virilio observes that a 'siesta' of consciousness and a decline in existence follow from denying 'the ideal hierarchy of the crucial and the incidental, because there is no incidental, only dominant cultures that exile us from ourselves and others' (1991: 37).

It is not ourselves that we find in images today, it is our desires and the manufactured markers of our identity that we encounter as other and that we attempt to integrate into consciousness. When the image had become sufficiently ubiquitous to provide a major part of experience, and the discourses which position the self in relation to the image had become sufficiently divorced from the local and from the elaboration of personal history to appear as the world, consciousness could then search for itself in the systems of images as it had once projected itself into the symbolic world grounded in local interaction. However, the self does not emerge only through an implication in ongoing social activities, but appears also as the solipsistic subjectivity predicated by an apparently self-referential world that is simultaneously intimately familiar and completely alien.

A study of the image allows us to explore different ways in which the self can relate to the world in a mediated way. Fundamentally, the image allows a form to be interposed between consciousness and the world, and this form differs from the abstraction of verbal language. This form may stand for some thing in the world as a sufficient knowledge of it to give familiarity and recognition. Most people know what the Grand Canyon, or the Great Pyramids, or the *Mona Lisa* 'look like' even though they may never have seen the original. In fact, after a lifetime of seeing images, the original may appear overwhelming, shocking. One is often totally unprepared for the complex reality and the overwhelming detail of seeing something *in situ* for the first time. It takes some time and contemplation before we can integrate the real into our understanding, but the image stands for a compacted version of the world, a flattened miniature that should convey the totality of our relationship to the world but which never succeeds in so doing.

Image and identity

The thrust of the development of the image has always been toward producing something that could stand in place of the real. The *telos* of this trajectory has been not to produce something that supplants the real, but rather to produce something that changes our relationship to what is, our relationship to being itself. Three key moments emerge that highlight this trajectory, enough to trace its path: the emergence of the image as a point of transition between self and other, the fixing of the image within discourses of identity and explanation (such as astronomy, biology, social sciences), and finally the development of the image as an interface linking consciousness to desire and identity.

The image today occupies a variety of positions within our personal and shared social consciousness. Ubiquitous, inescapable, at once fundamental and ephemeral, the image has triumphed over all other representation in the last 100 years of human history, in large part due to the rise of mass production. The reign of the image is both a tyranny and a release from the bondage of writing, for images are infinitely more dense in meaning than the written word and have an immediacy and an almost imperative modality in our perception of them, such that the importance and function of the written word has been dramatically altered in a relatively short space of time. The written word itself appears increasingly as image, a process accelerated by the social institutions associated with advertising and by the domesticated version of copy writing: desktop publishing in which the word appears as image on the screen. One may alter size, fonts, color, all at a whim, arranging the text on the page to conform with the several lessons acquired from advertising copy. In the education industry, DTP has led some students to produce papers with far greater attention to appearance than to substance; paragraphing, multiple fonts, subheadings, cut and pasted material, precisely justified left, right or center on the page: these and other legerdemain of layout were unthinkable prior to the word processor.

The influence of advertising in transforming words into images invades nearly every aspect of my life. As I write this, the desk upon which the computer screen sits is fairly covered with written words that function more as corporate logos, as identifiers, than as words. The mouse pad educates me at a glance to 'what you can do with degrees in communication and information studies'. The printer, the screen, the keyboard, CD games, each proclaims in a single evocation its existence, origin, familiarity, reliability, and quality in staccato bursts of vision that I instantly recognize and that in my contemporary, modernist aesthetic I can largely ignore.

These are not words for me; they are images. I do not read them as I would a book or a letter or even a child's crayon scrawl on a doorframe. The discourses that would frame for me a book, or even a literate phrase, as a particular sort of work (history, fiction, reference, philosophy, childish expression) are completely absent. There is no author in a meaningful sense of these images, and my relationship with them does not lead to extensions of thought or argument: they are not objects for contemplation. The limitations of their meaning are established not through the author function (Foucault 1984), nor through genre, nor through any of the other techniques used commonly to limit the proliferation of meaning. Words converted to images rather absorb their meaning into the form of the image. When I see the image 'Canon', I do not read words but see trademarks and indicators of function. Similarly, the mouse pad, though densely covered with tiny printed fantasies of various career options provided by a particular degree, is not something to be read. I am drawn to scan it as I would an advertisement pasted to a wall. Only its persistence on the desk, just beneath my hand, draws my eye to examine the greater detail.

What, then, is an image? The basic property of the image is to transfer identity or some part of it from one being to another through representation. The word 'image' is closely related to the idea of imitation, the state where one thing brings to consciousness some of the characteristics and features of another thing. I look at the image, a particular font and arrangement of the letters 'C-a-n-o-n' on the printer, and the history, tradition, and qualities of the corporation, as these are known to me through advertising and through my own experience, are invoked. Perceiving the logo in this way differs dramatically from how my consciousness would treat the word 'canon'. In the case of the logo, the image displaces the word from language, limiting the available meanings and the connections that I might make from them. In the case of the word 'canon', literary and theological discourses are immediately invoked, linking my consciousness through language and history to a far-ranging possible field of thoughts. The image establishes an identity, an origin and source of itself that it stands in place of; it represents something that is not present. The image stands in perception for that which is not present, an IOU from the domain of being.

The direct eidetic function of the image, to bring something to consciousness by standing for the absent thing, establishes not only the absent thing but one's relationship to it as well. The new context of the thing as image, the represented thing, presents the relationship between consciousness and the thing in a new form. Rather than the consciousness confronting something that has equal status as a being in the world, the *created* image has a subservient position to both consciousness and the world to the extent that the image emerges as an expression of consciousness acting through language. In the process of constructing the image of something, one constructs also the relationship that one has with the represented thing, and this remaking of the relationship allows that relationship to be changed.

Indeed, the fear of hubris involved in representing some beings or things, and so attempting to control them, is a likely reason for the prohibitions against representing god in some religions such as Judaism or the representations of any sentient creature in Islam. It is also the basis of some forms of magic. It is not the thing being represented that is changed; one does not change either being or god by making images of them. A caribou remains a caribou regardless of whether one has made an image of it. However, the technique of creating the representation makes possible a change to one's relationship to the thing. The new caribou, represented, is the distillation of the idea of the caribou, set into a visual language, arranged so that its relationship to the creator of the image is altered: no longer completely independent, the represented caribou is associated with the painter in ways the physical caribou could never be. The relatedness between the person and the world in some cultures is much more direct and explicit; for example, the animal being hunted gives itself as food, and this gift is acknowledged in various ways. These relationships of obligation and reciprocity that already existed between the world and the person could, however, be manipulated, symbolically transformed. In order to ensure that both participants, the human and the spirit, were present, the spirit could be represented. This is explicitly the case in the Navaho making of drypaintings.

Drypainting and the invocation of the other

The creation of an image, perhaps more than any other technology of communication, demonstrated the ability of human beings to freeze the unfolding moment of the world, much as writing froze the unfolding moment of the word. In the case of Neanderthal cave paintings of animals or hunting scenes, the pictures are hidden deep within the recesses of caves where great effort would be required to reach the place. The places where these sorts of paintings of great bison, deer, the actions of hunters, and similar images would be painted by torchlight onto walls were perhaps not meant to be viewed again or seen by the uninitiated. We do not know if the images were, in fact, ever meant to be seen again at all. Rather, it is possible that the purpose of these paintings lay in the act of creating, the magic of making the representation.

A similar disregard for the permanence of the image may be seen in the sandpaintings of some southwestern tribes of Native Americans. Complex and elaborate designs, highly stylized, are created by pouring colored sand onto a smoothed dirt or sand surface or upon a skin lain upon the ground. In the Navajo rites, the image is destroyed both by interacting with it in the course of the rite, and ritualistically at the end of the rite. Preserving the image in any permanent form was largely prohibited, even by threat of death (Wyman 1983 [1952]: 9). While the Navajo were not, by and large, nomadic people and had the permanent settlements that would have permitted them to preserve representations had they so chosen, the creation of the image was, for them, not a thing to be saved. The image was not meant to preserve, but to bring an idea into being in a different form, to make visible in a representation aspects of the otherwise invisible relationships between the people and the universe.

The sandpaintings of the Navajo peoples of the American desert show a purpose for images and their creation that is alien to the mainstream of the Western aesthetic tradition. The sandpainting or 'drypaintings' (as other substances are used in their creation) are created by 'singers', men empowered to perform rites for the good of individuals or the tribe. Women are forbidden to perform these rites, or even to be present at some parts, not from a sense of chauvinism but to avoid prenatal spiritual contagion by an evil spirit. The singers are consulted especially in the case of illness, and one of their first tasks is to establish the cause of the disease or illness. For the Navajo, all things exist in balance governed by reciprocity (1983 [1952]: 15). Illness, misfortune, and most problems in life stem from a loss of this balance, and the job of the singer is to recognize precisely what forces must be set into order through the performance of a particular rite. Broadly divided into holyway rites and ghostway rites, numerous different rites with songs and paintings unique to that rite address different causes of imbalance. There are, for example, a waterway, used to cure diseases arising from the effects of nearly drowning or from injury by water; and a beautyway, linked to infection by snakes, causing rheumatism, kidney and bladder illness, and dreams of snakes (1983 [1952]: 57).

Once the etiology of the situation is discerned, a particular rite will be planned and will be announced to the supernatural and to humans by placing certain objects outside the hogen (the dwelling place) of the affected person; this is the 'setting out'. Then the ritual will begin and may continue for two, five or nine days. After a purification involving sweating and emetics, the singer will proceed to draw particular images of various supernatural beings, the 'holy people', and creatures with supernatural powers on the floor of the hogen. The images are drawn in certain relationships to each other and are often surrounded with a 'guardian' image, such as a rainbow guardian. Each drypainting, or *iikaah* in Navajo, is linked to particular songs. Wyman writes that the purpose of these images is threefold: to attract the supernaturals, to identify the 'sung-over-one' with them, and to serve as a path for the exchange of good and evil (1983 [1952]: 33). The image, again, serves a means of establishing identity and then transferring this identity to another thing.

Once a drypainting had been created to the satisfaction of the singer and of other elders who may be present, the Navajo believe that the supernatural beings will come to look at their portraits (1983 [1952]: 33) and that having arrived they will actually become the images and enter the dwelling in person. The holy ones, obligated by the images of them, restore balance and effect a repair of what has been disordered. Good will flow from the supernaturals, and evil will be transferred into the sand. For this reason, the painting materials must be removed after the rite is concluded. The restoration of balance is accomplished by the transfer of identity of the supernatural beings to the one being sung over. This person may sit in the picture and have bits of colored sand transferred from the image to his own body. He literally becomes the image, and as the holy ones are also the image, the sung-over-one becomes identified with them.

Drypaintings seduce the supernaturals into appearing and, through physical contact with the image now imbued with the being of the deity, the sung-over-one's relationship to the deity, and thus to the universe, is changed. The drypaintings thus act as altars more than as what we mean by the word, image, and it is within this function as altar that the deep, ontological function of the image reveals itself. We commonly think of altars in the purely functional sense of what they are: they are a sacred space where some activity is performed, the host consecrated, the hearts of virgins cut out, and so on. This misses the point. Altars are above all gateways between the spiritual and mundane worlds. They mark the places where the divine and the human may safely cross over from their respective domains and touch one another. The altar allows the divine to enter in a controlled and predictable manner, a way that does not destroy the mundane and that does not unleash the supernatural in its full power. Many religions from diverse cultures have strict rituals to ensure that the one is never face-to-face with god and that god never appears in undiluted form. The image brings us into relationship with being in ways already normalized and codified in language. When Moses asks for the name of god so that his people may address him, god says, 'Tell your people that I am.' Other translations have it: 'Tell your people I am that I am.' God does not tell Moses I am this or I am that; he never identifies himself with some thing. Rather, god says only that he is. The divine is the dimension of pure being, and one cannot directly enter the domain of pure being without destruction. Consciousness must have the reference points of self-awareness and its relation to language to establish a relation with the world; therefore, being must be mediated for consciousness to continue to exist separate from it. The other cannot exist for consciousness as it is.

The required distance between consciousness and being is derived from an intermediary in the form of technology. Images are created through a technology, a *techne*, and this constitutes an attempt to manipulate symbolically one's relationship with the domain of being. The creation of images in the Navajo rituals is, of course, only one of several possible functions of images. What is key here is the attitude of consciousness toward the image. The purpose for which the image is created emerges out of the need of consciousness in that setting. The Navajo wish to bring the divine into the physical through a series of transfers of identity from the image to the deity to the sung-over-one. In this process, the image is destroyed, but the benefits of the identification continue after the ceremony. Neither consciousness nor the supernaturals are transformed in any enduring way: they meet, exchange, and separate. At no point does the supernatural become the object in front of consciousness, but the supernatural does effect a change in the relationship of consciousness with the world. This is the main purpose of the ritual: to restore balance and harmony in relationships.

The Navajo approach to the creation of the image has some similarities to the approach of creating Byzantine icons. Monks would create the image while engaged in religious contemplation and prayer, and the icon exists more as a testament of the artist's spiritual contemplations than as a work of art. After the Byzantine period, in European religious cultures, the image functions quite differently, and all images bring about an identification whereby objects exist for contemplation, examination, and recording. This fact suggests a rather different relationship between consciousness and the world, and it makes possible the confusion of the image with the real.

Time, narrative and the image

If an image allows us to alter our relationship to the world of the supernatural, it also allows us to alter our relationship to the world as real or true in subtle ways. In the aesthetic choice of choosing one set of details over another, this perspective in preference to that one, the meaning of the image and, theoretically, one's relationship with the thing being represented are transformed. Through artistic representation in the middle ages, artists commonly conflated the time frame of the subject matter with their own, depicting figures of religious or historical significance in the clothing and settings of the artists' own worlds. This recasting of details into other settings was not viewed as a deception or distortion, it was simply a way of bringing the present and the past together in representation, making the past at once familiar and present. It was also a way of writing the present into the great historical narratives and events of the past.

Time and real were manipulated in other ways in the image as well. The standard posing of people for portraits through the middle ages was the frontal pose, a tradition that continues today in wedding pictures, family portraits, and many snapshots taken to commemorate events. The aesthetic effect of pose is to eliminate temporality from the picture. Bourdieu notes that 'in every aesthetic, frontality means eternity, in opposition to depth, through which temporality is reintroduced, and the plane expresses being or essence, in short, the timeless' (1990: 78). Compressed into the surface of the image, the faces of Jesus and Justinian stare out of the surface, frozen forever in an abstract moment. What mattered was precisely the timelessness of the picture and not the conveyance of time or of a moment. A consequence of the particular philosophies of Christianity which focused on the eternal and spiritual in contrast to the mundane, this aesthetic worked to extend the image as idea by linking it with symbolism and iconography, and through the image, the viewer was led to a renewed understanding and appreciation of the divine.

One's temporal relationship to the great, the divine, the eternal was recreated in the act of viewing the painting. The eyes flow from detail to detail, the mind moves through the symbolic depths conveyed in deeply coded, highly iconic complexities that to the modern mind make many Byzantine or medieval paintings seem abstruse or simply cluttered. Lacking the aesthetic code which would position us toward the work and guide us through its meanings, we find the pictures do not work for us as they did for the savants of the era in which they were created. Many things are different, certainly most today do not understand the coding of symbols in these works, but our relationship to the world has changed as well, particularly the way we experience time, and this relationship to time is captured in the images of every culture. Virilio (1989: 35) writes that 'all art is like death, an inertia of the instant', that is, the way that the moment is captured in art reflects the attitude of consciousness toward time.

In early Western representation, a linearity of time competes with the fixed moment. Stories unfolding in strip fashion adorn Egyptian temples and Greek vases and continue appearing in Western art through that most amazing strip story, the Bayeux Tapestry. Through 72 different panels, this work depicts the events leading to the death of King Harold of England and his replacement with William of Normandy in 1066. Near contemporaneous with the events, the tapestry guides the eye through one after another episodes in the history without any consistent representation of time. One scene depicts Harold seated on his throne while a comet, the 'hairy star', blazed in the heavens above him. This ill-omen, in this case Halley's Comet, portended disaster or catastrophe. So in an early form of foreshadowing, the present scene evokes a future moment, one already in the viewer's past, the Norman conquest of Harold's England. The use of time is most clearly seen in the sequence depicting the building of William's flotilla. One image shows trees being chopped down which overlaps a representation of ship hulls being constructed, and finally, this image overlaps, however slightly, the representation of ships being pulled to the water. The importance of these events overshadows the duration of the moment: we see not time but the effect of action through time, the traces of time as a product of events.

In a work such as the Bayeux Tapestry, each frame constitutes an episode, a single moment or series of moments that compresses the flow of events through time into a fixed image. This is a common technique for showing the passage of time in medieval art; pictures representing different moments occupy the same frame of the picture. Although multiple exposures of a photograph may achieve the same effect, we still tend to see the images as separate frames or moments.

One problem, though, is that the images are necessarily an interpretation, and even the moments chosen as well as the details included or left out reveal a series of human decisions that ensure that the tapestry cannot be 'taken as read' and understood uncritically. Uncertainty pervades our understanding of the piece. The question of who made the work necessarily invokes the question of whose point of view of that history is being represented. We have no framework to guide our reading of the tapestry and arrive at a belief that one or another version is necessarily true. Being a work of art, the tapestry unabashedly presents its version of this history as the true story, the one to remember, and it has compressed into its telling all the information that the commissioner of the work, whether Bishop Odo or someone else, wished to include. As such, the work presents a Norman view of the events leading to William's conquest of the English: cosmic portents, secret histories, moral justifications, practical plans.

Time in this work is multidimensional; the current moment reflected looks both forward to outcomes and back to justifications, and the current moment is thus blurred with slippage. We cannot even grasp the current moment of a panel as image; we too must invest in its perspective on time and bring our own histories to the reading.

With our perspective and the invocation of other histories, we are in a position to challenge the work. It is a work of art, from our perspective, but it is also a work of propaganda that seeks to influence not the world but language. The tapestry does not adjust one's relationship to the real Harold or the real William, but it changes the way that they are positioned in our understanding of history. The treachery of Harold in breaking his oath to William justifies the invasion and subsequent regicide. Certainly the Greeks and Romans had recorded their great deeds and triumphs of conquest and combat, but they limit themselves to depicting the crucial moment, Achilles carrying off Ajax, and so on. The Bayeaux work deliberately attempts to tell all the pertinent details of the story from beginning to end. It is a writing of history in a pictorial form, and as such, the tapestry speaks not to its contemporaries but to the future and is an explicit attempt to alter the way that the future will view the past. In so doing, the work reveals an early way of compressing time and the complexities of the moment for the specific purpose of extending one perspective of time into the future.

Patrick Geddes and the camera obscura

The problem with viewing the world is not that it won't stand still, but that the world is too complex and sudden to take in at one glance, and by the time one looks again, the world has changed. In the real world, one's attention wanders from point to point, always at the risk that what is important to see, what is revealing, might be missed while one is looking elsewhere. It is impossible for consciousness to anticipate with certainty what is important to notice in any given moment. The importance of a moment derives from what one has chosen to perceive, and this derives from the structuring that he or she is attempting to place on the moment. There are two ways of seeing: broadly, taking in the whole field of vision, and narrowly, focusing on some particular detail. Both are important, but they are, from the standpoint of perception, mutually exclusive. To limit the amount of visual information that one must process mentally, a simple technique is to reduce the visual field in size and collapse its three dimensions into two. This is precisely what the camera obscura, and later the photo, accomplish.

The photograph does not capture the attitude or relationship of consciousness toward the object. Rather, the photograph instantly reorients the object of the gaze into new aesthetic positionings for consciousness. Bourdieu noted that 'because of its subordination to a machine, photographic art allows that transfiguration of the object by which we are accustomed to recognizing artistic creation' (1990: 78). This is only partly true, however, for certainly the photographer has a determining part to play in the setup of the camera, the choices of angles, exposure, depth of field, and so on. The camera image is not subordinated to the machine, but it does introduce discourses and ideas associated with the machine into the aesthetic of the image.

Replicability, standardization, mass production – these characteristics of the machine had certainly been applied to images before, but the camera altered the process of making images and so the way in which images were to be viewed. The camera is a kind of machine, and once the problems of making photos consistently had been resolved and popularized by George Eastman with the Brownie camera in 1888, 'choice, freedom, aesthetic evaluation [were] transferred from the process as a whole, where it might take place at any moment, to the initial stage of design' (Mumford 1952: 82). The Brownie was preloaded with film at the factory; after shooting the roll, the consumer would send the camera back to the factory, the images would be processed, the camera reloaded, and the entire package returned. The making of images thus evolved from processes closely associated with the crafts of drawing and sketching, through a phase of artistic development and experimentation (which continues in photographic art), to a machine for producing, without training or indeed much thought, instant art for the masses.

In the beginning, though, the ways in which photography would be practiced and understood were by no means clear. Several competing discourses at different times and places located photography in relation to the ideas of the times, and among the most persistent of these were the discourses of documentation and rationality extending from the Enlightenment. In 1793 a statue of reason was enthroned at the cathedral of Notre-Dame in Paris, an extreme statement of the same philosophy that led Diderot and the other encyclopedists to attempt to incorporate all worthwhile knowledge into books. While the power of the old religious and aristocratic orders was being eclipsed by a faith in progress, steam power, techniques of mass production, and ruthless capitalism on a global scale, the social philosophies encapsulating these beliefs found expression in a whole range of activities extending from medicine and penology to education and urban planning. These beliefs found expression in art as well, especially in the emergence of the new realism and the abandonment of allegory and myth in painting and sculpture. Rational beliefs were the order of the day.

Most importantly, the new sciences that had emerged in the seventeenth and eighteenth centuries provide the material means for the photographic process. Alchemy had become chemistry. Work in chemistry had since 1737 demonstrated that some substances respond to light, although the reason would not be known for many years. This fundamental discovery was coupled with a new interest in looking at the universe born from the recent astronomical work. Above all, the formation of professional organizations, such as the Royal Society created new communities of researchers, not only familiar with the work of others in their own world but acquainted with the entire sweep of science. The age of the expert had not yet emerged, and the true scientist of the eighteenth and nineteenth centuries was often active in several fields. Sir John Herschel, for example, was known as an astronomer, a chemist and a biologist, and he had an active interest in the formation of photography.

In the 1500s, the idea of the camera obscura was elaborated into a fairly common device. A wall in a darkened room could be illuminated with the image of what was outside, although inverted. To turn the image right-side-up, a simple objective lens could be fixed to the pinhole. From the image in a room, the size was reduced to fit in a box or cylinder with a pinhole in one side. The incoming light would focus on a sheet of translucent paper or thin skin placed between the hole and the viewer. This device was commonly used by artists as an aid to capturing scenes for drawing. The great advantage of this miniaturized version was its ability to reduce three-dimensional space to a two-dimensional surface while preserving the apparent proportions of the scene.

A few camera obscuras still exist. One, located in Edinburgh, Scotland and once owned by Patrick Geddes, is situated in Outlook Tower near the castle. A mirror inside a gondola reflects the light down through a series of focusing lenses and onto a concave white surface. Through mechanical controls, the mirror can be rotated, elevated, and depressed, allowing various views of the surrounding areas. This particular camera obscura was built in the 1850s as a curiosity and tourist attraction. Significantly, this was about the same time as photography was being introduced. Already in Edinburgh and elsewhere, photographers such as Robert Adamson and D.O. Hill had begun to exhibit photographs of scenes about the country as early as 1840.

However, the experience of the camera obscura is quite different from that of a photograph and differs even from the experience of watching a video. In the 1850s, the difference between photos and the camera obscura must have been even more pronounced. The images move as do the objects in the outside world, though in a reduced scale and in two dimensions. We would now say that the view occurs in 'real time'. Colors appear saturated while edge lines and proportions are very clear. Both contemporary photos and the camera obscura share an extremely deep field of focus. All objects, of whatever distance from the camera, appear within the same plane with the same degree of clarity. One knows that, because of the rules of perspective, there is depth to the scene being represented, but one cannot perceive depth in two dimensions. As a consequence, the image in the camera obscura appears oddly removed from reality, compacted and distilled.

It is no accident that the camera obscura in Edinburgh would have been owned at one time by Geddes, one of the first great modern town planners and a figure of tremendous influence on zoos, pedestrian walkways, green spaces, and all of the other factors that we like to believe make our cities livable. Geddes was already formulating his philosophical attack on the most extreme aspects of Enlightenment philosophy and sought to restore a balance between experience, the inner life, and economic and technological rationalism divorced from humanistic values. From the Outlook Tower, Geddes could see the whole of the old town of 'Auld Reeky', as Edinburgh was then known. The smoke from coal fires in homes and factories, made more pungent by open sewage and rotting organic filth of all kinds, made nearly all cities hellish places. The old town of medieval closes and ways, punctuated by the newer tenements, was in the nineteenth century largely inhabited by working people and the poor, the wealthier people having moved down the hill to the newly constructed 'new town'. Geddes not only envisioned the reintegration of the city by encouraging the return of the middle classes to the city center, but also helped to redesign the old town to make it more inhabitable. From his vantage in the Outlook Tower, itself a seventeenth century building, Geddes could view most of the city; and with the aid of his camera obscura, he could represent the living city as an image, alive in ways that maps, plans, and even photos could never be. He sought to create in his visitors a 'synoptic' view of the city, seeing the city as a whole, as Aristotle had urged (Geddes 1968 [1915]: 13).

Indeed, the Outlook Tower camera was one part of a larger project undertaken by Geddes, his 'Index Museum' (Meller 1990: 110). Kitchen points out that the tower was to be a laboratory, 'for it was here that Geddes grew fully to realize the importance of the process of a comprehensive survey as an integral part of planning for the future' (1975: 139–40). The view from the camera was to be the beginning of a journey through Geddes' museum that would locate one within the scientific, cultural, and philosophical understandings of one's being in that place at that moment in Edinburgh. Geddes would race people up the winding steps to the tower, and out onto the balcony that provides a panoramic view of the surrounding countryside. Visitors then would be led into the darkened room, and gathered around the table upon which the image would be presented (1975: 130–1). Geddes himself described the purpose of the camera image, writing that it 'harmonises the startling landscape, near and far' and thus serves 'as an evidence for what is so often missed by scientific and philosophic minds, that the synthetic version to what they aspire may be reached more simply from the aesthetic and the emotional side, and thus be visual and concrete' (1968 [1915]: 321).

Thus, Geddes saw that the experience of viewing the image could lead to seeing the world in an integrated way, as a whole. This conception of the whole would then allow the mind to perceive other kinds of wholeness. After witnessing the city from the camera obscura, guests would be led again to the flat roof with its views of the city. The contrast between the darkened room with its tiny image and the sweeping vista of Edinburgh's surroundings from the Pentlands to the Kingdom of Fife 'was to Geddes a symbol of the change from the artist's view – the aesthetic and emotional view – to the limitless panorama, impossible to absorb at one go, of the geographic or scientific view' (Kitchen 1975: 131). The great challenge for Geddes, and the purpose of the Index Museum, was to integrate the scientific and the aesthetic along with their respective constituent disciplines. After this introduction to the place and a few lectures by Geddes on meteorology, geology, geography, history and so on, the guest would be led into a room with one small chair to meditate and absorb what he or she had learned (1975: 131).

The aim of the museum was illustrated in a planned stained-glass window called Arbor Saculorum, which symbolically represented the evolution of knowledge, all branches growing from common roots but separated by the 'mists' of specialism (Meller 1990: 106–7). The Index Museum would thus be a study center teaching the interlinkage of all forms of knowing, and as guests descended they would be directed through various exhibits, each floor being dedicated to an area of knowledge: the Edinburgh room with its models and photographs that formed the basis for Geddes' city exhibitions, the Scotland and Great Britain rooms, a floor devoted to Europe, one to language, and the ground floor devoted to 'the Orient' and general anthropology.

The use of the camera obscura in the Geddes' Index Museum reveals the extent to which the image emerged into existing knowledges and aesthetics. The rules for composition governing perspective and the arrangement of objects in the picture had grown for 400 years from the work of Brunelleschi and others. By the time the photo emerged, the discourses establishing what the picture should be were common knowledge in those classes having access to education and artistic exposure. Geddes tried to take the function of the image to the next step, to use the ability to transform a complicated, three-dimensional real world into a simplified aesthetic one in order explicitly to integrate this unique perception of the world with the other forms of knowing available. The aesthetic view could in an instant create the relationship between consciousness and the world, *in the context of knowledge and language*, which he believed to be the essential condition for a meaningful study of the world. Geddes wrote:

> Children and artists may see more than the wise, for there can be no nature study, no geography worth the name apart from the love and the beauty of Nature, so it is with the study of the city. (1968 [1915]: 321)

The world so perceived does not exist truly separate from the person but becomes emotionally and psychically a part of consciousness, a part of the self. Through such perceptions, one creates himself or herself in the world in a context that structures feeling and thought. Geddes' aim was to use this process to increase one's awareness of the world and of one's place in it; however, without this awareness, one's perception of the image could easily be confused with a perception of the world. An aesthetic awareness of the process of under-standing the image is necessary if one is to avoid the mistakes of seeing the image as the world or of believing that one's feelings, which the image evokes, are caused by either the world or the image rather than resulting from the conventions by which the image is read.

The dimensions of thought and feeling were for Geddes dependent not upon the object or the individual but upon the relationship that could be built between them through knowledge, that is, through language. Geddes, just as all other early experimenters with the camera image, relied on a familiarity with the discourses of art and science already present. In 1854 Charles Nègre would state explicitly the historical dependence of photography on art:

> Photography does not form a separate, barren field of art. It is only a means of execution … which serves the artist by reproducing, with mathematical precision, the form and effect of objects and even that poetry which at once arises from any harmonious combination. (quoted in Daval 1982: 41)

Thus there is something of a paradox in the emergence of the photographic image: it offers a new way of seeing the world that is at the same time reliant upon pre-existing knowledge about the rules for representing the world. It is, then, hardly surprising that those groups and persons with long-standing habits of working with representations and models of the world, artists and scientists, should so often have been involved in the early history of photography.

Photography and Meaning: the Stability of the Image

Among the pioneers of photography, one finds primarily two groups of people: scientists and artists. Although each group was concerned with truth, the main contention between them was whether that truth lay in the rationalistic and, later, positivistic methods or in the artistic and emotive experiences of the world. In the end, the distinction between the two would become blurred.

The creations of systems, whether scientific, philosophic, social, or artistic, arise from the specific cultural dynamics of their time and place, and as such, the same inventions and ideas often break out at several places at the same time. Newton and Leibniz, for example, each developed independently of the other a mathematical calculus within a year. When the Wright brothers flew their first plane, numerous other persons were working on the same problems. As discussed in the previous chapter, breakthroughs in thought and invention that succeed – and many do not – emerge because of compelling social need, the convergence of technologies, and the social and economic conditions to support their development and use. The social need in photography developed from the growing culture of the rational fascination with documenting the world as it is, as object. The technologies that converged were both technologies of science, which made the physical practice of photography possible, and technologies of art, which laid the foundations for the realism that photography could so ably provide to representation.

The emerging technology of photography

Thus, three methods of photography emerged nearly simultaneously in France and England. The scientist and inventor J.N. Niepce, in addition to developing an early model of the internal combustion engine which he called the 'pyrolophore', had succeeded in capturing an impermanent image as early as 1816. In 1822, using a pewter plate covered with bitumen of Judaea dissolved in lavender oil, Niepce succeeded in capturing a permanent image. Seven years later, he was joined by an artist of some acclaim who had worked for years developing new ways of representing the world and who in 1824 had obtained a patent for his illuminated models called 'dioramas'. L.J.M. Daguerre continued the work after Niepce's death in 1833, and plagued by financial difficulties, in part as a result of a fire that destroyed his dioramas and much research into photography, he was persuaded to sell his idea to the French government which presented it publicly in 1839 (Gernshein and Gernshein 1956: 24). The system was the daguerreotype.

Despite almost completely obscuring the work of another Frenchman, Hyppolyte Bayard, who had exhibited a system of capturing permanent images a month before the unveiling of the daguerreotype, Daguerre's method had several drawbacks as a practical system of photography. The system used copper plates coated with a silver halide that underwent chemical change when exposed to light. Mercury vapor would then be passed over the plates, creating an amalgam with the silver, and after washing, a fixed image of great clarity was revealed. However, the copper plates were expensive and dangerous to develop as mercury vapor is highly toxic. The exposure times were extremely long – up to three minutes depending on the light – and this limited the types of objects that could be photographed. The major drawback, though, was that the daguerreotype produced a single positive image from which copies could not be easily made. Nonetheless, the daguerreotype enjoyed considerable success on the Continent and elsewhere, particularly in those situations where only single images of stationary objects were required. An early use was the photographing of the monuments and buildings of France, commissioned by the French government; and in the US in the 1860s Brady still used the daguerreotype, in part for its clarity and in part because of licensing problems with the other major photographic system, the calotype.

In the United Kingdom, another system of photography was soon announced by William Henry Fox Talbot. He had developed a system of capturing images on paper in 1835 and, shocked by the news of Daguerre's system, he reported his new method, that of capturing images on a negative from which an infinite number of positive prints could be made, in a Royal Institution lecture, introduced by Michael Faraday, on 25 January 1839. He patented his method in 1841, calling the images so produced 'calotypes'. While the ability to make copies from one captured image was a great advantage, the calotype lacked the clarity and definition of the daguerreotype. Talbot, a true polymath in the fashion of his day, did not limit his work to developing a single system but sought ways of using photography to aid science. He is credited with making the first photomicrograph in 1841, and 10 years later used an electric spark in the first attempt to photographically capture a moving object (Daval 1982: 42). The genius of calotype for making multiple images was demonstrated when Talbot published the first book containing photographic images, *The Pencil of Nature* (1844).

As quickly as photography appeared, its products were incorporated not only into artistic discourses and practices, but into scientific ones as well. In its early manifestations, photography was indeed much closer to a chemistry experiment than to the creation of a painting or sketch. This confused origin accounts for the early confusion about the precise status of photography as either an art or a science. In fact, it was both, depending upon how it was used. As the practices of photography were taken up in different settings, the meaning of the photographs changed depending upon the uses to which they were to be put. An image of a person could be a social study, a family portrait, an exoticism, or an object of scientific study and curiosity. And it was not only people that were being photographed. The interests of science in stopping motion, in being able to present a precise and objective image of a moment, ensured that the new technology would find its way into nearly every field of investigation.

Talbot was joined by many august contemporaries in exploring the scientific uses of the new photographs. Jean Foucault captured a daguerreotype of blood at a magnification of 400× in 1844, and in 1852 took the first known photograph of the sun. The moon was first photographed in 1845. Sir John Herschel, already famous for his work in mapping and categorizing astronomical objects, was intensely interested in photography and is sometimes credited with first applying the terms 'positive' and 'negative' to the art.

The potential application of photography to astronomy was present from the beginning, for the problem of detailed astronomic observation and mapping depends on comparing subtle differences in a complex visual field between different moments in time. For example, the early sketches of Galileo showing the four largest moons of Jupiter relied on careful sequential observation of the sort to which photography would be uniquely suited. In addition to stopping the moment for closer study and mapping, photography captures the precise moment of observation in a form that others might examine. They could experience the same moment even if they were not present. The scientific habit of truth built upon replication of a moment was thus greatly advanced by the ability to hold the moment forever present as an object for study.

It was not only the moment in nature that scientists sought to arrest for study. The human subject and its infinitesimal gestures came under scrutiny from Charles Darwin with the help of the photographer O.G. Rejlander in 1872 with the publication of the book *The Expression of Emotions in Man and Animals*. Darwin sought to explore how expressions might have evolved, and the photograph allowed precise moments in the formation of expressions to be studied and compared. Photography began to enter other areas of science as a means of documenting and studying human appearance in madness. Dr H.W. Diamond, superintendent of women at the Surrey County Asylum, took photos of his inmates to demonstrate the various forms of mental illness. He presented his pictures to the Royal Society along with his paper 'On the application of photography to the physiognomy and mental phenomenon of insanity' on 25 May 1856 (Buckland 1974: 75). The truth of the image was thus established through the linkage to existing discourses of natural science and medicine and to the prestige of these sciences as well as the authority of their spokesmen.

As with astronomy, the pictures used by Darwin, Diamond, and others represented something real that had identifiable characteristics available for all to see and study. The world was no longer a matter of interpretation or personal experience. Anyone could see what the various forms of hysteria, catatonia, or dementia looked like. Of course, these pictures did not capture reality. As Bourdieu noted of the family portrait, they captured only

> an aspect of reality which is only ever the result of an arbitrary selection and consequently, of a transcription; among all the qualities of the object, the only ones retained are the visual qualities, which appear for a moment and from one sole viewpoint. (1990: 73)

The one point of view so represented draws the gaze to see through it. The sophistication of seeing the image 'as it should be', in the 'realist' way (Denzin 1991; Hall 1980), depends on the viewer acquiring the appropriate relationship toward the image, and this relationship can only be established from within the institutions, meanings, languages, and beliefs already constituted in the discourse that created the image. Such a nuanced approach to images is appropriate within highly specialist knowledges such as medicine, astronomy, and art, and the early methods of producing relatively small numbers of specifically mean-ingful images were appropriate for such situations. The camera systems which were available in the first decade of photography – heavy and difficult to use and develop – were no great impediment for these limited uses.

A further technological refinement was required before photography could become truly widespread, and this appeared in 1851 in the form of Frederick Archer's wet-plate process and the use of albumin print paper for the positive. The method was still cumbersome, requiring that the exposure be made while the plate was still wet, but the glass plate negative was capable of producing images of extremely high quality and in infinite numbers of copies. The mechanized mass production of photographic images became possible for the first time, and this opened photography to a variety of other institutions that had their own uses for the new method of making pictures. For the first time, high-resolution reproductions of great works of art could be made and distributed for study. Although still lacking in color, these copies could be printed in books and distributed for study by people who had never seen the originals and would perhaps never have the opportunity to do so. In addition to the art world, the governments of both England and France used photo-graphy from the middle of the century to document buildings, monuments, and places of historic or archeological significance. The English Ordnance Survey, which by 1867 filled five books, even made copies of its photos available for purchase by the public. These photos closely paralleled the pictures that were creating and defining the newly emerging fields of archeology and anthro-pology by extending the voyeuristic exoticism of the travelogue. The world, both far and near, was being documented in images, and these pictures were reaching increasingly wide audiences as they addressed ever more socially engaging topics.

The aesthetic context of early photography

The second major discourse that took charge of the foundling child of photo-graphy was art. As already noted above, the camera obscura had its origins as an aid to composition for artists for centuries preceding. Fox Talbot was using such a device to aid his sketching when he began to contemplate how to preserve the image (see Ward and Stevenson 1986; Lassam 1979). The photograph, though, quickly became both a major high art in its own right and the most popular means of artistic creation.

It is possible that the photograph would not have gained such popularity as an artistic medium without the cultural background of emerging expressions of realism in art and literature both on the Continent and in the United Kingdom. While an interest in the natural world had been growing in the arts of painting and sculpture since the fourteenth century, especially influenced by the works of Cavallini, Giotto, and Brunelleschi, much of the seventeenth and early eighteenth centuries had been marked by a neoclassical extravagance in art that sought to link the powers of the age with the greatness of the past, much as Renaissance artists had sought to recapitulate and borrow from the nobility of Greek and Roman art and architecture. The realm of the ideal was preferable to the realm of the real.

However, all this was changing. Painters such as William Hunt and the other Pre-Raphaelite artists in England had already begun to express their disgust with neoclassical painting by 1848 with the founding of their movement, and Henry Robinson, among other photographers and artists, was strongly influenced by their unconventional compositions and attention to detail (Harker 1988: 31–2). On the Continent, the French artists, notably Courbet, had stridently declared their interests in a straightforward art more cognizant of the time and place of its creation. In 1863, while Bradley and his photographic teams followed the battles of the American Civil War in their wagons, making daguerreotypes of both camp scenes and the dead, Manet was shocking the Paris art world with his nude painting *Olympia*.

The change of focus in the visual arts was paralleled in the literary arts as well. The novel had been borne of the English middle class and its values, and high art of the early nineteenth century was dominated by classical aesthetics and allegorical themes, but all that was about to change. In literature, the holy trinity of realistic writing in France, Balzac, Flaubert, and Zola, would throughout the nineteenth century turn the attentions of the reading public around the world to the everyday world, its problems, and their origins as aesthetic material. In Russia, Dostoyevsky and Tolstoy focused their attentions on the social, psychological, and spiritual dimensions of ordinary people, often caught in situations that illustrated the growing gap between people's lives and the social conventions and beliefs that structured their world. Perhaps most importantly, the novel sought to relocate the narrative point of view within the sphere of the individual person. 'The various technical characteristics of the novel ... all seem to contribute to the furthering of an aim which the novelist shares with the philosopher – the production of what purports to be an authentic account of the actual experiences of individuals' (Watt 2000 [1957]: 27). Rather than the truth of allegory and myth, the novel created literary truths that were closer to the English countryside than to the Elysian Fields.

Following Giedion, we could observe that the aesthetics of the early part of the century displayed already a conflict which is obscured by making too much of classicism. Giedion writes that 'Classicism is not a style; classicism is a coloring. Behind the shield of antique forms, two great conceptions clash: Baroque universalism (the English School; Louis XVI) and nineteenth-century specialization, with its trend to increasingly isolated forms' (1970: 337). As these two elements, universalism and specialization, were already united in one artistic form, it should not be surprising that each appears in photography, sometimes united in the attempt to forge a new classical aesthetic and other times splitting into its component parts, as, for example, in the photographs of Robinson as opposed to the photographs of Thomson.

The photograph thus emerged into an aesthetic world which was clearly ready for its unique characteristics. It should not surprise, then, that among the first subjects of photography are the same sorts of subjects which were increasingly represented in painting of the day: the ordinary. Talbot himself remarked that 'we have sufficient authority in the Dutch School of Art for taking as subjects of representation scenes of daily and familiar occurrence. A painter's eye will often be arrested where ordinary people see nothing' (quoted in Lassam 1979: 17).

Although Talbot did not see himself as an artist, artists began to see the application of photography. David Hill and Robert Adamson were among the first to use Talbot's calotype to photograph in Edinburgh, Newhaven and other places as early as 1840. Among their photos are many subtle compositions of the streets and common folk. Hill's and Adamson's photos of street life were much in keeping with the traditions of painting and were seen as art. Hill was already well established as a landscape painter when he took up photography, and his gift at composition was derived from his familiarity with the conventions of that art. Their photographs were a mix of genre work, documentation of historical and local scenes, and portraiture; they hoped these would prove popular, for their first intention was to make photographs that they could sell either singly or in subscription.

One of their most enduring works is drawn from a series they planned but never completed of 'The Fishermen and Women of the Firth of Forth' and is entitled *The Letter*. One woman sits reading a letter while another looks down at her and a third stands by. A simple composition which still works as an artistic photograph, the picture had a special interest for their clientele. Ward and Stevenson explain that 'at a time when many Scots emigrated and died abroad without seeing their families again, letters had an importance they have now lost, and a picture of this kind had a strong emotional appeal' (1986: 154). A further factor was the introduction of the Penny Post in 1840, an event which opened the mails to ordinary people for the first time. Social conditions, in this case migration and the novelty of the post, contribute to the formation of an aesthetic by helping to form the emotional timbre of a people and through increasing interest in particular objects and topics.

The work of Hill and Adamson thus helped to define and focus feelings and impressions of the time around the images that they took. This was nothing less than the introduction of an aesthetic sensibility grounded in the objectification of the local as an object of artistic contemplation. In 1846 Dr John Brown expressed his delight in the new ground they were breaking: 'These clean, sonsey, caller, comely, substantial fishwives – what a refreshing sight! As easy, as unconfined, as deep-bosomed and ample, as any Grecian matron' (1986: 154). In addition to people, Hill and Adamson turned the environs of Edinburgh into scenes of artistic importance that could compete with anything from the Continent. In their calotypes of Greyfriars churchyard, for example, they experimented with simple Gothic drama in the placement of characters and the use of lighting, as well as capturing the ornate art of the tombs and monuments.

In France, Bayard, receiving only 600 francs from the government for his inventive work, took up the *art* of photography, exploring the aesthetic that his paper negative system and Talbot's shared. While the daguerreotype produced stunningly clear images with a silver cast to them, each picture being ornately framed as an individual work of art, the paper negatives were 'coarse in their tonal effects, better at rendering broad masses of tone than fine detail' (Schaff 1996: xiv). The problem was not so much that the images were blurry as that they were uneven in their clarity and tone, a characteristic often blamed on the quality of the paper, and a great many people attempted refinements to the process. Still, Talbot and Bayard (as well as others) explored what the new medium could accomplish. Many of the pictures in his *Pencil of Nature* were picked precisely to accomplish what Talbot believed would be the great addition of his technique to art, that is, to 'introduce into our pictures a multitude of minute details which add to the truth and reality of the representation' (Talbot, quoted in Lassam 1979: 18).

Between 1846 and 1848, Bayard composed what is perhaps the first modern photograph to explore the new possibilities of the art, the *Colonnade, Church of the Madeleine, Paris*. In this picture, he did not try to capture the church within the surroundings as a total, realist composition. Rather, Bayard abstracted aspects of its design, its lines and its shadows into 'geometrical principles in a fragment' of its appearance (Jammes and Janis 1983: 26). This picture would have been inconceivable at the time in painting, relying solely on the ability of the camera to compress the play of line, shade, and field into a single image. Although anticipating cubism and abstract expressionism in its realization, Bayard's *Colonnade* was a departure from his more usual pictures and from those of his contemporaries. Most photography stayed with established genres and conventions: portraits, architecture, landscapes and still life. Among the most popular were illustrated travel books (especially books of the Holy Lands of the Near East) which had accustomed large audiences to illustrations in the forms of engraved renderings, but the photograph provided a realism and subtlety of detail that no engraving could rival.

In contrast, the pictures of Henry Robinson deliberately strove toward creating an almost mawkish representational style. Sentimental in the middle-class Victorian fashion, his more creative photos show his attempts to popularize the ability of photography to create images which would evoke intense emotionality and so sell. In addition to his main activity of portraiture, Robinson also experimented with renderings of popular scenes, such as four albumin prints of *Little Red Riding Hood* (1858) and photographic drama. Through 1858 he developed his most famous and controversial photographic construction, *Fading Away*. The work represents the final moments of a young woman dying of the most artistic of nineteenth century diseases, consumption. The picture is composed of five separate negatives, assembled in a montage to produce a finished, complex composition. While assemblage worked well as a technique (and was widely used by his contemporaries), the publication of this piece caused serious complaints from people who felt that they had been deceived by what they had thought was a single composition. A photograph was, after all, supposed to show the world as it appeared, but on 2 July 1860 the editor of the *British Journal of Photography* wrote, 'Absolute truthfulness of representation is not a necessity of photography' (Harker 1988: 28).

The application of photographic truth to society

Even if a photo were absolutely 'truthful', the question remained: what did it show? Were there, for example, regular relationships between the surface appearance of things, which were captured on a photo, and their qualities and characteristics which established the function and position of people and objects in social narratives? Dr Diamond's paper presented in 1856 appeared within a growing medical and criminological discourse which emerged from the 1740s and after and which eventually culminated in the pseudo-science of phrenology and the belief in a relationship between the appearance of people and their psychology. If their assumptions were correct, photographic records and documentation would validate a new science built upon the physical features of criminals and lunatics. Thus, photographic record keeping was instituted in French prisons from 1872 and these pictures were attached to index cards listing characteristics of the incarcerated as well as details of their physical description, place of origin, etc. (see Mattelart 1996: 234–5).

The public health and social reform movements, originating in the United Kingdom in the 1840s, contributed to this objectification as well, for they took as their object the extreme social other, the working poor. In order to convince both Parliament and the middle class of the dire need for social reform, Dr George Bell, Dr Edwin Chadwick, and others undertook the task of describing the lives of the poor. Bell urged that 'these places must be seen', but he lamented that 'no description *has*, because none *can*, be given of the interior of a low Edinburgh lodging house. It defies the graver of Hogarth, the pencil of David Scott, so familiar with nightmare horrors, the pen of Dickens, and the tongue of Gutherie'. Writings such as these made the poor both an object upon which some actions were required and an object of aesthetic contemplation: Dr Bell even quoted Dante's *Inferno* (Canto III, v. 22) in an explicit invocation of the language of literary horror. Through using the literary discourse, Bell reveals that his problem in description is an aesthetic one and that his idea of aesthetics is not separable from the social. The poor live like the dead in hell; one can hardly imagine a comparison more alienating. Bell's distinction of the poor as others is at times explicit in his prose; he notes that the dwellings of the poor 'are as repulsive as the class which inhabits them, and they are as difficult to describe' (1849: 6).

An aesthetic and rhetoric of the horrors and repulsiveness of the poor quickly became a popular artistic sensibility within photography itself. While Hogarth had famously made engravings of the depravity and degradation of the cities in the mid eighteenth century, the photograph could produce what the engraver could not: the promise that the images were in fact true. By the 1870s photographs of the poor and of their lives were introducing the explicit images of 'paupers, beggars, vagrants' and their 'masses of rotten, rat-haunted buildings' (1849: 6). Photographers such as Robert Amman were recruited to document conditions in slum areas of Glasgow and other cities. John Thomson's book *Street Life in London* (1877), with its photographs of cripples, the poor, and the crowded and dirty streets, sold for 1s 6d (Buckland 1974: 76). Thomson had begun his career capturing exotic street images in Singapore and China, photographing the unusual habitation, dress and appearance of the inhabitants, and these photos had proved popular among the English middle class. However, the exotic, alien, and other lay not only across the seas but often just a few streets away from the comfortable homes and gardens of the middle class.

It was not just the reformers who purchased books such as *Street Life*. A prestigious medical journal, *The Lancet*, praised the work as providing vital information for 'the sanitarian, the citizen, and the philanthropist' (Ovenden 1997: 88). Several discourses were thus converging in this work, and Thomson's book was built partly upon previous publications, such as Mayhew's *London Labour and the London Poor* (1864), as well as upon woodcuts made from daguerreotypes, such as *Criminal Prisons and Scenes of Prison Life* (1862). Thomson was ahead of his time in his use of the woodburytype process for reproducing his images directly from glass negatives. This new method of inexpensively reproducing photographs greatly enhanced the quality of the images, as well as lowering the price, helping to stoke a public appetite for such books.

As with the slums, the extreme otherness of the insane was an image from which the nineteenth century middle class could scarcely take their eyes. They sought out the decrepit, the dirty, the shocking in their cities almost as sideshow amusements. Sunday visits to Bedlam and other asylums had long been popular entertainment and were illustrated by Hogarth in *The Rake's Progress*. The photograph, however, allowed the poor and insane in the context of their conditions to become objects of contemplation from within the homes of the middle class, and as objects, the poor could be acted upon. The surface of the image, bolstered with medical and scientific theories and wedded to aesthetics of difference, provided absolute proof of the difference of the poor, helping to establish both their identity and the identity of the middle class as something quite different from what the pictures showed. Voyeurism is, apparently, socially acceptable if the object of interest evokes feelings of disgust rather than a more direct pleasure. By the end of the nineteenth century, slumming in pictures was a well-established form of entertainment masquerading as the reformer's interest in the wellbeing of others.

The great problems which the poor presented were the threats to social order arising from their demands for equality before the law, the threats to public health arising from their way of life, and the need for a sober, reliable workforce. Edwin Chadwick, Matthew Arnold, and Thomas Carlyle, to name a few, all argued along these lines. In thus becoming social problems, the poor became the shared object of social sciences and reform. In transforming the poor into an object of contemplation and an aesthetic, the specific histories, social relations, and economic realities which created all classes of society were neatly excluded. Who could argue with the undeniable truth of the squalor and depravity into which the poor had sunk and which the surface of the photograph demonstrated so clearly? While extending vision into new places, the photograph collapsed reality into the view presented at that moment.

Photography from the mid 1800s lent to some of the scientific and social discourses of the day a method of documentation which mimicked their purported objectivity. From this relationship, photography would become a tool for creating an aesthetic of social reform, which the later photos by Riis and others would increasingly popularize and which would develop in support of the muckraking journalism and social reform movements in the US (see Alland 1993). However, phrenology and physiognomy soon died out as sciences; this particular relationship between the surface appearance and underlying reality had proved untenable. What had been established was a *social* aesthetic associated with the photographic image. One now knew what the poor looked like, how they lived, and one knew as well how to view the photographs of them. Hogarth's engravings mocked, but the photograph held up the poor as objects of contemplation, and this helped to define and document the relationship of the middle class to the poor. In real ways the photograph altered that relationship as well: accompanying civic and social surveillance of the poor, photography stabilized social identity as appearance and linked it to specific modes of action.

The stability which the discourses of art and science lent to photography, and which photography lent to those discourses, was thus short-lived. While portraiture grew through the middle of the nineteenth century to be one of the most lucrative avenues for photography, thus demonstrating that many people had no problems accepting the 'truthfulness' of the image, the photograph was demonstrating that its great power lay in its imaginal quality, the ability to present a shared social 'real' about which people could think, feel, argue, and marvel which did not, in the end, have an equivalent status in being. The object could not return the gaze; surveillance is one-way. The identity that the image promised, the objectivity promised by the mechanical camera, could not deliver the real, but it could provide a substitution embedded in aesthetics and discourses that consciousness would have trouble separating from real experience.

With Bell's pronouncement that the poor are not conscious of their misery, the entire reformist attitude toward the poor is crystallized. If the poor are not aware of their condition, one may define it for them, and one may thus define the poor (see Stallybrass and White 1984). Dialogue between the self and the world ceases when the meaning of the world is already given. In just the same way, the photograph compacted the real in ways that made it easier to grasp, and it provided a kind of reality to people who would never actually see what was represented. What was important in photography was not the real but what the representation meant and how it was used in different contexts. To accomplish this, the photo had to simultaneously 'truly' represent reality and displace the real with the meaning of the image.

Most importantly, the totality toward which the photographic image pointed was not a totality of experience or understanding but was finally grounded in how one viewed the image as a kind of science or a kind of art or a combination of each. Knowing how to position the image in a taxonomy of understanding or within an aesthetic system revealed what one was to think or feel about the image. In either case, the new image provided an object which had not been there before, a newly uncovered being, created by technology, which had its own status in the world and its own ontologically independent relationship to consciousness. It could reference the real, but it had become something else. The form that this relationship would take in the new uses of photography and in its mass production and dissemination helped to create the new social reality of the late nineteenth and the twentieth centuries. Photographers took the pictures, but the middle class, and later everyone else, saw the world through them.

The elaboration of precise aesthetic and interpretive systems, that is, social framings for the subjectivity of the dominant view, was well established by the end of the nineteenth century. The new mass production of the newspapers, facilitated by advances in printing technology (such as halftone printing), ensured the ubiquity of the image within the cultural landscape. The multiplying numbers of images guaranteed the success of such a system through its very commonness, through its own vulgarity, for 'sheer superabundance [the reproduction of the photograph] undermined old habits of careful evaluation and selection' (Mumford 1952: 94–5). The new world of the image – and soon of the cinema, the picture magazine, and television – was created simultaneously with the creation of individual psyches which were well accustomed to the fleeting glance, the flickering image, and which were capable of taking in everything important in a glance. Long before the soundbite displaced political rhetoric, the image had formed the objects around which a new subjectivity was expressing itself. The ancient act of representation as a technique for establishing relationships with the world had transformed into a negation of the world and the substitution of the image for the real.

FOUR

The Rise of a Literary Epistemology:
The Social Background of Self

Memory is finite by nature. Plato recognizes this in attributing life to it ... A limitless memory would in any event be not memory but infinite self-presence. (Jacques Derrida 1972: 109)

The Advent of Print

Books are not memory

It is commonly believed that the book is an extension of memory, an exteriorization of it. Yet what the book stores is not memory, not that which previously existed only by being ingested, chewed, ruminated upon. To say that a book holds memory requires a major redefinition of how the word was used prior to printing. What would be stored in entertainment, in magazines, in the news? What memory is stored in the images of the cinema or the magazine? The apparent memory conveyed in these forms carries little of knowledge with it. People generally turn to these forms not to find the traces of the past, the recollection of what has been, but rather to gain a purchase on what is now, to share in a social subjectivity of the present. To see these media as devices for memory collapses all the forms of reading which people may bring to texts into one mythic version of reading drawn from the origins of printing.

What is interesting about early studies of the effects of media, such as those conducted by the Payne Fund studies of Blumer (1933) or Munsterberg's (1916) examination of the psychology of film, is not the finding that people model themselves upon media, but that the media do not directly transmit memory or the reality of the past but instead form a part of the background of perception within which people perceive their actions taking place. Neither do these media freeze moments of reality for 'transmission' from a sender to a receiver, as implied in the Shannon and Weaver model or in its subsequent elaborations. Rather, as Luhman (2000) suggests, the 'memory' portrayed in the mass media is instead a field of accepted, recognized and taken-for-granted statements and beliefs about reality. Moreover, these statements selectively present some views of the world while ignoring others, and those views which are presented appear already contextualized as moral judgments.

As discussed in the second chapter, memory was in medieval times inextricably linked to moral development guided by the structures of monastic society, and meditative reading took place in this context. In the same way, the medieval text was a complicated product of many minds and voices often appearing on the same page in glosses, annotations, notes, and references which might or might not be copied in the scriptorium into subsequent transcriptions. A hierarchy of appropriate meanings, relations, and values, drawn from the social contexts of reading, guided the reader to internalize the text along particular lines. The medieval book did not store meaning that could be extracted as a singular thing, for reading was visibly, physically, and phenomenologically a shared, complex experience. The spread of printing allowed ideas to be shared but the context of that shared experience was increasingly unlinked with the individual person's wider social environment. Reading and writing became parts of a private realm which became independent from a world in which ideas on paper had to be 'published', that is, made public.

The self-presence brought about through memory, the attendance of consciousness to its internal recall of prior experience, differs from the recording and accessing of external traces of signification, although the two processes are related. In both cases one is self-present, but with memory one's attention is engaged in a complex of emotional and psychic states that are bound up with the act of recalling. In reading external significations or records, one perceives the world ordered not by personal experience but through signification. Almost everyone has had the experience of confronting some drawing or bit of writing that he or she has created which upon subsequent examination seems completely alien, foreign, and as if it had been created by someone else. Language teaches us to think in particular ways, and the imprints of images and words provide us not with a *memory of* the world but with a point of view, a *subjectivity towards* the world which arises out of the given assumptions about the world as well as from the language we use to describe that world. If in the contemporary view the world in which nature is given is already the created world of culture, then one stands at risk of confusing the languages and grammars in which the world 'presents itself' with the reality of the world in itself. One risks falling into an unreflective nominalism.

Certainly, some parts of the world are social and linguistic, constructed and shared. This shared linguistic world begins within the family, who impart one's language, and extends through peers and into abstract realms. At this remove, one may sense the presence of mind, but the living, breathing aura of a person is absent. What one finds in the practices of reading is not the memory of a person or a people but the track of a mind through domains of language.

Thus, the contemporary view of the memory of humanity being stored in books (or in other media) is already a metaphor which transforms the notion of memory into something like culture. Such a transformation reveals the extent to which one commonly accepts the culturally contingent and created subjectivity with which he or she sees the world as uniquely one's own experience and memory. Given this confusion, we should not be surprised to find that people continue to discover their experiences, emotions, ideas, and fantasies already given in objects in the world. Everything in the world becomes an object of reference for the self and for consciousness as it locates its subjectivity in the experience of cultural forms which, given their organization as a seemingly natural world of meaning, pass as memory. Such was a major social function of art in the nineteenth century: the representation not of the world as it truly is but of a consensual set of narratives about the world which might be held to be 'true' in providing a cultural perspective based on particular relations of power along the interconnected lines of race, class, gender, education, and so on.

When art ceased to live up to this function, it was, in the eyes of some, a form of insanity and betrayal which could only end badly. Thomas Carlyle in the *Latter-Day Pamphlets* (1850) wrote:

> The fact is ... the Fine Arts, divorced entirely from truth this long while, and wedded almost professedly to falsehood, fiction and such-like, have got what we must call, an insane condition: they walk abroad without keepers, nobody suspecting their bad state, and do fantastic tricks. (quoted in Giedion 1970: 363)

Carlyle's concern was not with the failing function of art as an intellectual project but with the collapse of the social and moral consensus which he believed art (and other intellectual endeavors) should provide. Yet Carlyle's belief in the necessity of art to morally educate and guide was in some ways an extension of the same beliefs which led critics in the seventeenth and eighteenth centuries to deride the novel and other 'diversions' as corrupting of the family, of domestic labor, and of women in general.

Still, the possibility of such a shared narrative or set of histories on a national (or international) scale depends upon a dispersed population of people having access to the same body of literature and having similar overall strategies toward reading and interpreting this material. Individual differences of interpretation, of course, exist between readers, but such general issues as genre, authority, and reliability had to be socially constructed and articulated through philosophical, social, and industrial expressions. From these shared understandings could grow institutions such as science and literature as well as new expressions of religion, nation, and self. These provided not truth or 'putative laws', which are 'simply heuristic devices, useful in the discovery of the supposedly real nature of the mechanisms and objects', but 'orientation to a model or analogue' (Shotter 1993: 151). Such institutions grounded power in concrete forms, and simultaneously they provided stable points of identification for the construction of self and for other social relations at a time when these were undergoing radical transformation and change.

From the late seventeenth century on, the once firm realities of place, of land, of the *domus*, and of country were being lost to new representational ones: nation, the conjugal family, the corporate, the city. In every area of society, the world had to be reconstructed around new forms which were sympathetic to and which helped to create and stabilize the requirements of the social for individualistic, economically motivated and defined identities. The technologies for achieving this construction of a shared social in new forms required the building of an infrastructure of literacy, the history of which traces one part of the history of modernism.

The book as signifier and sign

The practices of early modern reading, that is, reading after printing and prior to the development of large-scale industrialized production of written matter, developed quickly, supported by a variety of social, institutional and philosophical changes in European society. As these developed, they guided a new kind of consciousness into being, a consciousness that saw its world and the domain of valuable experience in external, manufactured, socially constructed words and images. The rapid spread and growth of printing and the large number of books which appeared within a very short period of time supported and were produced by a belief in a series of fictions and narratives about the world, metaphysics, truth, self, and the state. Yet, the one truth that most of the major beliefs shared was an unshakeable acceptance that an empirical universe was knowable, describable, and that the same laws which governed the world and the cosmos could profitably be put to use governing the social as well as the personal. The appearance of the world became more and more symbolic, and this trend was what drove many sixteenth and seventeenth century scholars to attempt to read the 'book of nature' in ways that seem naïve and a bit disturbing today (see Hudson 1994). Somewhere in the world was truth which could be gotten by the right method, and this truth would finally render the subject transparent, producing the pure object, the true world, as it was.

The medieval text was not the creation of a single person, although an 'author' might be recognized as worthy of imitation (Carruthers 1990: 190). The medieval text was 'a polyphony of voices' transmitted in a single document (Le Saux 1996: 11). The printed book, through a variety of mechanisms, limited the voices which could be heard to one: the author. This process was by no means guaranteed by the technology but evolved in a process of negotiation between writers and publishers.

The rise of printing raised several issues. Among these was the final dismissal of the belief that a finite number of books existed, that one could read virtually everything worth reading. Indeed, a number of things which many would hold as not worth reading found their way into print. Eisenstein (1984: 94) notes the common 'perusal of scandal sheets, "lewd ballads", "merry bookes of Italie", and "other corrupted tales in Inke and Paper"' which had become accessible and whose sale augmented the income of printers. Within 100 years following the deployment of the printing press in Europe, the death knell of reading as meditation and as a way to truth had been sounded. Books now established a knowledge which was clearly outside the personal consciousness and which could never again be integrated into one's entire moral and intellectual being.

Moreover, the book became a signifier itself which represented not only a repository of information, descriptions, narratives, and instructions but also the location of beliefs and ideas in a tangible form. The mere existence of a book on a particular topic indicated to everyone who encountered it that particular ideas were present to be read. Febvre and Martin write that:

> the printed book is at least tangible evidence of convictions held because it embodies and symbolizes them; it furnishes arguments to those who are already converts, lets them develop and refine their faith, offers them points which will help them to triumph in debate, and encourages the hesitant. (1976: 288)

Thus the printed book was both a resource for ideas and a social marker of their existence. From at least the fifteenth century, the book was also a status symbol (see Engelsing 1973).

Widespread printing enabled the rapid spread of current ideas. In 1517 Luther himself expressed surprise at the speed with which his theses circulated and the range of people who read them (Eisenstein 1974: 239). Intended as a call to a debate within a limited circle of academics and scholars, their publication and dissemination indicated the extent to which literacy and interest in scholastic debate had spread. The metaphor of a circle is misleading, however. Printing spread not in a widening *sphere* of influence but along *lines* which retraced the links of commerce and power. From Mainz, the technology of printing quickly spread to Amsterdam, Rome, Paris, London and a host of smaller places which lay near centers of commerce and learning or along the routes between them. Books were expensive to manufacture, difficult to transport, and easily damaged by water; there were immediate advantages to reducing the amount of transport involved in getting the product from the press to the purchaser and the reader.

However, there were other factors which limited the location of presses. The proximity of a paper supply was important in the centuries before canals and railroads made inland transportation reliable and economical. Further, the making of paper requires a copious supply of fresh, clear water with a low mineral content to avoid discoloration. Early paper was made completely from rags, especially discarded clothing, and not surprisingly the supply of rags was most steady near cities, and their collection was often a monopoly enjoyed by paper manufacturers.

The greatest use of the book as signs was to come from historians and others who sought to establish a break with the past, a separation from what had been before. While there had been numerous revolutionary forces emerging throughout Europe from the mid fifteenth to the late eighteenth century, Protestantism and the new bourgeois philosophies were to prove the organizing centers around which modern society and the modern self could grow. Protestantism marked the beginning of proliferations of schismatic breaks within Christianity which previously had been contained either with brutal repression or with incorporation into the hierarchy of the Roman Church. Simultaneously, a new middle class was creating itself and its wealth out of shrewd economic exploitation of colonial holdings and mercantile and manufacturing enterprises domestically. In France, England, and America, traditional justifications of the power of the state and the sovereign were increasingly under attack and in need of defense. The divine right of kings to rule, argued by Jean Bodin (1530–1596), and the absolute right of the state's enforcement of the social contract, argued by Thomas Hobbes (1588–1679), reflected the extent to which the legitimacy of existing forms of state power had come into question. This question would be answered, although somewhat provisionally, with the head of Charles I in 1649. Indeed, the contractual nature of the sovereign's relationship to his or her people had been raised years before with the Declaration of Arbroath in Scotland in 1320 seeking to limit the excesses of Edward II (Magnusson 2000: 187–9), but the civil power seriously to challenge the notion of divine right did not catch hold until other supporting ideas of the individual person's place in society and the nature of the social contract itself were in place.

The Protestants, the scientists, the new middle class, the political revolutionaries – all had a stake in drawing a historical line between what had been and what was to come, and this line needed markers and signs to establish symbolically and socially the idea of their new age. Printing was one of the great markers. Johns writes that:

> The 'printing revolution' as we now know it is thus the product of a later, political revolution. It was a retrospective creation forged with tools selectively chosen from the arguments created by eighteenth century historians of the press for other purposes. It was designed to serve as the indispensable cusp separating Descartes, Bacon, Newton, and modernity from corruption, superstition, ignorance, and despotism. (1998: 374)

In much the same way as Socrates incorporated the myth of Theuth as an origin of writing, subsequent generations invented a myth of origins for the press. The fact that people could do so no doubt combined elements of a newly emerging sense of nation which the press helped to bring into existence with changes in the social relations between genders, classes, and estates. Printing had been in existence in China, Japan, and Korea for half a millennium, and even movable type had an older origin than the 1430s story of the Mainz goldsmith Gutenberg, but the attribution of a single moment of invention to the lone genius proved irresistible. Further, this myth of origins helped to solidify the perception that there had been a break with the past and a new age was being entered.

Early modern technologies of the book

The printed book, when read scholastically or professionally, was read in silence – and increasingly, as the numbers of readers grew, in isolation. Many non-scholars' experience of literacy still had a strongly oral component. In addition to the literate villager who might read to others, public readings of books were common, at least for the middle class, through the nineteenth century. Yet the process of silent reading which had emerged in late medieval times was implicated with other changes taking place to produce not only a new psychology of reading but a new psychology of existence. One characteristic shared by many of the changes taking place through the Renaissance was a tendency toward inwardness, privacy, and personal responsibility for one's self. The worlds of the inner, private self and the outer public world become increasingly well defined and to a large extent define one another.

Paul Saenger's (1997) work on the origins of silent reading traces the development of particular technologies of physical textuality which supported changes in the way that readers engaged what had previously been a shared activity. He writes that 'psychologically, silent reading emboldened the reader because it placed the source of his curiosity completely under personal control' (1997: 264). While what one read might be personal, social forms of literature were becoming increasingly well defined. The derivation of those interpretations approved by the hierarchy of clerics and scholars had been guided by the social practices of reading; dictation and *lectio* ensured that the written word did not become too personal or private, and so they 'buttressed theological and philosophical orthodoxy' (1997: 264). Writing and reading had become private activities, and these changes were reflected in other sites of knowledge and other parts of society. It is important, again, to stress that these changes occurred together and that, while silent reading and the increased availability of books did not in themselves produce new ideas of the private self, they supported and fostered it, creating a series of activities in which the private self could be developed.

The self, of course, depends upon social interaction to create, reinforce, and develop it, and reading became for many people for the first time in history a part of the social activity in which the meaning and place of books in one's class, one's gender, and one's family were negotiated. Selective social spaces within the home library allowed for collective readings, and a popular entertainment among the middle class was readings in small groups (Raven 1996: 199). Middle-class women especially were often involved in reading in ways much more varied and empowering than merely consuming novels, and in addition to being a leisure activity, reading aloud with small groups would be integrated into domestic work (Tadmore 1996). The practice of reading in public even developed as a commercial and social enterprise through the nineteenth century. Charles Dickens and Samuel Clemens both enjoyed considerable popularity as public readers of their texts, and in this way both advertised their printed works and supplemented their income. Still, there was a growing number of people for whom reading was an asocial activity, something which took one away from the physical presence of others and into the abstracted realm of the society of letters.

Changes in other parts of society saw an increasing need to bring what had existed for millennia as private acts into the domain of the social, or to be more precise, within the surveillance of the institutional. Among these was marriage. Marriage had existed for most people in much of Europe as a vow spoken between a man and a woman. In the act of speaking, the bonds were made real with a force that only a society deeply immersed in orality could impose and recognize. 'If the words of marriage *had* been spoken, it was believed that a real marriage existed until death in the eyes of God' (Gottlieb 1993: 72). By the time of the Council of Trent (1545–1563), the authority of the spoken word in marriage was recognized only to the extent that it had been properly acknowledged by authority of the Church, that is, witnessed by a priest who was also now required to record the event. 'The changes in weddings in the sixteenth century did not diminish the force of spoken words, but church legislation sharpened the requirements for the circumstances in which they were spoken – a step that seemed revolutionary at the time' (1993: 73). Simultaneously, the familial keeping of records in a Bible marked not a diminishing of Church power but an extension of it into the home. 'Where functions previously assigned only to the priest in the Church were also entrusted to parents at home, a patriarchal ethos was reinforced' (Eisenstein 1974: 251).

The authority of the printed word helped to create new kinds of authority and power as well as new kinds of physical places and activities. The new, increasingly crowded, public world brought about a demand for a separate space wherein the growing interior arts of reading and writing could take place. No longer the purview of the singular genius slaving alone, a place separate from the social was increasingly the creative space wherein the great activities of the new intellectuals could take place unsullied and undisturbed by everyday life – or such was the fiction portrayed by Michel Eyquem de Montaigne (1533–1592) who claimed he 'withdrew to lay his head on the breast of the learned Virgins in calm and security' within his library. In his essay on the three commerces (III.3), Montaigne writes of his need to separate the activities he undertakes in his library from the mundane ones. In his library, he writes, ''Tis there that I am in my kingdom and there I endeavor to make myself an absolute monarch, conjugal, filial, and civil; elsewhere I have but verbal authority only, and of a confused essence. That man, in my opinion, is very miserable, who has not at home where to be by himself, where to entertain himself alone, or to conceal himself from others' (Montaigne 1952). The separation that Montaigne sees of book knowledge from common intercourse concerns the development of his private self, his inner self-perception: 'Others study how to raise and elevate their minds; I, but to humble mine, and to bring it low; 'tis vicious only in extension.'

Montaigne sought to develop thought and learning while yet keeping touch with the world about him, an activity only possible with a strict segregation of erudition and experience. Learning draws one away from 'a thousand to whom my fortune has conjoined me, and without whom I cannot live'. And thus he calls for the cultivation of a soul that 'knows both how to stretch and how to slacken itself'. He envies those who 'can render themselves familiar with the meanest of their followers, and talk with them in their own way'. The method of achieving this balance is through 'temperance and composedness'. 'We have, for the most part, more need of lead than of wings.' The new, increasingly common book learning and the fashion of learnedness had the power to tempt people away from themselves and from their lives: ''Tis in my opinion, egregiously to play the fool, to put on the grave airs of a man of lofty mind amongst those who are nothing of the sort: ever to speak in print.'

Sherman (1996) draws a more comprehensive picture of the library in Renaissance England as a sphere which is selectively public and which serves a different end. For his evidence, he examines the most extraordinary library of John Dees, who was, among other things, Elizabeth's astrologer and who has been proposed as a model for Shakespeare's Prospero. In addition to holding over 'three thousand volumes, in twenty-one languages, representing virtually every aspect of classical, medieval and Renaissance learning' (1996: 64), Dees' library was the site where he both performed scholarly research for pay and maintained a robust traffic of visitors.

As with printing houses of the time, a well-stocked library would often be a meeting place for scholars, students, public servants: in short for virtually everyone who had an interest in the compilations of writing which were growing increasingly large and unwieldy. Dees' library was not the private space of contemplation that Montaigne had written of but much more of a workshop, putting into practice the Elizabethan ideals of placing knowledge into public service. While not a lending library in the modern sense, Dees' library served as a place for negotiating the boundary between textualized knowledge and the public needs; it was not a dividing line between public and private but rather served as a 'permeable membrane' which 'let certain people, texts, and ideas in, and kept others out' (1996: 74).

Thus, Montaigne's introspective view of the library as a place of withdrawal from the social and familial is at odds with the purposes ascribed to Dees, in that Montaigne focuses on the experience of the library as a phenomenological dimension, while the description of Dees' library explores more of the functional aspects of this space within a social realm. This contrast reflects the emerging paradox of reading and of the place of written knowledge within the social. The individual person's pursuit of increasingly focused reading required, perhaps, a retreat from the social, but at the same time the uses of written information and the inscription of the ideas in books upon the social were becoming increasingly public. It is perhaps not too much of a stretch to describe Dees' library as a prototypical research laboratory where knowledge has application, and Montaigne's library as a seminary where knowledge fosters the development of the inner, private self.

Although reading may have taken place in silence and often in private, the activity taking place in Dees' library gives the impression that it was something more like a modern laboratory than a retreat or storehouse for books. Here the authority of books was woven into new activities and uses which extended the influence of the book by combining old fields of study (such as cartography) in new ways. This joining together of diverse sorts of knowledge to achieve practical ends was precisely the purpose of scientific and literate societies which emerged through the seventeenth and eighteenth centuries to bring new kinds of social and epistemological orders to the burgeoning number of texts circulating in London, Paris, Amsterdam, and elsewhere.

By the eighteenth century, one need not have his or her own collection of books, even if one had the money. Booksellers had begun to organize circulating or lending libraries on a subscription basis from the 1740s in England, thus increasing their turnover and helping to augment profits coming from sales. Circulating libraries expanded greatly during the eighteenth century. The number of circulating libraries grew from 20 in London in 1760 to over 200 nationwide in only 40 years, and within another 20 years over 1500 libraries were supplying more than 100,000 regular and 100,000 occasional users (Raven 1996: 175).

Certainly the social world of reading dramatically changed through the sixteenth and seventeenth centuries. Increasing numbers of texts created the possibility of a large body of literate people. The diffusion of written materials of all kinds ensured that even those who could not read were influenced both directly and indirectly by writing. However, the book was not a form of social memory and could not be truly thought of as one until its position as a reliable source could be trusted, and this took some time. As books were mass produced (even if printing runs of individual titles might average 500 copies), any mistake was rapidly promulgated. A shortage of good quality woodblocks and later metal plates meant that early images were not necessarily accurate or trustworthy (Eisenstein 1979). The problem of reliability was rectified by a growing attention to the production of the book, predicated in part by greater reader expectations of veracity as well as by technological improvements in the development of woodblock engravings, copperplate etchings, and later lithography. Such changes contributed to the understanding that books could represent the real in some ways, but what part of the real was to be represented and what these representations meant were still not clear.

In short, those social conditions that guaranteed the position of the medieval text were insufficient to justify the printed text within the new social and cultural settings into which it was emerging. Just as silent reading and minuscule writing had speeded up the medieval practices of literacy, so printing would refine reading as a practice even more, requiring greater attention to the form of the text on the page which would in turn guide the eye quickly through the printed words. While the incunabula had closely mirrored the appearance of the manuscript, printing rapidly developed its own organization of the page with new typefaces, running heads, and other techniques to make reading easy and quick. Latin fonts won out over the heavier Gothic ones, producing a page that was lighter and a text that was easy to scan (Houston 1988: 211). The amount of material for reading created a demand for those innovations which improved the readability of the text.

Distribution of materials

The production of books and printed matter of all kinds could not have arisen without the distribution systems to spread them throughout the reading world. From the beginning of publishing and printing, lines of distribution and sales in the forms of booksellers and stationers created networks of dispersion extending out from the printing shops. In a short time, these lines of movement began to create loci of social power and prestige. Early booksellers might travel to fairs, as had the sellers of woodblock prints before them. They also went from village to village, town to town, selling what they could carry to the inhabitants. Pictures of the saints, illustrations of biblical scenes and songs were all popular. One technique for selling copies of songs was for the salesman to put on performances of tunes and then offer copies of the songs for sale.[5]

Booksellers quickly rose to prominence and social power themselves, and were linked closely with printers. The ownership of the book as an object was tied to the amount of real capital which was invested in its manufacture. A publisher would have to obtain a work, purchase the paper and ink, and invest the labor in setting the type and conducting the print run; then the book would have to be bound, distributed, and sold. Subscriptions taken out before the work was begun was one way in which publishers tried to guarantee their income. Plagiarism and unauthorized copying were widespread, as the basic issues of ownership were transformed in ways similar to the changes brought about by the internet. The question had not yet been resolved of who owned the printed book: the author or the printer? Was it the investment of financial capital or the investment of intellectual material that bestowed the most power and control over the text? The Stationers Company established power on the side of the publisher. The author's name was more important than the author's labor in the early economy of the book, and this accounted for much of the widespread piracy of texts that was common well into the eighteenth century.

Booksellers and publishers explored a variety of new areas of writing, and women writers as well as readers were increasingly common in the seventeenth century (Bernard 2001; Tadmore 1996). Household books and cook books as well as fiction, art, and history were among the genres read by women during this time. Other audiences were explored and created in the printing of low-cost editions of popular works, chapbooks, which produced profits in economies of scale rather than quality, and these marked the tendency toward profit-making strategies which would characterize mass production in general.

Still other sources of revenue for the industry came from pamphlets and broadsheets generated by all sides in religious and political conflicts across Europe as they sought to influence popular attitudes and sway the loyalties and affections of the people. These exchanges amounted to the first propaganda wars as Catholics and Protestants on the Continent and in England vied with each other for the control of public discourse. Later such contests would take place between the Royalists and Parliamentarians in the English Civil War, between various factions of Protestantism, and in various provinces of later Germany in the early nineteenth century. Publishers were not always committed to the positions held in their printed material, and some would profit from producing materials for both sides of an issue or even of a revolution (Bernard 2001: 4–7).

Social Formations of Literacy

How, then, should one regard the book after the advent of print? The woodblock print and later the printing press are the first widespread uses of mass production in Europe. As such, if there are general effects deriving from a technological development, they should be present in printing, and to some extent they are. Mumford (1952: 67) observed that the printing press was 'one of the earliest pieces of standardized, increasingly automatic, machinery', and the history of printing is to a large extent a history of the machine age. Although the railroads, telegraph, and factories are more emblematic of the machine age in popular imagination, the press has an older history. While certain standardizations were necessary even in the medieval manuscript, the printed book ensured standard-ization within a print run with all copies exactly the same. This production of identical copies, argues Eisenstein (1979; 1984) made possible a culture of people who could organize their lives and thoughts in similar ways because they had, nearly simultaneously, the same texts in front of them.

Social formations of beliefs and practice require mechanisms for creating symbolic unities among people. The emergence of discourses of modern medicine, science, manufacturing, and indeed of social class was predicated upon commonalities of thought, speech, and belief which had to be con-structed and shared throughout society. The dramatic reorganization of European society in the sixteenth and seventeenth centuries challenged more than the Roman Catholic Church. An influx of wealth from the new colonies in the Americas, Africa, and Asia, as well as a growing middle class riding on the tide of increasing mercantile trade and manufacturing, contributed to the transformation of the old social order into the beginnings of the modern.

The book constructs a shared culture, that is, a group of people who share ideas because they read precisely the same thing. While certainly readers did not, and do not now, derive exactly the same meanings from a given text, specific reading practices and new technologies of the text helped to build the epistemological structures which limited the possible signification of words. Thus, even if readers did not bring identical sets of practices, beliefs, or interpretive schemata to a text, their relationship to the text was increasingly given through other structures such as genre, purpose, author, and publisher.

The early modern uses of the book emerged with the systems that could sustain the production and distribution of millions of copies of books, pamphlets, broadsheets, and other material. These systems were not only essential for getting books made and delivered into the hands of readers, but also integral parts of the emerging social, economic, and political structures of modern Europe.

Publishing culture

In the first 100 years of printing, there was something of an explosion of texts with the same sort of disorder of materials one finds after a blast. Febvre and Martin (1976) estimate that, from 1450 to 1500, between 10,000 and 15,000 titles were produced. Assuming small print runs of 500 copies, this still amounts to around 7.5 million books, pamphlets, and other works. In the eighteenth century alone, an estimated 55 million books were printed in

England alone, consisting of over 100,000 titles (Kernan 1987: 153). Watt's (2000 [1957]: 36) survey of the literature suggests perhaps 250,000 regular readers of newspapers and a book-buying public that numbered tens of thousands in the early eighteenth century. Even by the end of the century, though, only a few hundred book titles would likely be printed in a given year, excluding pamphlets.

What was published was anything commissioned or that which printers and booksellers thought they could sell. Many people read 'promiscuously' as Milton advised one to do. Those forms that organize bodies of literature had largely not yet emerged. Once the market for Bibles and religious texts had been saturated, other types of materials were rapidly produced to sate the appetite for reading that this same growth of materials was itself creating. A literate public requires a collection of books to come into existence, and the new literate individual, who could draw upon the experiences, information, and literate forms that were being created, was creating new forms of thinking and reading while reflecting the new forms in thought and behavior.

While much has been made of the indubitable influence of the book in the spread of Protestantism and the stability which a rapidly produced canon of literature lent it, from a social point of view the explosion of do-it-yourself books on a range of topics was as important. Education itself became a project which did not require one's attendance at university or at the monastery, at least in some subjects. The appearance of grammars and texts in the classical languages supported a surge of interest in biblical scholarship and in linguistics. Latin, Hebrew, and Greek as languages expected of learned people, as well as the translation of the Bible and other works into national languages, helped to foster the independence of interpretation which would be one of the hallmarks of the Protestant Reformation. Catholicism stressed lay obedience while the Protestant scholar had more motivation to develop his or her own readings of the holy scriptures (Eisenstein 1974: 249).

Among the other DIY areas of publication, music was first printed in 1501, but early print runs would have been small and aimed at professionals (Boorman 1986). After about 1540, polyphonic music began to be widely published in performance scores for both amateur and professional musicians (1986: 223–4), thus suggesting that print had some relationship to the development of a popular interest in polyphonic (as opposed to folk) music and the spread of musical ideas. Luis Milan's *El Maestro* (1535) was patterned on Castiglione's *Book of the Courtier* and promised to teach anyone to play the vihuela (a forerunner of the guitar). Castiglione had written that the gentleman must be acquainted with the practice of music, but Milan proposed actually to teach one to perform music. In the late seventeenth century Thomas Mace, an Englishman, would publish *Music's Monument* (1675), an even more comprehensive work covering not only the playing of the lute, but also such previously hard to learn craft practices as the correct manner of tying fret strings onto the neck of the lute, the type of knots to use, and so on.

Books such as Mace's did not just expose people to a set of ideas and illustrations. They presented a complex texture of information woven into the form of detailed instruction which one previously would have acquired from social interaction with other people. These fragments of previously embodied knowledge – anecdotes and stories, bits of ephemeral information which are not immediately understandable as part of the practice of playing music but which reflect a part of the culture of musicianship – become learnable. As such, these books are empirical, practical, and provide a substitution in written form for that acculturation which would normally have taken place within a group practicing a particular activity. While one would not necessarily have acquired the same level of skill or the same degree of knowledge as was obtainable from a teacher or class, what one did get was a degree of substitution for that knowledge with which to augment what else one might have already known.

Histories also proved extremely popular in early printing. Julius Caesar's accounts of the civil wars were big sellers, as were the histories of Herodotus, Thucydides, and Tacitus (Febvre and Martin 1976: 283). For the first time since the Visigoth invasions and the subsequent collapse of the first Roman Empire, these works were widely available not just to clerics but to nobles and literate commoners alike. What amounted to a mythology of the origins and development of classical and biblical antiquity was increasingly shared among the literate as a common set of stories which linked them together not just as Frank or Saxon but as members of a larger community. This invisible state owed part of the idea of its existence to the failing Holy Roman Empire which linked all of Latin Christendom into a loose unity, but with the shared histories as a common story stock, both individual identities and local structures of social class had links to each other on the basis of this shared mythic past.

The knowledge which was now available became as well a marker of what a learned gentleman had to know: Greek and Latin, certainly, as well as the stories and subject matter of Aristotle, Cicero, Livy, Juvenal, and so on. These amounted to a historical foundation upon which the new cultures of Europe were being built. What would become the 'high culture' of the nineteenth century bourgeoisie was formulated into a canon of lay classics scarcely 300 years earlier.

The underpinning of a myth of classical origins became necessary precisely because the seventeenth and eighteenth centuries had undertaken the process of splitting themselves off from the period which had gone before, and nothing signified the split with the physical certainty of the book. The political changes in England and France marked a shift in power from the crown to less historically ancient social forms (the parliament, the assembly), and these were paralleled by the transition of religious government from the highly centralized medieval Catholicism to the local and even individual responsibility for interpretation of scripture and hence salvation. The rise of scientific societies as well as manufacturing societies undertook to maintain both profits and moral probity (as in the stationers' societies). Governments also saw the importance of having a defining role in the new literatures, not just through legislative activities such as the Licensing Act (1643), but also in producing their own version of the events of the day. The English Parliament initiated printing on its own in 1641 at the start of the Civil War and engaged in what amounted to a propaganda war with the Royalist press (Bernard 2001: 3).

All of these social changes constituted revolutions that had to be in place before the 'printing revolution' could be established as a historical fact with certain historical meanings. Johns writes that:

> The printing revolution as we now know it is thus the product of a later, political revolution. It was a retrospective creation forged with tools selectively chosen from the arguments created by the eighteenth century historians of the press for other purposes. It was designed to serve as the indispensable cusp separating Descartes, Bacon, Newton and modernity from corruption, superstition, ignorance, and despotism. (1998: 374)

No institution in England signifies the origins of this revolution more than the Royal Society, but it only constituted one part of the creation of this myth of a historical break.

The new truths of science

From its founding around 1645, the 'Royal Society of London for Improving Natural Knowledge' (its entire and proper name) sought to eliminate whole domains of knowledge from the enterprise to which it believed itself dedicated. Formed by a mix of scholars, manufacturers, and the polymaths so common prior to the age of expertise, the society extended the Elizabethan impulse to apply knowledge in useful ways, and to achieve that end, other kinds of knowledge must be excluded. This was:

> a condition laid down in Robert Hooke's original memorandum on 'the business and design of the Royal Society', namely, its engagement not to meddle with 'Divinity, Metaphysics, Morals, Politicks, Grammar, Rhetoric, or Logick'. (Mumford 1964: 115)

This exclusion of religion and the liberal arts from what were seen as more practical pursuits not only influenced the development of the scientific method but contributed to the dismissal of the personal, interior knowledge which had constituted truth from antiquity through the middle ages. And Hooke's injunction neatly established the 'truth' of science by eliminating from consideration any self-examination of the methods or findings of science except from standpoints of science, profit, and perceived usefulness. In short, 'this reservation not merely discouraged the scientist from critically examining his own metaphysical assumptions; it even fomented the delusion that he had none and kept him from recognizing his own subjectivity' (1964: 115).

Books accompanied and helped to support changes to the ways in which truth was established. Being at one remove from the person, books placed an abstract distance between the author and the reader, a distance which grew with the number of books one encountered and the skill with which one could read through them. This distance fitted well with the new science of the early

Enlightenment and with the distance its proponents sought to place between their practices and beliefs and those which had gone before. In discussing Condorcet's view of printing, Chartier expands this role of the book:

> Intellect against passion, enlightenment against seduction: the second effect of printing is the substitution of evidence based on reason for beliefs drawn out by rhetorical argument. The certitude and irrefutability of the truth, conceived according to the models of logical deduction and mathematical reasoning, are thus fundamentally differentiated from the ill-founded convictions imposed and reinforced by the rhetorical art of persuasion. Finally, through printing, the truths thus established can be revealed to all. (1995: 9)

The existence of the modern sciences was thus dependent in two ways upon printing and the book. First, the book produced the evidence in linear argument often accompanied by diagrams and increasingly accurate and clear illustrations; and second, the book transmitted these ideas among people whose practices would be informed by what they read. 'In early modern science ... the book was by all means a medium of observation, voyage and experiment, which not only provided a solid frame of reference but lent (through the authority invoked in the reference) considerable argumentative force' (Sherman 1996: 73).

The regimentation of ideas through reproduction in the printed book reflected well the scientific practices of shared, verifiable knowledge. There was considerable overlap between the traditional 'scientific' practices and the new. Even in the seventeenth century Newton continued studies and experiments based on alchemical practices, while older approaches to medicine such as herbalism would still invoke astrological principles as the bases of the character of plants, animals, and minerals. In medicine, the classical descriptions of anatomy and physiology from Galen's time and before had been derived at a time when the body could not be dissected and empirical observation was less important than the fit of a theory into the overall epistemology of the time. It is generally true that ideas are accepted which fit most comfortably with other beliefs of the time. A hundred years before Newton the stunningly detailed artistic renderings of anatomy such as Andreas Vesalius' *De humani corporis fabrica* (1543) not only provided what were among the first widely distributed and accurate representations of human anatomical features but reflected a growing focus with the human body as organism. Also published in the same year as Vesalius' work was the equally influential book by Copernicus, *De revolutionibus orbium coelestium*.

While the works of Galen and Hippocrates had unified medical thinking in the middle ages around their authority, new texts constructed their authority not simply around tradition but also by combining the old method of truth with a new empirical methodology. The scales did not drop from the eyes of doctors and scientists overnight, however, and the new sciences constructed the institutional forms which would solidify their discourses in practice and language, ready to occupy the positions left by the deaths of their predecessors (Kuhn 1970).

The literary establishment

In addition to the new sciences, a new liberal arts, a community of writers and philosophers, specifically sought to shape the practice and reception of literature. The production of literature had been at odds with the perceived role of the gentleperson from the seventeenth century. The work of writing placed one under some degree of control of the publisher, and this 'constrained a gentleman's defining freedom, making writing not fit work for a gentleman' (Johns 1998: 176). A writer's work would commonly be abridged or edited if it had been commissioned, thus removing control of one's own words. This was certainly the case of the early 'diurnals', the forerunners of the modern newspaper. Introduced from Amsterdam into England in the 1620s, these publications depended upon the reader's belief in the writer's credibility, and to increase this trust 'they were … the genres that first developed rhetorical procedures to project authenticity in the domains of print to the highest degree' (1998: 174). No doubt such 'procedures' were necessary. John Cleveland had written about reporters: 'To call him an Historian is to Knight the Man-drake.' He continued, 'In summe, the Diurnal-maker is the antemark of an Historian' (cited in McKeon 1987: 48).

Among the popular material for such diurnals were descriptions of events in which the reader could not participate. Descriptions of executions were popular fare, as were the confessions of those being executed. The scaffold speech of Charles I was a popular seller (Bernard 2001: 5). Such publications supplemented the popular printings of the likenesses of important figures of the day, the king, and later Cromwell, in addition to depictions of celebrations, affairs of state, and battles (see Eisenstein 1979). Especially during the Civil War, pamphlets from both sides of the conflict were widely printed and distributed. As with the Reformation of the previous century, such materials contributed to the formation of a public who shared common perceptions of events to the extent that they shared the same information. Whatever the meaning of a given publication or picture for the individual person, larger and larger numbers of people were participating in the same symbolic space and consequently they shared a common experience of the published expressions of thought.

Writers and propagandists needed the booksellers to produce and disseminate their works, while publishers or booksellers needed writers, who were often unhappy with the constraints of working for a publisher. In this tension are represented two sides of another conflict which in the long run was to prove as sweeping in European society as the Reformation and which was at least as important in shaping the future of modern culture, and this was the decline of aristocratic influence in the face of a rising, monied, middle class. In several areas of writing and publishing economic and social reflections were taking place of what McKeon (1987) identifies as an epistemological crisis. The social transitions appeared not only in contests about the ephemeral creative power of the author versus the physical power of the publisher but also in the emergence of various forms of literature that changed the ways in which various forms of truth were legitimated. During the seventeenth and eighteenth centuries, as McKeon notes,

> the general discrediting of aristocratic honor ... was accompanied by the accelerated mobilization of social, intellectual, legal, and institutional fictions whose increasingly ostentatious use signaled their incapacity to serve the ideological ends for which they were designed. (1987: 133)

In other words, one of the social fictions which had underpinned the structure of European society held that nobility originated with birth as an essential, inherent, and inherited quality. The forces of the developing bourgeoisie challenged this notion on every front, and the old orders of social truth, transmitted and legitimated in fictions of all kinds, began to alter to reflect new understandings of social deference.

The position of the bookseller in society was hotly contested because it was on the rise in importance. Watt notes that owing partly to the decline of patronage, 'the booksellers, especially those in London, had achieved a financial standing, a social prominence, and a literary importance' which gave them a virtual monopoly over 'all the main channels of opinion, newspapers, magazines, and critical reviews' (2000 [1957]: 53). On the one hand, these early representatives of the trades (already quite different from the medieval guilds) were portrayed, generally falsely, as pirates and thieves, that is, as mercenaries who would do anything to produce a profit, and with this reprobation the whole of profit-making activities was cast as disreputable, certainly as beneath the gentry. However, most revealingly, the status of booksellers and stationers was also criticized on the basis of the control which they exercised. 'The character of the "bookseller in general" mattered because contemporaries were convinced that it prevailed in determining what appeared in print – what could be bought, sold, borrowed, and read' (Johns 1998: 147). Dr Johnson, writing in the *Adventurer* in 1753, commented that 'the appearance of writing was formerly left to those who, by study or appearance of study, were supposed to have gained knowledge unattainable by the busy part of mankind', while at the present time, people of every profession and calling were writing with abundance (cited in Watt 2000 [1957]: 58). While such a situation presented some real problems for those engaged in winning propaganda wars, the underlying social tension leading to such accusations reveals as well a recognition of the importance of controlling and defining the popular printed discourse and a growing concern that the control of letters was going to fall not to the aristocracy but to the trades.

The publishers in the sixteenth and seventeenth centuries were tradespeople and among the first successful middle-class manufacturers. They possessed money, if not on the scale of the landed aristocracy, but they lacked the historical legitimacy of nobility. While the aristocratic order increasingly relied upon books and other printed material, the dissemination of information favored here the revolutionaries, as it had in the Reformation. Qualitative characteristics and criteria of status were being held to a similar empirical test as was applied to the physical world. The pragmatic test of the new formation of power was to be applied in the English Civil War and later in the revolution of France. What had begun as a conflict of 'land' versus 'trade' in the 1600s had, by the eighteenth century, become the new social conflict of 'landed interests' opposed to 'monied interests' (McKeon 1987: 166). The series of changes around social status was for McKeon one of several 'categorical instabilities' which posed a series of problems in meaning which were to become 'central to modern experience' (1987: 20).

The articulation of this problem took place in representing the challenge of the middle class to the power and status of the gentry, and such a challenge would require attacks on the legitimacy of their social and moral power. These took place in many areas of society, but the meaning of the new social order was still to be decided. The novel was thus a kind of popular social philosophy which expressed in concrete ways the pressing problems of social change:

> The problem of the novel was formulated to mediate … not questions of truth and questions of virtue in themselves so much as their division, their separation from each other. And the fact that the novel originates when it does signifies that it is in this period that the separation of these two realms of thought and experience comes to be felt most acutely. (1987: 419)

The virtues of the new individual were not to be found in society which, reflecting the values of the old order, had to be opposed in a similar operation to the separation of Protestantism from Catholicism. Rather, the virtues of self lay within a plain and simple humanity, and the legitimation of written description such as travel narrative is to be found in 'the private virtues of honesty, sincerity, naturalness, and integrity that guarantee the perspicuous observation and documentation of truth' (1987: 104). One saw the virtues of the Protestant middle class presented in fictional forms. The protagonist of the novel was no longer the noble person endowed with virtue by birth but the middle-class individual struggling against adversity and corruption. 'The movement for moral reform … tended to be mainly supported by the middle class, who fortified their outlook as a group with the assumption that their social superiors were their moral inferiors' (Watt 2000 [1957]: 166).

These problems were to be resolved not so much by the scientific community, certainly not by the aristocracy as it had existed, but by emerging philosophical and literary circles which from the seventeenth century on would assume growing control over the meaning and place of literature. Such were the forms that the 'philosophical radicalism' took when the revolutionary impulse which created the emerging middle class began to settle down, changing from an energy of transformation to one of continuity, stability, and the respectability of power. Certainly, much of the literary activity from the late seventeenth century on consisted of 'attempts to establish and make believable a particular kind of literary truth' which presented 'the new role of the writer as a struggler with meaninglessness' (Kernan 1987: 161). This was precisely the sort of fiction that Johnson and Boswell constructed for themselves and which others would follow, although the meaninglessness would appear in differing ways as modernity developed. In a more subtle way than expressed in the pamphlet wars of the seventeenth century, the organization of literature into classes and genres contributed to the emergence of new criteria for truth.

Thus, hardly a century after the Royal Society began giving form to the sciences, groups such as the Literary Club were bringing together Goldsmith, Gibbon, Boswell, and others who were creating a standard genre through a systematic theoretical review of literature, that is they 'sorted out true literature from the literary apocrypha of ephemeral mass-cult trash the printing press spewed out daily' (1987: 159). Johnson, in addition to producing what was probably the first edition of Shakespeare's plays as literature, sought through projects such as his *Dictionary of the English Language* (1755) to uncover in language an order 'underlying the particularities and confusions of actual usage' (1987: 187) to reveal what he called 'a fabrick of the tongue'. There was still the possibility of a secret continuity of language which lay behind the surface. These activities shifted control of the meaning and value of writing away from the booksellers and publishers and toward the intellectual elites who now sought to define the forms, aesthetics, and purposes of literature.

The interaction of the booksellers, the authors, the reading public, and a growing and self-conscious literary culture helped to stabilize the cultural forms of printing. As these forms gained recognition, the implied contract between the producers of these forms and the consumers fixed particular relationships between style, form, genre and content, thus generating the recognizable types of literature and readers which characterized the eighteenth and nineteenth century literatures. Ian Watt's study of the novel raises the theory that various forms of emerging 'realism' formed the bases around which the techniques and tropes of the novel were developed. Among these changes were inversions of the meanings of the words 'original' and 'realism'. Watt writes that 'from the mediaeval belief in the reality of universals, "realism" had come to denote a belief in the individual apprehension of reality through the senses: similarly the term "original" which in the Middle Ages had meant "having existed from the first" came to mean "underived, independent, first hand"' (2000 [1957]: 14).

Through the eighteenth century writings of philosophers such as John Locke and David Hume, and influenced as well by the growing focus on parti-cularities of life and nature derived from the new empiricism, the word 'realism' came to connote something more like a particular view of experience. 'The various technical characteristics of the novel ... all seem to contribute to the furthering of an aim which the novelist shares with the philosopher – the production of what purports to be an authentic account of the actual experiences of individuals' (2000 [1957]: 23). By the same token, 'originality' reified the singular experience of the unique point of view which, on the basis of other artistic criteria, was now privileged as true. One great fiction of the novel, then, borrowed from the great fiction of empiricism: that the view derived from a particular subjectivity represented reality as it was. To suspend disbelief about this form of representation was to accept it as valid not only consensually but empirically. With the prose forms of the eighteenth century, fiction emerges as a statement about the appearance of the real in much the same way that science emerges as an explanation of the real.

Middle modernism and the invention of another rupture

The constructing of a literate *episteme* was another social site where the definitions of power and meaning were fought out. It took place in an imaginary geography not of Platonic forms but of economic and social practices inclined toward resolving philosophical and epistemological differences within linguistic domains. The development of modern individualism in philosophy and practice following the Reformation traced one fault line along either side of which various forms of social power were arrayed. On the one side was an elite consensus about meanings and forms and the uses of reading, and on the other side were ever growing numbers of people who, lacking stable relations within the industrial, urban social world, created identity, pleasure, and a sense of their fit in the world out of the public discourses of print.

The seventeenth and eighteenth centuries established their legitimacy by positing a rupture with all that went before, and in adopting this strategy, they helped lay one of the templates of modernity. While an ancient or medieval reader or writer would seek to link him or herself with the epicycles of history that repeated endlessly, and after Christianity in subordination to the biblical temporal line, the early modern defined the age with newness. It would take some time before this idea of narrative, temporal, and experiential separation would permeate the culture, and as it did, the continuous sense of time linked to the past appeared increasingly as a mysticism. Thus, at the transition into the industrial age, Blake (1757–1827) could ask, 'And did those feet in ancient time, Walk upon England's mountains green?'

By the beginning of the nineteenth century, all of the social apparatus was present for the creation of a mass, shared, language and literature which would help to produce new definitions of social identity and relations as well as an ideological viewpoint consistent with capitalism, empiricism, and the abstractions of time and place which would fit well with the modern, urban, disjointed social and which legitimated the roles of experts of all kinds in running the social. The mechanisms were in place to create a 'reading revolution' (Chartier 1995: 17–18).

Many of these changes would accelerate with further social and technological innovations in the nineteenth century including mass public educational campaigns to raise literacy levels, a proliferation of popular newspapers, and improvements to the technology of manufacturing.

Those genres, forms and techniques for stabilizing meaning, the author, and the narrative perspective developed well beyond their original environment of a relatively small number of relatively wealthy people. The novel form as well as the diurnal could become popular only as they became affordable. This was accomplished through the introduction of new techniques of printing as well as through improvements in transport which lowered production and distribution costs. It was not until 1800 that the Stanhope press was made entirely of metal, and the screw press, used since Gutenberg's time and which was an adaptation of the older wine press, was not surpassed for another decade until Clymer's improvements. The Koenig flatbed cylinder press, patented in 1811, was the first significant advancement in the mechanism of printing and greatly increased the speed of production to something around 1000 pages per hour.

The same social processes which made possible the steam-driven cylinder press produced the wealth and leisure time enabling the middle class to purchase and read books. These processes also contributed to the creation of industrial cities throughout Europe and the United States as masses of people were concentrated in the production centers to operate the mills and machines. The great migrations of peoples in the middle to late nineteenth century from Europe to the United States had early precursors in the Irish potato famine migrations (1841–1851) and the Highland Clearances of Scotland (1750–1850) which emptied rural areas of people who would populate the slums and factories of Edinburgh, Glasgow, New York, Boston, and elsewhere. Such disruptions severed or at least severely strained traditional links between people, their community, and their heritage, and they posed as well a threat to the social order of the emerging bourgeoisie. In a sense, the migrating millions shared with the middle class a lack of a stable social framework within which identity, values, and beliefs could be relied upon and maintained. This uncertainty would have generated a social need for the early mass media of the nineteenth century which were able to provide in print what was either missing altogether or in danger of being lost: a shared public language and the participation in various forms of literate culture.

The linkage between the scientific knowledge and the literary forms was articulated in class, wealth, and connections to state power which were still only slowly undergoing transitions from hereditary aristocracy to social status based on economics. The rise of a middle class as the new power was solidified through their identification of models of social knowledge which would generate wealth and simultaneously produce the mechanisms for disseminating this power through the social realm. Once one has identified empirical, consensual evidence as the highest form of rational truth about the world, it is a small step to envision its application to all areas of the social as did the Saint-Simonists of France and various social reform movements in the United Kingdom and later the United States. The limitation of the caucus for that consensual meaning to the middle-class, white, males of property was not yet a philosophical problem in the formulation of the eighteenth century democracies.

The origins of the code of mass media

In the origins of the 'reading revolution' are located most of the economic, technological, and epistemic forms, in however embryonic an appearance, of the mass media. It matters little if a revolution taking 300 years can truly be called a revolution (Briggs and Burke 2002: 22). For those commentators and historians of the years following the introduction of printing, and for us, the interrelated changes both to the *episteme* of Western culture and to the institutional forms which underpin the discourses of a society appear as a dramatic transformation even if some developments took years to penetrate the culture. With new technologies of producing texts, growing numbers of people who became literate as a consequence, and philosophical undertakings which attempted to stabilize the meanings of texts, the social world which followed increasingly located, identified, and expressed itself in literate sources and forms.

These same practices and institutions, sometimes appearing in modernized configurations and sometimes in creakingly ancient ones, continue to create the stories, histories, social identities, and scientific explanations of the world. They provided the narrative structures of much popular drama, established the criteria of realism and representation, and created templates for thought, feeling, and behavior. The story form of the English novel set the standard practices which continue to govern realist fiction in writing and in cinema. The representations of fictional characters in techniques established by Richardson, Fielding, Austen and others create the models with which people compare themselves and their lives on television and in film. Similarly, histories of the great inventor working alone to change the world reinforce the mythologies of individual control over one's self and one's world, mythologies which built upon while simultaneously rewriting the Protestant narratives of salvation.

In a sense, then, one can see developing, through the seventeenth century practices constructed around reading, the sort of Kantian transcendental subjectivity or 'illusion' which Luhman (2000) suggests as the field of the mass media in general. He writes that one may speak of the reality of the mass media 'in the sense of what *appears to them*, or *through them to others*. According to this understanding, the activity of the mass media is regarded not simply as a sequence of *operations*, but rather as a sequence of *observations* or, to be more precise, of observing operations' (2000: 4). In the creation of consensual definitions of what would constitute science, or literature, or newspapers, those influential persons in the early knowledge business established a 'code' of the system of mass media which distinguished information from non-information (2000: 17), that is, they established the boundaries of the separate literate discourses which the social institutions would reinforce and extend.

These literary processes constituted a social memory not in the sense that the individual became self-present in the information of the system. This development would only come later. After an early period of radicalism and change during which the media helped to create and publicize new forms, they settled into patterns of maintaining the structure of the society which they had helped form and which reflected the values and taken-for-granted beliefs of those in control of the media. With the emergence of a media of the masses in the nineteenth century, information became less something that was transmitted between people who had it and people who did not. Now trivialized into genres, into easily recognizable forms and tropes, mass-produced information painted the taken-for-granted but thoroughly important background against which the everyday takes place (Luhman 2000: 65ff.). Mass media create a 'depth of texture' in culture which lends authenticity and believability to what is seen and recognized as the setting of reality (Krug 2001: 407–8). However, the mechanisms for this process and hence for the general function of the mass media as information systems were already present by 1900.

Included within the 'information systems' established in the eighteenth and nineteenth centuries were common-sense, taken-for-granted values and beliefs promulgated by the authors, literary societies, and booksellers who saw themselves as a class largely through its construction as a epistemological form. The creation of the 'self' also created the 'social' in the particular forms which each took.

> Hypostasized over against the individual, 'society' slowly separates from 'self' as 'history' does from 'literature', a ponderous and alienated structure whose massive impingement on the individual paradoxically signifies the latter's autonomy, the very fact of the individual's 'rise', as well as the subjection of self to this greater power. The autonomy of the self consists in its capacity to enter into largely negative relation with the society it vainly conceives itself to have created, to resist its encroachments and to be constructed by them. (McKeon 1987: 419)

However, the same mechanisms which created the possibilities for the appearance of a social stability also laid the seeds to undermine the very processes of that stability.

Reading practices created a tension between knowledge as a social activity and knowledge as a personal meditation and experience. The possibility of subjective truth and understanding created a space in which the social consensus of knowledge could be debated and challenged. As groups of people who did not share the values and beliefs of the new establishment came to demand enfranchisement in society and government, the middle class construction of self would be stretched and distorted beyond recognition. Could the new ideas of self be extended to all? Could the shared forms of the middle class create a social world that could encompass the working class as well? These questions would occupy much of social debate and reformist thought for the next 200 years.

FIVE

Building the Divided Self: Letter Writing

The public sphere comes into existence whenever and wherever all affected by general social and political norms of action engage in a practical discourse, evaluating their validity. (Benhabib 1992: 105)

Augmenting Human Existence?

A common fallacy about technology is that it necessarily augments and extends human capabilities. In this view, popularized in advertising hyperbole ('Better living through chemistry'), technology is both the magician, pulling endless rabbits from his hat, and the magical boon itself. This fallacy arises from assuming that all forms of technology are comparable and that human actions in relationship with them are similar; they are not. From their original forms, tools do extend the human body and its capabilities. The hammer hardens and extends the fist. The lever multiplies the strength of the arm. However, there is a point at which tools become machines, and machines are, by necessity of their operation and their interdependency within other social systems, of another order of complexity (see Mumford 1963; Illich 1973).

The machine is not a tool but a part of a system, and it must be used in particular ways. The machine no longer maintains a direct connection with the actions and the world of humans. The machine is a sort of slave (Illich 1973: 11) that performs the same series of tasks over and over again, reliably, efficiently. Our relationship with the machines and with the world in which they operate for us becomes that of master and slave. Norbert Weiner (1954) noted that automatic machines were 'a precise economic equivalent of slave labor', and he warned of the economic consequences of that relationship. There is still the moral dimension: that the machine should work for us and we should enjoy the benefits without thought or consideration, that is, without moral involvement in the process. Our involvement consists solely in our position as masters in the relationship.

Removed as we are from direct experience of these machines and the systems which drive and support them, we know only their products. Our knowledge of the world created through and for technology is very limited. The operation of a steam engine remains a mystery to most. The principles of internal combustion might be understood in basic form by those who have dismantled a lawnmower or overhauled a Chevy short block V8, but the days are long past when one could understand and repair one's own automobile. How much more is this true of computers than of cars! How many people understand, however roughly, the physics of semiconductors? How many understand binary logic? Such knowledge is not only esoteric, it is unwanted. Such knowledge is unwanted precisely because it extends one's consciousness outside the master–slave relationship, and it is usually dismissed with a remark such as: 'How is that going to help me operate a computer, drive a car, etc.?' It is in this narrow sense of performing some limited activity in isolation from other activities that machines augment or improve human activity or 'intellect'.

Thus, it is not the 'essence' of technology that separates us from a part of the world but rather our relationship with the world as mediated through technology. If technology in the form of machines, devices, and systems will act for us, performing our will in the world, then we are at that point freed from having to know about or be responsible for that world. The machines will take care of it for us, and if there is an unexpected or undesired outcome, the problem is technological, an issue of tinkering with the machine. Our concerns are directed elsewhere: to the products of this relationship or to what we may do with these products. This is the point to which the augmentation of the human intellect is directed. It seldom speaks to the fundamental relationship between people and technology but enters later in the development. While proclaiming that everything has changed, modernist technological tinkering addresses not the process itself but only the form of it. The photograph is a new, improved way of capturing and remembering one's life. The computer improves the way that we conduct business, write, play, and share information with others. Superficially true, both statements neglect examining underlying issues such as the place of conducting business in life, the meaning and symbology of remembering one's life, and the kinds of games we play. More to the point, both statements posit an ideal of the true which is unexamined and which illustrates the creation of a *de facto* class system.

This system takes shape first in the formation of social ideas which are concretized in structures that enshrine and communicate (in the ritual sense of the word) the values, rhythms, and relationships of the class division. The class system is seen early in the literacy divide and later in the digital divide between those who were admitted to the master class and those who were excluded. However, the most pervasive and influential markers of this class division are less well known. The social divisions of the technological class system do not exactly recapitulate the economic class system, setting one group against another. Rather, the master–slave relation between self and the world tends to be recapitulated in all relations. While helping to structure conditions of commonality between people (and uniformity in the world) the logic of technology simultaneously undermines those kinds of thought and feeling which could provide the connections between individual persons. The master–slave relationship fundamentally destroys the reciprocity and recognition of the other necessary for humans to orient themselves either to the world or to other people.

The Technological Self

The context

People learn their orientation to the world in various ways. Some of these are formal and explicit, as when the English middle class cultivated letter writing as a social skill in the eighteenth century or when one takes a course in computer usage at the local vocational college. Most of our understanding of our world, that is, of all the things that really matter and that help us get through the day, are acquired in much more subtle and unrecognized ways. Bourdieu (1977; 1991) refers to this process by which dispositions to actions, values, thoughts, behavior, language, and affect are structured in the individual as the *habitus*.

The habitus of people is acquired throughout life from a multitude of linguistic, physical, and communicative moments. Without compelling or determining behavior, the habitus gives one 'a sense of the game' (Thompson in Bourdieu 1991: 12). Bourdieu writes that 'the "choices" of the habitus ... are accomplished without consciousness or constraint, by virtue of the dispositions which, although they are unquestionably the product of social determinisms, are also constituted outside the spheres of consciousness and constraint' (1991: 51). That is, there is neither freedom nor constraint in the habitus because that behavior or value which is being inculcated reflects structures from outside the habitus and outside the commonly acknowledged social world.

Relevant here are those aspects of the social world that are quite literally embodied through this habitus and that are easily identified in the myths of progress, justice, and the good surrounding technology. The purpose of the machine is ostensibly to free human beings from drudgery, danger, and the monotonous toil required to build our world and manufacture our goods. The working class would be eliminated. However, this promise is almost never realized. The computer was thought to offer the potential of the 'paperless office', an environment in which workers would move effortlessly and seamlessly within the new resources, knowledge and information. The steam engine would provide limitless power to drive the machines of manufacture. The other devices of technology would likewise assist us in our pursuit of the good life.

The reality was different. The steam engine did drive the factories, railroads, and steamships, but it imprisoned hundreds of thousands to wage slavery in inhuman conditions. The computer did eliminate the need for some aspects of physical record keeping, notably in information exchange, but it also presented new templates for conducting human activities based on very particular kinds of rationality, reliability, and uniformity. Such models fit closely with the needs of industry and capital. Contemporary machines are creating new templates which are in keeping with the changing structures of the contemporary world. Our habitus reflects the order of the technological world.

The current societies in the industrial, Anglo-American world require that individual people have a self which is oriented not to the rhythms of the steam engine and the order of armies and factories but to the newer orders of society. The contemporary self is oriented to the formation of values, desires, and patterns of action created in the context of a post-territorial, post-disciplinary, fragmented and unstable social world. The creation of the post-industrial self requires the modification of the bourgeois self which preceded it. Some parts of the older form are amplified: an idea of private interiority, the sovereignty of one's desires, and so on. Other characteristics of the older self are excluded, devalued, and eliminated.

All societies have ways of integrating their members into the formal and informal rules and beliefs; however, few societies have been as successful as this one in establishing and creating demands for the formation of selves which are as fundamentally unstable as are our own. We have learned how to construct elaborate selves around complex and collective symbolic referents within mass, industrialized societies, but these referents themselves are unstable, leading to the formation of selves that bear little resemblance to the self that emerged in the early modern middle class, though both the eighteenth century self and the contemporary self came into being through transformations of the habitus that were to a large extent negotiated through the use of new forms of communication technologies. Initially, the early modern self was poorly defined and vaguely formed, but the values and rules that were elaborated to govern and characterize the middle class eventually came to find institutional support of such penetrating thoroughness that they became the taken-for-granted social norms for Anglo-American society in general. The habitus of the contemporary society owes much to the templates for thought and interaction established in writing and reading, particularly as these formed the practices and infrastructures of the social intercourse in letter writing. Today, however, letter writing as a social form for defining and testing self and for linking the self to the emerging world of manufacturing capitalism is a dying art. Yet, the modern self acquired many of its basic characteristics from the world created in the eighteenth and nineteenth centuries, and before examining the mechanisms from which the modern self emerged, we should first consider some of its key characteristics.

Aloofness and withdrawal

George Devereux has suggested several characteristics of the contemporary self which are also 'major schizoid traits systematically fostered by our society' (1980: 224). Some of these we are already acquainted with: aloofness and withdrawal. This is the ethos of 'cool' and is, indeed, necessary in a world of hyperstimulation; one cannot respond to, or even notice, every stimulus without becoming a nervous wreck. The self is pulled back from the world, held in abeyance. The world as it exists can be experienced only at speed, at a distance.

At times our separation from the surrounding world is both psychically and physically extreme. Driving in automobiles, within a crowded, high-speed pattern of traffic, we are isolated from the physical and psychological world of others. We replace it with the radio, tape, or CD, creating a surrogate social world according to our desire, but finally, encased in our glass and steel shell, we are alienated from the natural as well as the human world. Augé describes such travel as 'reminiscent of aerial views' and observes that 'main roads no longer pass through towns, but lists of their notable features – and, indeed a whole commentary – appear on big signboards nearby' (1995: 97–8).

Our expressions of self in the car are those of the private domain, such as singing along or the acting out of primal territorialities as in road rage. The setting through which one travels is both ahistorical and without substance. No one wants to know distance or what lies between here and there; the pertinent question is, how long will it take? There are moments of dizzying disorientation when one realizes that one could be anywhere: Australia, America, England, Germany – only minor clues (road signs, vehicle types, tree silhouettes, if one is very observant) give the setting away. The experience transforms the place into a space and finally into speed, velocity, motion.

The speed of our motion on the motorway and in our own world hits us with a deluge of visual perceptions. We are, in Auge's terms, presented with an 'overabundance of events', part of which derives as well from the paradoxical opening of space through its contraction. As the world becomes 'smaller' and more visible, it also becomes more knowable, at least in theory. We have a considerably greater access to images and descriptions of formerly exotic places, as well as a greater capacity to actually travel there, than previous generations. The downside of this contraction of the world is the degradation of the space in front of us. We find that 'getting closer to the "distant" takes you away proportionally from the "near" (and dear) – the friend, the relative, the neighbor – thus making strangers, if not actual enemies, of all who are close at hand' (Virilio 1997: 20).

The 'information superhighway' is an apt metaphor for contemporary communications precisely because so much of that communication takes place in systems in many ways analogous to highways and to the experience of driving within them. Such technologies are complex systems which require reformulations of thought and perception in order to live within them. One's attention is highly exteriorized, focused on the signals and events which occur in that strange, neologistic experience of 'real time' which replaces both the interior subjective experience of time and the capitalist commodification of time in newspapers, the timeclock, and the billable hour. New values arise to produce new hierarchies of importance: speed triumphs over the texture of a moment or a place, order supplants serendipity and chance, and a certain number of failures (often catastrophic) are accepted as inevitable.

Segmentalism

Another tendency is toward segmentalism or partial involvement in the world. Devereux writes that 'most transactions in daily life are extremely segmental, implying little or no total personal involvement' (1980: 224). Much of contemporary interaction takes place in service relationships, for example with the store clerk or salesperson, and neither requires nor has a place for affect or attachment. Related to this limited involvement, a depersonalization of others takes place. They exist for us only as partial people, as representations of their functions. Any similarly competent person might do as well for us in any given setting. 'This depersonalization is further reinforced by the social demand that one should be impersonal, unemotional, reticent, inconspicuous, average, neutral and the like. All these demands amount in the last resort to saying: "Never mind who you *really are*! Just *behave as expected*" ' (1980: 223).

Devereux also identifies the tendency toward dereism, that is the distortion of the real in favor of a model already held of how the world should be. Thus, it does not matter that the policies of the West create dissention, poverty, and conflict in the developing world; the West is acting out of the highest possible moral reasoning and evidence to the contrary is simply dismissed or not noticed. Dereism is closely related to the blurring of a distinction between the imaginary and reality. 'Our pseudo-rational society insists that we accept a schizophrenic split: that we keep our equilibrium with one foot firmly planted among the transistors of an electronic brain and the other in the revivalistic church around the corner' (1980: 229).

These tendencies appear individually as categories of experience, but they appear in the world not singly but together in mixtures of alienated, eroticized, disaffected, and temporally fragmented selves. To illustrate, the characteristic that Devereux refers to as infantilism is manifested in adults taking on the subjective position of the child who believes his or her self-world to be immediately accessible to others. Merleau-Ponty writes that, 'for him men are empty heads turned toward a self-evident world where everything takes place' (1962: 355). From such a standpoint, one's differentiation from the world is simply the reduction of the world to objects related to gratification.

Devereux does not and nor do I assert that the modern world is mad or that the modern self is inherently insane. The analysis above suggests only that the contemporary self is positioned within social and cultural demands that cannot easily be reconciled with the classic liberal ideology of the self determining, responsible, atomistic, and hedonistic self which continues to be enshrined in popular mythology, much of Christianity, and law. The self within capitalist society is inherently divided; empathy, emotion, and positive affect are difficult to manifest in a world of service and object relations. Still, there are multiple, workable kinds of selves and a number of people who, despite the cultural tendencies, manage nonetheless to develop fairly integrated selves. There is also evidence (psychiatric, pharmaceutical, and otherwise empirical) that considerable numbers of persons have neuroses or other disturbances that are at least exacerbated by the tendencies just described. Kovel goes so far as to write that 'wherever an individual is in the class structure, she/he will necessarily be exposed to profound splits in personal existence' (1981: 58).

The suggestion here is not that individual people have no self-determination or that contemporary culture creates schizophrenics. Culture creates the conditions, the tendencies, the median values, as well as the mechanisms for teaching them and for policing their use. Louis Sass (1992) strikes a good balance. He writes that 'it is not hard to see how a number of [schizophrenics'] core traits (the asocial turning inward, the lack of spontaneity, the detachment from emotion, the hyperabstractness, the anxious deliberation and cognitive slippage, and the exquisitely vulnerable sense of self-esteem, for example) might be exaggerations of tendencies fostered by this civilization' (1992: 370).

Historical bases in capital for the modern split

These traits had a useful place in an earlier culture, that is, in the emerging world of modernism in the eighteenth century. Scientific and capitalist thinking both benefit from a deliberate disengagement with the world, a distancing of emotions. 'To separate labor from other activities of life and to subject it to the laws of the market was to annihilate all organic forms of existence and to replace them by a different type of organization, an atomistic and individualistic one' (Polanyi 1957: 163). Capitalism in its emerging powers drove much of the abstraction of the world and the concomitant splitting and distancing of the self. Joel Kovel (1981) clearly articulates the relationship of the modern self to capital. Capital, in its attempt to 'universalize the sphere of the economic by separating human activity from its outcome', immediately devalues the world into things, into resources, and other people into either competitors, rulers, or commodities. 'A personal side and a thing side, made by human activity but each apparently having a life of its own, seem to wander separately through the totality' (1981: 56).

Time, nature, and other people are severed from their groundings in human perception and become abstract characteristics linked to production. This had been a characteristic of liberal philosophy and views of psychology. J.S. Mill, Locke, and others had held that 'social arrangements affect individual human nature only superficially. They are additive and artificial' (Girvetz 1966: 43). Bentham had extended this atomistic view of humanity to his understanding of community and the common good:

> The community is a fictitious *body*, composed of the individual persons who are considered as constituting as it were its members. The interest of community then is, what? – the sum of the interests of the several members who compose it. (Cited in Halévy 1955: 500)

The self thus severed from others and from nature becomes aware that it is separate; the individual splits off parts of his or her self as the activities which engender and create the self now exist in separate spheres of life and no longer have a connection with each other (Kovel 1981: 58–60). Those activities, now split off, can be treated as if they are simultaneously metonymic for the whole of human existence and quite independent of human life. While useful for certain kinds of abstract rationalism, the cost of such a split of the world is a diminished affective attachment to the world. George Devereux writes that 'Society operates most efficiently for business – or for mass activities – and most destructively for the unfolding of Man by narrowly circumscribing the scope of his affective transaction' (1980: 224).

The Letter

The containment and differentiation of affect and the splitting of the psyche into commercially useful and commercially non-useful segments required the development of specific technologies of self. These emerged in social practices, beliefs, and the institutions which framed them. The creation of a new and radically different social order required the adherence to new beliefs and views of the world, even if these seemed directly to contradict both personal experience and the received wisdom of the ages. The emerging bourgeois sensibility also privileged a considered, highly structured presentation of self. This self had to be strictly monitored and adjusted, above all by oneself, to ensure a fit with the social model of proper and respectable life. In the eighteenth century there was an intense concern among the emerging middle classes with the proper conduct of self, the proper presentation of self, and in the following century there was also a great concern with imposing many of these traits upon others. Such social engineering quite naturally would foster an orientation to the newly privileged patterns of language and discourse. This would appear on the perceptual and affective levels as 'the presence of intensified forms of self-consciousness and various kinds of alienation' (Sass 1992: 37).

In addition to being a site of intense self-scrutiny (rewriting and recopying of letters was common), the culture of writing letters was clearly an extremely important public arena for the dressing, make-up, and promenade of the self through settings of family, business associates, and others with whom one had a 'social' relationship. The concern for assuming the proper form of self in the eighteenth century was to a large extent expressed and commented upon in letter writing. Indeed, letter writing was the most popular form of written self-expression open to most people until the late twentieth century and the development of e-mail. As such, the process of letter writing and its location within social and cultural forms are key to understanding the technologies that were available for this expression of self. We may also examine here the relationship between capital and technology manifested in the institutions and government organizations and the subsequent emergence of the postal system.

In the specific field of communications, limited but highly structured activities mediate values from one area of society to others. This process is not a transmission but is more accurately seen as the creation of conditions requiring the new values and the providing of the physical material and means of acting in accordance with the new values. Most commonly, and especially in the case of the post, models for demonstrating particular values emerge in a social context which requires people to write and to respond to the letters of others. In general, what are modeled are the needs and activities of power manifested by government, business, and other institutions. Activities which these aspects of society conduct for their own purposes create social systems which are reflected by communications and which then find their way to the level of individual persons. At this personal level, the phenomenology of personal experience, that is, one's own sense of his or her self, changes in accordance with the systemic activities so introduced. One sees this pattern repeated throughout the development of modernist society, producing elaborations of business and military or bureaucratic values within the activities and selves of ordinary people.

The postal systems in Britain and America

The book and the rise of the publishing industry created one form of technology linked to language, and in so doing a new shared consciousness was created on a massive scale throughout the industrialized world. People were implicated in the meanings, uses, and forms of the mass-produced word. However, most people did not produce many written words themselves, and if they did, most had no efficacious way of getting them to others. The written word tended to come from the industrial production of words and language.

While people have written letters to each other perhaps for as long as writing has been used, a system which would allow them to send their writing to others and have a reasonable expectation of timely delivery, that is, a system of mail, was slow in developing. Such an enterprise required an organizational power which transcended the individual person, the local community, and even the country. Who could develop such a system? Who was interested? Governments were naturally suspicious of the private transmission of information. The newspapers could be widely read and monitored, as could broadsheets, and even in the eighteenth century there still existed the idea that personal letters were more reliable and trustworthy than the notoriously inaccurate and political courants which continued from the previous century. Information in a paper or broadsheet was public and could not be easily used to transmit secrets. The transmission of letters was another matter. Personal communication held the threat that plots and conspiracies, aimed at overthrowing the existing government and state religion, might be organized in secret, as indeed they were.

There was also no widely based demand for a post which in the beginning would justify the expense in road building and bureaucratic infrastructure. While there are examples of memorable personal correspondence – one thinks of the letters of Héloïse to Abélard – the personal letter was a rarity or oddity for most people until the early eighteenth century. 'Memoirs, diaries, and family record books were the main vehicles of private writing in the late seventeenth and eighteenth centuries' (Foisil 1989: 327). Letters were less important. Most people, even those who might have some degree of literacy, had little reason to write letters prior to the great migrations of the nineteenth century. Even if one wrote, to whom would such letters be addressed? At a time when few traveled more than a few miles from their homes, one's circle of acquaintances tended to be local and based in everyday life.

Some of the same factors which hindered the development of a postal system also hindered the physical movement of people. Paved roads were a rarity, and even highways in Europe were little more than dirt paths that could become quagmires with rain. Bridges or ferries might exist at key crossing points, but smaller rivers and streams would require fording. Although the Romans had constructed a network of roads of high quality through much of Europe, by the sixteenth century most of these had fallen into disrepair. At any rate, the Roman system was not sufficiently extensive to provide good internal communications within most European countries.

The growth of the postal system

The letter was always private and carried the aura of a communication which, if not intimate, was at least personal. Widespread letter writing developed, then, within a growing privatization and importance of written language, at least in the upper classes (see Chartier 1989: 124). These private letters had always been conveyed by hand, delivered to a traveler bound for a destination near the recipient or dispatched with a slave. This practice had its origins apparently in the ancient Near East and Greece, and the personal messenger bearing the letter was believed to impart something of the presence of the sender, the *parousia* (Bazerman 2000: 17–18). By the thirteenth century or so, there were others who, as societies grew in complexity and diversity of labor, had a need for the exchange of ideas and information. Universities, trade guilds, banking houses, some towns, and merchant organizations all had need of some regular lines of communication, and each developed limited methods for distributing letters and other documents among their constituents.

Governments, however, had long had postal systems, as the command and control of widespread lands required ways of getting information and transmitting orders. From Xerxes through the Romans to Charlemagne, imperial rule demanded empire-wide communications. The Royal Post in France was instituted under Louis XI in 1464 and was open to private citizens provided they had obtained permission and were willing to pay for the privilege. The Holy Roman Emperor Maximilian ordained a day and night horse post from 1491. Administered by the von Taxis family, this post continued in operation until 1867. Systems such as these generally operated only within a country, and were by and large reserved for government communications. However, these early postal systems did serve as models for what was to follow.

With the growth of international trade and finance throughout Europe and into the new lands of America, Africa, and the Far East, businesses required increasing communications. News of commodities, information about shipping, as well as simple tracking of shipments all contributed to the development of an informal postal system developed and run by merchants. Having already an infrastructure of acquaintances, agents, and transportation, the merchants were well positioned to develop both the physical infrastructure and the increasingly codified writing and reading forms for letters. In England, the continental merchants' system was called the 'Strangers' Post' and was commonly used for international communications. Until nearly the English Civil War, the merchant post was all that was available to English merchants, and it was widely used.

The case of England presented special problems. Even before the death of Henry VIII, England was under threat from France and Spain, and the aristocracy believed there were plots everywhere. Private communication, particularly coming from overseas, was viewed with suspicion. This concern was borne out when Mary Stuart was discovered to be receiving and sending secret letters from the French government and her co-conspirators against Elizabeth I. Nonetheless, it was under Henry VIII that Brian Tuke was appointed Master of Posts in 1512 and given the charge of maintaining relays of horses for conveying the government mail. This plan of maintaining fresh horses every 10 to 15 miles provided the term for subsequent mail systems, for each stop was called a 'post'. To send something with all possible speed, then, was to send it 'post haste'.

Despite the establishment of the post riding system, the speed of delivery had not significantly changed from Roman times. In the Roman post, a letter would take seven days from Sicily to Rome, one month from Britain to Rome. Under the system of Tuke, a letter from London to York took three to six days. The great speed trial of the era occurred in 1603 when Robert Carey rode from London to Edinburgh to inform James VI that Elizabeth was dead and he was now king. Carey rode post from London, departing between nine and ten on the morning of 25 March and arriving after bedtime on 27 March. He had accomplished the memorable average speed of seven miles per hour (Robinson 1948: 22). One technology used to help identify and eliminate delays was the dated postmark introduced by Henry Bishop, the Postmaster General of Charles II. Some improvements were seen, and by 1700 a letter from London to Bristol would take almost 17 hours, and a letter from London to Glasgow only around 42 hours.

Charles I opened the posts to public use in 1635 with the establishment of the Letter Office of England and Scotland. Postage was, however, expensive, being assessed on the bases of destination and the number of pages. The expense was paid by the recipient, a condition that was also true of the early American postal system. As the British postal system was made more centralized, it was also made more efficient. Ralph Allen revamped the northern routes, eliminating London as a hub through which all mail was sent, thus greatly speeding delivery through the north of the country. On 2 August 1784 John Palmer saw the first of his post coaches run a trial route. These coaches professionalized the staff, provided a uniform, and greatly improved the reliability as well as the speed of mail delivery (Robinson 1948).

However, the great democratizing process of the English mails came in 1840 with the local Penny Post. On 6 May 1840 the first Penny Black adhesive postage stamp was inaugurated, and a simple letter could be sent anywhere within the United Kingdom for one penny. The number of letters sent through the Royal Mail in the UK doubled from 75.9 million in 1839 to 168.8 million in 1840 (Daunton 1985), though most of this increase was certainly merchant post and some portion of that had previously circulated by older means. This innovation also removed the recipient from the responsibility of paying for the letter, whether it was wanted or not. Consequently, many more people began writing, and there was a concomitant increase in sales of stationery, pens, paper knives, and stamp boxes. There were also reductions in prices as economies of scale evolved and industrialized production increased. In England, for example, the price of steel pens (or more precisely the nibs), which were a significant improvement over the quill, dropped from 18 shillings per dozen to four pence per gross between 1803 and 1838 (Hall 2000: 93). Envelopes began to be used as postage was no longer assessed on the number of pages, and by 1843 Christmas cards began to appear.

These innovations in the postal system took place in the midst of the very large migrations of Irish, Scots, and English both within the United Kingdom and abroad to America and Australia. Displaced by a combination of famine, industrialization, and government pressure for resettlement, millions of people were separated from their home communities and their families throughout the century. There was, thus, considerable social pressure for a rationalization of mail services to bring them within the reach of larger and larger numbers of ordinary people.

Overseas migration remained a barrier to communication, however, and postage was prohibitively expensive for most people until nearly the end of the nineteenth century. Although the idea had been advocated since at least 1846, a standard rate for overseas postage would not be set for another 50 years. Within the Commonwealth, Canada was the first to introduce the Penny Post to Britain in 1898, forcing other countries to follow suit. In addition to uniting separated families and aiding business correspondence, communications in the late nineteenth century were in general believed to possess the power of uniting people. Elihu Burritt, an American who campaigned extensively for a single, affordable international postage rate, believed that the Ocean Penny

Postage would 'link all nations in trade and peace'. To help promote his campaign, he distributed envelopes with slogans such as: 'The World Awaits Great Britain's greatest gift – Ocean Penny Postage'. Another read: 'An Ocean Penny Postage is wanted by the world and will be a boon to England'. His most eloquent, though, was: 'All ports will open up, friends will greet the happy arrival, and there will be no more enemies' (Hall 2000: 101).

He was neither the first nor the last to believe that improved communications would foster understanding and peace. The same would be said about electricity, about the telegraph, and even about aviation. I am told that the same argument is even made about hamburger chains ushering world peace with their spreading franchises. I suggest that such naïvety is not founded in the belief that talking or writing will necessarily allow for the negotiation of differences. Rather, in believing that the other will take up one's forms of communication, one also commonly assumes that the other will also take up the associated values and ideals. Such a view attributes far too much power to the medium and far too little power to the contexts, discourses, institutions, and lived activities from which the communications emerge. Nonetheless, letter writing, having played a major part in the formation of bourgeois selves and society, seemed imbued with the power to similarly transform whoever else would take up the practice, and this power would be developed and tested through the late eighteenth century.

The letter and the narrative self

In order to better appreciate the several purposes to which people put the letter and the post, it is necessary to examine some of the uses as well as the evolution of using personal letters. The letter had always been a link to others from whom one was physically separate. Personal letters were common for all classes in Rome and Greece (Bazerman 2000: 18). Even if one could not write perhaps more than one's name, public scribes or amanuenses would, for a fee, write a letter dictated by the sender; and for another fee, another scribe might read the letter for the recipient. As such, there is no reason for supposing widespread literacy at more than a basic level (and the same remained true until at least the end of the eighteenth century). Just as the use of the computer does not premise understanding or 'computer literacy' in any meaningful way, the use of letters does not imply that people were psychically involved with what was on the paper.

A fascination with the power of the new form and its uses – which included letters to the gods, letters to the dead, prayers, moral romance, and erotica – no doubt helped to fuel the practice of letter writing. Each of these phenomena constitutes an exteriorization of thought and self for the letter writer. The writer is creating a relationship with the absent thing by sending a part of his or her self in the form of a letter, and the recipient of the letter obtains a part of the sender.

Even letters from Roman soldiers stationed on Hadrian's Wall in the north of Britain to their families elsewhere on the island reveal the humanity that such sporadic contact keeps alive. The idea and remembering of the absent other in letters, perhaps especially in the mention of the trivial events of everyday life and plans, provided physical evidence of one's continued existence in the language community from which one came. One had physical evidence, often crafted by the living hand of the writer, phrased in that person's unique idiolect, that one still lived in the words of family. Even the primarily phatic content of the Christmas card conveys acknowledgement that one exists for others. How much more powerful would be the words of a mother, father, son or daughter from whom one had been long separated, in a form in which one could not hear the voice but still read it.

Similarly, to write a letter was to have another person in one's mind and thoughts. It involved an orientation of the present here and now around the imagined existence of the other in the physical act of writing. To receive a letter was to be held in the abstract linguistic formation of the writer. As discussed in Chapter 2, the act of perception leads to the necessity of language to recapture that part of one's being which is being lost to the perception of another. The act of writing, then, as a reciprocal relationship between two people not physically present, creates the construction of narrative selves which are present in their words and their chirography. Such a relationship may be formed to maintain communality, to act in supportive ways as in business, or it may be used in the construction of a social identity as a member of a class. Within the eighteenth century, numerous guides and the social practices themselves educated the gentry and the 'middling' classes into how to present themselves in writing letters, particularly the familiar letter. Through the act of writing letters, one learned to create an epistolary persona and to present oneself in writing to others within specific, well-defined social relationships.

Within the context of gentry and the bourgeois, the letter became a marker of one's manners and breeding, that is, a key marker of one's place within the social. 'In practice, letters served as a badge of membership in elite society' (Whyman 1999: 19). The letter locked one into a web of reciprocal responsibilities to respond, and it conveyed in its form, content, and style numerous markers to be studied, contemplated, and commented upon. For writers such as Richardson, letters were 'documents demanding extraordinary time and attention', and as such 'they were one of life's central activities' (Zirker 1966: 75). Letters, particularly the 'familiar letter', required that one cast letter writing into the form demanded by the prevailing beliefs and structures of thought and conduct.

In the origins of the primary form of social correspondence prior to the 1800s, the merchant letter, the forms of letter writing were implicated in the complex web of social and economic relationships which were necessary for the conduct of business. Through much of the eighteenth century, merchants operated by intricate combinations of social and economic relationships. A form of this social/business hybrid continued into the twentieth century. There was thus an overlap between the need to convey specific sorts of information of a factual nature and the need to convey information about persona, about reliability, and about character. The reporting about a person and his character thus was deeply imbedded within the rules for bourgeois conduct of business. In many ways, the two blended together in the creation of the genteel persona, a replacement for the now displaced aristocratic aura. One's character was now indicated by one's education, attention to the details of literary conduct, standardized spelling and other markers of the use of proper forms. 'When merchants articulated intentions and defined situations, they did so within the matrix of possibilities and constraints posed by the genre and narrative conventions, symbolic repertoires, discourses, and vocabularies that they mobilized and reworked in their letters' (Ditz 1999: 62).

The epistolary persona was required by common assent to possess credibility in the social. It had to be stable enough to be recognizable and trusted, and this stability was acquired primarily through the use of formulae. As such, conventions for writing in this form emerged through numerous popular texts from the early eighteenth century forward, containing advice on how to write an epistolary self using forms and conventions provided along with exemplars to help regularize spelling. Whyman (1999: 34, n. 103) lists works such as John Constable's *The Conversation of Gentlemen Considered* (1738), Henry Care's *The Female Secretary* (1671), and *The Lady's Preceptor* (1743). Just as letter writing eroded gender barriers, requiring women to learn to write in this form, class barriers were also challenged. Samuel Richardson's *Letters Written to and for Particular Friends, on the Most Important Occasions* (1741) promoted letter writing as appropriate for all classes and all occasions, an essential skill for anyone aspiring to refinement (Dierks 2000: 32). Dierks also observes that between 1750 and 1800, there were nearly 400 imprints of penmanship manuals, spelling books, grammar books and dictionaries. Austin (2000: 52–5) argues that, at least in some places, as early as the 1790s 'ordinary working people' engaged in regular correspondence with family members and friends and that they employed self-help books such as George Fisher's *The Instructor: or Young Man's Best Companion* to help in achieving proper form of address, spelling, and observance of decorum.

In the eighteenth century, the 'familiar letter' emerged as a form. This new template for the letter form placed a premium on personal emotive response, and it changed the conventions for expressing feeling. 'Modelled on idealised conceptions of unmonitored, freely flowing conversations among friends, the emerging protocols of the familiar letter demanded candor and self-revelation, the central signs of which were "ease" and "immediacy" of voice' (Ditz 1999: 69). The emergence of this voice might well add to the increasing acceptance and use of the epistolary form in novels. Ditz continues that the epistolary creates 'the illusion of a privacy that permits the play of unobserved communication, establishing the textual equivalent of a fourth wall between third party readers and those engaged in dialogue without self-conscious reference to an observing audience' (1999: 69). One should note that this description of epistolary communication also describes the acts of voyeurism and some other forms of scopophilias.

Modern letter writing began as a bourgeois activity in which the newly emerging modern self was problematized on the individual and the social levels. The intense self-scrutiny of manners, behavior, and social responsibility which appeared in both letter writing and fiction from the mid 1700s demonstrates the extent to which people needed to discuss the meaning of changes in these aspects of society. By the mid eighteenth century, letter writing was sufficiently established as a cultural form to support the growing narrative form of the epistolary novel. Within the context of changing ideas about fact and fiction, history and literature, and the formulation of self within a new set of values and meanings (see McKeon 1987: 27–8), the legitimacy of the letter helped a new fictive form to come into existence in support of the new kinds of selves and the problems they faced.

Significantly, the letter was a medium of composition open to women, and as early as the seventeenth century some authors of writing manuals were explicitly recognizing women as authors of letters and hence involved in various aspects of social decorum, moral judgment, and decision-making. While it was still largely improper for a bourgeois woman at the beginning of the eighteenth century to be an author in fields other than domestic ones, she could write letters, and by the end of the century she not only could write books but was also catered to by publications aimed specifically at women and to their sphere of life. The division of labor in society along gender lines, as well as along other lines, was partially renegotiated during the process of constructing, painstakingly and with great attention, a reality which could, ultimately, be taken for granted.

The impact and power of the personal letter for a person isolated from his or her linguistic community, from those with whom one has a history linked to one's origin, can be profound. For people such as soldiers fighting far from home, for prisoners isolated from people who can express caring for them, for the family member away from home, the letter was the only form of contact that one would have with those persons and situations from which one was severed. In such settings, letters could become highly valued treasures to be retained, reread, carefully hidden, or proudly displayed. There was, then, a physicality to letters, a material existence through and within which one had a proven existence with another. Private and familiar, the letter maintained the relationship to the other within one's mind through its physical existence. The letter conveyed the reality that another world continued to which one still had attachments, that the other person is more than memory.

The letter as technology thus teaches people to create and to maintain one kind of split in the self, a split between those with whom one is physically present and those from whom one is physically separated but emotionally and socially attached. The ability to maintain this sort of split and the ability to develop it into an ongoing personal and social reality is essential, for it maintains the web of relations in which one is implicated even if these relations are not present. Chartier et al. observe that 'the goal of letter-writing was to cement, maintain, and extend the bonds of social life and solidarity' (1997: 15).

The role of the letter in maintaining psychic contact between people continues today, though in a diminishing fashion. The telephone, text messaging, and e-mail offer alternatives to the posted letter which change the importance of the message in various ways, and to a large extent they have come to replace it. As an example, one might consider the love letter composed by hand in opposition to the electronic text espousing love (I leave out the telephone here). The love letter is a composition which draws on the ancient techniques of rhetoric, poetry, and poesie; that is, the words and phrases are crafted to create a unique physical object, an artifact or *techne*, which, being sent into the world of another person, will convey not information but a reordering of that person's world. In a personal letter, one communicates not primarily information but a part of oneself which, as the eighteenth century bourgeois knew, was already deeply implicated in a range of social activities and beliefs.

The Post and the Rise of the Public

In the new lands of America, the postal system initially followed the English example. In 1639, Richard Fairbank's tavern in Boston was made the repository for overseas mail, following the English example of using taverns and coffee shops. The postal routes followed trade routes, and key crossroads, ports, and meeting places were central to the distribution of mail. One significant difference between the English and the US posts was the material commonly sent. 'Prior to 1775, the heaviest users of the postal system had been merchants active in overseas trade' (John 1995: 27). Merchants and some ordinary persons continued to send letters, but a major use of the postal system in the US quickly became the transmission of newspapers. Just as in England, merchants, bankers, and just about everyone else who had an interest in the affairs of the day met in public houses and coffee shops to discuss the news. The American situation, however, presented a much more dispersed public with less frequent access to cities and the regular press.

People in politics, power, and business might have reason, occasion, education, and the money to use the mails. However, many barriers stood between ordinary people and the writing and posting of letters. The cost of paper and ink, the costs associated with receiving a letter (as the recipient continued to pay), the absence of a reliable postal system, and a general lack of any need for letters hindered people's adopting of letter writing. The occasional letter of importance, such as informing a family of a death or birth, might be sent, but this was the exception and not the rule. As a cultural form, letter writing may well have been 'the least practiced major mode of cultural expression in early America' (Gilmore 1989: 380). Gilmore points out that the material production of furniture, headstones, and other activities far outweighed the use of post. Some personal writing might be used to disseminate information, but preserving information, i.e. making copies of documents, was much more common as late as the 1780s.

In the US, the places for the delivery of post, that is, public houses of all kinds, became also places where ordinary people might meet to learn the news. Post was delivered not to homes but to such public houses or to specially designated post offices. Given the scattered rural population, trips to collect the mail, including the newspapers, were few. Farmers would commonly wait until a need for provisions arose, so minimizing the number of trips required. A full day might be required to make the journey to and from the post over the inadequate and sometimes non-existent roads. Not until the end of the nineteenth century and the introduction of Rural Free Delivery in 1896 were the rural farmsteads and up to 50 per cent of the US population introduced to regular delivery to their homes. Delivery to homes in selected major cities had been available for an additional fee since the early 1800s, but widespread application of the service did not appear until the Civil War, and this practice was not commonly used until near the end of the century. Similarly, street collection boxes had been in use since 1858, and the combination of delivery and pickup effectively destroyed the post as an institution for public gathering. In the US, however, some parts of the tradition of public houses continue. For example, they are among the few places where public notices of government laws regarding immigration or the draft as well as the 'FBI Most Wanted' posters continue to be displayed even today.

Prior to the postal delivery and pickup services, newspapers awaiting pickup by their intended recipients would commonly be read, often aloud, by others. Papers were even sometimes publicly displayed for this purpose. The post, as a public distributor of gossip, news, and rumor, not only provided what people talked about, but became a significant reason for people's gathering together in the first place. In contrast to urban centers, where political affiliations or commercial interests formed the bases for such public gatherings, in more rural settings the topics of such gatherings had much to do with the news itself and the reason for the gatherings was the common source of staples of all kinds.

Habermas (1991) notes that such sites of social organization and discussion provided not a model of democratic equality, but the concretized social idea of it. He writes that *Tischgesellschaften*, salons, and coffee houses all organized ongoing public discussions among private people: 'They preserved a kind of social intercourse that, far from presupposing the equality of status, disregarded it altogether'. Of course, this social was already a closed society and one's fitness for membership had to be demonstrated. However, within that social setting, a kind of wide-ranging equality prevailed. 'Laws of the market were suspended, as were laws of the state. Not that the idea of the public was actually realized in earnest in the coffee houses, the salons, and the societies; but as an idea it had become institutionalized and thereby stated as an objective claim' (1991: 36).

Ordinary people implicated in the web of activities associated with letter writing undertook themselves this institutionalization of the idea of the public. In seeking to create themselves in a new form, they were also conscious of creating a new social order with the same stroke of the pen. This was perhaps the only moment in Anglo-American history when 'the public' and 'the people' were the same thing, for people directly represented themselves publicly without mediation (see Barnhurst and Nerone 2001: 7). The coffee houses may have been the venues where people gathered to discuss the newspapers, but even early papers were highly reliant upon private letters. Hall notes that

> when Benjamin Franklin took over the *Pennsylvania Gazette* in 1729, he appealed to 'gentlemen' to send him 'private letters' to print in the newspaper. Franklin was assuming that men of a certain social class would posses distinctive 'Information'. He wished, in other words, to link up with an existing network of exchanges that, occurring as they did among the members of an elite, bridged the public and the private. (1996: 155)

This bridging of public and private worked both to influence the conversations, relationships, values, and actions of people and also to extend the voice of these people to increasingly wider audiences. Ditz draws the dual influence clearly: 'As mercantile correspondence disseminated information about men, markets and imperial policy ... it complemented and extended ... the reach of the face to face conversations that took place in coffeehouses, taverns, wharves, and commercial exchanges' (1999: 70). These letters literally spanned the British Empire and the world. Ditz continues, 'simultaneously, the material contained in mercantile letters was reincorporated into those oral conversations. Often they functioned literally as an extension of coffeehouse talk as their recipients read them aloud or pinned excerpts on bulletin boards' (1999: 70).

The 'objective claim' of equality of which Habermas spoke could only be *realized* in the creation of an infrastructure which would allow all persons to be full participants in the public discourses of the papers though reading and to an equal degree through letter writing. In actuality, this could never take place, for the public so constituted outside the narrower interests of class and business could not hold together. The middle class in England defined itself oppositionally against the working class whose boundaries were most clearly established politically in the Reform Act of 1832 and economically in the Poor Law Reform Act of 1834 (Polanyi 1957: 166). Yet, within New England there was perhaps enough linguistic and philosophical uniformity to at least allow the *idea* of a public to take root and flourish (see Hall 1996: 93).

Nonetheless, the opening of the public's participation or at least knowledge of social affairs was closely linked with the development and spread of the networks required for manufacturing. In the US this took the form of road, canal, and later railroad construction, all of which were intended primarily for the transport of commerce: raw materials, physical resources, crops, and so on. The transport of mail, which had become increasingly important by the middle of the eighteenth century, was generally adapted quickly to the new technologies of movement. Although the first railroad steam engine in the US, the *Stourbridge Lion*, only had its first run in 1829, by 1832 the Post Office was granting allowances to its stage contractors to use the new railroads for the transport of mail. And within three decades, the organized transport of destruction and carnage of the American Civil War helped to initiate the explosion of railroad mail carriage and sorting in the US as well as the extension and use of telegraphy.

Formations of a social truth

Once the technologies for the external construction and presentation of self had been developed, it became possible for these selves to be implicated in systems of meaning which operated apparently independently of the self and its immediate lifeworld. Books had begun the process but lacked the immediacy and volume to saturate people's worlds. Letter writing established both the fact of an externalized self and the technology for generating it. The ingredients for the modern self still missing are the mechanization of the means of producing the externalized self, and the thorough reworking of the structures of knowledge and belief that could orient this new self overwhelmingly to the social at the expense of the personal and local. Both of these missing elements were elaborated through the nineteenth century and were already well established by the time of the critiques of Weber and Veblen.

What had started with the bourgeois as a fairly local phenomenon was extended through the world via the routes and technologies of communication. The merchant and later manufacturing networks of social influence, supported when necessary by military force, spread the modern social order through the classes of Britain, across the seas to colonies in America, Australia, Canada, India, Sri Lanka, and elsewhere. Of course, the farther one travels from the center and the more people who are included in the society, the less the social functions around the rules of conventionality grounded in a reasonable expectation of the values, beliefs, and sense of commons. Large groups, empires, and multinational institutions of all manner require a managerial and organizational elite.

The rise of a new social class to dominance, the bourgeoisie, was a kind of social revolution touching on all aspects of society and culture. These people and the institutions which they founded and operated redefined all of the ideas that had gone before about truth, art, beauty and, perhaps most importantly, the relationship of the individual person to the social. The bourgeoisie used various forms of liberal philosophy to demonstrate the ideals of a social world in which personal self-determination rather than a rigid caste system governed the social activities of people and established the goals toward which people might strive. These goals were, however, already predetermined as exemplars of middle-class virtues. In a way, there was a tendency toward the unity of self and culture which, paradoxically, was sought through technologies of self and communication better suited to the fragmentation of both the self and the social.

Part of the process of creating this new world was to redefine some social activities and to appropriate others. Stewart Home (1991) identifies one consequence of the process of transformation that occurred in the seventeenth and eighteenth centuries. He writes that 'as a revolutionary class, the bourgeoisie wished to assimilate the "life" of the declining aristocracy. However since the activities of the bourgeoisie served largely to abolish the previous modes of life, when it appropriated the concept of art it simultaneously transformed it' (1991: 43). In replacing the aristocracy, in creating new forms of power and control which supplanted the aristocratic view of timeless truth and innate, inherited rights, the new institutionally sanctioned truths of science, Protestantism, and liberal justice, supported by the control of the literary establishment and publishing business, asserted the values and world view of the bourgeoisie. In thus raising some new values as inherently more true than the old values, there is an implied 'assertion that bourgeois society, and the ruling class within it, is "somehow committed to a superior form of knowledge"' (1991: 43). All of the processes of making truth and transmitting it are thus vouchsafed to the bourgeois.

It is thus no wonder that, as noted above, one of the first major uses of the printing press was to produce propaganda pamphlets. The leading writers and thinkers of the time were expressly aware of the need to modulate the popular language and thought in ways favorable to the new social order. The values of the new middle class did not have the weight of history behind them, and thus required some additional legitimation. As with other social revolutions which replaced not just rulers but the entire social framework and belief system of an age, some degree of serious re-education of the people was needed. New stories were called for, new values, new beliefs, and all of these had to become part of the background, taken-for-granted understanding of how truth and justice operate. New literary forms, mass education, social reform movements, all gained their power to define the world to new generations from a compelling social need to create a coherent world view within which most people could be taught to live.

From within the 'truths' of Protestantism, science, and the new mercantile and industrial groups, other values necessary for the efficient functioning of the bourgeois also emerged. Further, as this society industrialized through the late seventeenth and early eighteenth centuries, as factories and mills sprang up and as the products of manufacturing became more common, the character-istics and needs of the machine and of the manufacturing process had to be translated into social values. Just as the materials of the planet had become resources, raw materials for the furnaces and looms, so the people who would work in the factories and ultimately consume the products of the factories were conceptualized and represented as a mass of workers and a mass of consumers. They lived in planned housing, in tenements especially constructed near the mines and factories. Educational programs addressing both the mind and the soul sought to elevate the workers from depravity, drunkenness, and finally unreliability to sobriety, literacy, and law-abiding stability. In short, the social values of the factory owners were written small for their employees as a standard of behavior to which they should aspire.

The organization of the masses around the values of the bourgeoisie did not, however, strictly follow the social philosophies of liberalism. The values of the machine process also began to manifest themselves in the same principles of organization: uniformity and regularity became social virtues, as did the psychological structuring of minds and emotions best suited for optimal efficiency and highly segmented social divisions of labor and consumption. The factory provided a template for social thought and action, and it became the model which was subsequently used in many areas of society, including schooling. Because the virtues of the machine were empirical, observable and 'true', they could be improved by rational processes of design and analysis; and if the machine could be so improved, why not the social?

Epilogue

Letter writing provided a model for the learning of a specific technology which was wedded to social values, and letter writing as a social skill and technology was not supplanted until the advent of the internet. The telegraph proved especially useful for governments and business, but it was too arcane for most people to use and its infrastructure never reached the homes of more than a few. Despite the claims made, the telegraph was never really the 'Victorian internet'. The telephone, which emerged scarcely half a century later, also did not replace the letter or offer a set of social skills comparable to those of letter writing. The telephone introduced the idea of instantaneity to personal communications, and through it most people encountered the physical reality of being a node on a network. However, though certain manners of telephone behavior developed in business, in answering the phone, in the (often abused) observation of privacy on party lines, the telephone was always a private form of communication unlinked from the broader social world. Only the cell phone and telemarketing truly succeed at making telephony an integral part of one's daily functioning.

Thus, it is the world of computer interaction which is the natural successor to the world of letter writing. All of the major elements of making a new form of self through the application of technologies reappear in the use of this new domain. As a direct form of communication, some aspects of the internet promise a new era in which people can remake themselves in accordance with new social structures of politics and desire. In the exploitation of this new form, sites appear such as MUDs, MOOs, chatrooms, etc., but these are quite different from the coffee houses and salons of a previous time. These are not physical places where distant communications are discussed, but virtual places consisting of more communication. Rather than operating as the public houses of the eighteenth century, they are analogous to writing letters about letters one has received.

The bourgeois world and the bourgeois self were illusory, elitist, patriarchal, and, being inherently unstable, were short-lived. Parts of them continue to function as aspects of people's selves supported by fragmentary discourses and institutions. However, oriented as they are to different times, places, and contexts, they cannot unify into either a public or even a coherent symbolic whole. The old class divisions of power and wealth still continue in different forms, but the new class divisions are oriented around our being in multiple times and places, and this undermines the kinds of attachments between people which would be necessary to create a public. Neither do we have the public places where we might discuss the meaning of news in the presence of others. Still, however, there are the desire and the dream inherent in the internet to recapitulate that moment, perhaps apocryphal, when it was possible for the people to appear as the public without mediation. This is one great, unrealizable myth of electronic communications: that a medium such as the internet, which is immediately accessible to all, can become the site within which people turn their private concerns into public ones.

SIX

Technology, Truth, and the Military-Industrial Complex

The world has arrived at an age of cheap complex devices of great reliability; and something is bound to come of it. (Vannevar Bush 1945)

The Establishment of Social and Mass Truth

Truth is never a simple matter. For our purposes here, I will hold truth to be the socially consensual agreement about the symbolic ordering of the world. If transcendent truths exist, they are outside language, unshareable, and thus must be taken as matters of faith. The truths with which I am concerned here are the truths of the world, the agreed answers which each culture creates for itself about the good, the true, and the beautiful. As such, the truths explored within this chapter are socially constructed. This kind of truth protects and ensures power: only certain people within certain institutions can define the world.

Foucault (1988) demonstrated how this process created definitions of madness, sexuality, and many aspects of the modern self. Foucault (1980) explained social power as an articulation of knowledge/power; that is, as the ability to create and use certain kinds of knowledge simultaneously with the power to define the subjectivity of others and to establish the ways in which the world may be discussed. As these dominant linguistic and symbolic formations are taken up in ordinary language, in schools, in the common-sense reportage of the newspapers, in law and in the mythologies of everyday life (Barthes 1972 [1958]), they in turn define people's beliefs, expectations, and social definitions. They define what is included and what is excluded from the shared social reality.

This complex of meaning-making we may define as discourse. Following Edwards, I use the term, 'discourse' 'to refer to the entire field of signifying or meaningful practices: those social interactions – material, institutional, and linguistic – through which reality is interpreted and .constructed for us and with which human knowledge is produced and reproduced' (1996: 34). Thus, in order to transform a society from a feudal, aristocratic, agricultural form to a capitalistic, liberal democratic, and industrial form, changes had to occur at all levels of the social, and new definitions of the individual had to be created, transmitted, and internalized as personal subjectivity.

Every society has what Steven Shapin (1994: 245) calls 'centers of judgment' by which he means a group of people, operating in institutional settings, who have the power to define scientific and social reality, that is, to define what is true. Traditionally, the centers of judgment in liberal, Anglo-American countries have been religion, science, and various aspects of government. Although these institutions are interlinked in many ways, each speaks to its own domain of truth: the truth of god, the truth of the physical universe, and the truth of power as expressed in various ideas of law and justice. Such ideas are conveyed and expressed within the society through supporting institutions and people: police, proselytes, and the press. The dominant ideas of truth and reality form the bases of the taken-for-granted stories and everyday truisms.

These domains of truth-making are not clearly separated one from another. Science, politics, religion and other areas overlap, one becoming now more important than another, more influential, or more reasonable. However, it is also possible for different domains of truth-making to join forces, combining in ways that transform what was there before. Thus, persons operating in the political domain may seek to justify their values and actions by linking these with a different order of symbolism such as religion, or they may invoke the historical-mythic symbology of country, calling forth the spirits of long-dead heroes who fought in utterly unrelated battles. Thus wrapped in the trappings of religion or with the flag, any idea so contained becomes more than it was and, if it does not slip into bathos, may expand to encompass a significant part of the symbolic whole of a people and a time.

In general, in the nineteenth and early twentieth centuries, two forms of truth emerged, and these marked the transformation of the symbolic order of the new social world and so also a transformation of the self. The philosophical bases of this new social truth had long been established, but the technologies and infrastructure required to bring them into being had not matured until the mid nineteenth century. Central to one major truth of the social world was the metaphor of industrialism itself.

Public Knowledge in the Nineteenth Century: Communicating the Social Order

Certainly, as Chartier observes,

a 'reading revolution' took place in the second half of the eighteenth century. Its forms were readily apparent in England, Germany, and France: the expansion of book production, the multiplication and transformation of newspapers, the success of small formats, the fall of book prices (thanks to pirated editions), and the expansion of reading societies (book clubs, *Lesegesellschaften, chambres de lecture*) and lending libraries ... Described as a danger to the political order, as a narcotic (Fichte's word), or as a disordering of the imagination and the senses, this 'rage for reading' profoundly impressed contemporary observers. (1995: 17–18)

Books and the habits of reading and writing which had developed in the eighteenth century were simply inadequate to document and mirror the changes in social relations and social formations brought about with the implementation of industrialization. The earlier forms of reading were predicated to some extent on the availability of various texts at specific moments and places. The pace of industrialization and the migration of peoples, the transformation of family, and the mutation of people's social relations had transformed the social settings and relationships around which the bourgeois self was formed. Arising from the loss of the old world and the apparent mutability of everything in the new world, the emphasis of temporality shifted from the traditional and enduring to the modern, the rational, and the immediate. This change from duration to topicality was precisely what the industrialized print and news organizations of the mid nineteenth century were in a position to produce.

A part of the regularizing function of the early papers, that is, through the mid seventeenth century, was simply a product of regular publication. While pamphlets had been widely used since the advent of the press, the papers were 'creating a weekly anticipation or dread of the discussion in a way that irregularly produced pamphlets never could do' (Williams 1999: 116). By the end of the nineteenth century, the newspapers would have created what Innis could call 'the monopoly of time'. Papers possessed all the features necessary to be, if not initially an authority, at least a source worth taking seriously. They had places and dates of publication, and the editor/printer was generally known. There was not yet an issue of truth, as the early papers did not seek to put their own version of the news in print. Barnhurst and Nerone write that 'Colonial printers received correspondence and culled other sources, print or oral, to fill their pages; they did not actively report the news, and they rarely inserted their own voices in the newspaper' (2001: 15).

However, the issue of truth was in some ways inseparable from the press at least since John Peter Zenger, editor of the *New York Weekly Journal*, was put on trial for his criticisms of Governor Cosby. Acquitted by the jury because his 'libels' were true, Zenger's case marked not so much a turning point in the role of journalistic truth as a new level of intensity in the papers' role in public political debate.

At a time when much of a person's news of the world was learned either from correspondence or from conversations that might be several times removed from any first-hand knowledge, hard information about the world was hard to come by. Williams writes that:

it did not seem to matter so much whether the printed 'truth' were actually true or not; what seemed to matter was that American writers and readers believed that printing was one of the best ways to undo false reports. As a result, a great body of correction literature was published; the printing industry became ever more essential as a sort of moral force for publicizing what was good and right. (1999: 130)

This sensibility of what was 'good and right' depended largely on the ideals of middle-class merchant culture. The colonial papers modeled their prose and their forms on the English papers such as Addison and Steele's *Tatler* (1709) and *Spectator* (1711).

The purpose of the papers was twofold. Certainly they fulfilled a vital position in politics and public debate, and they conveyed information which affected trade and commerce, such as news of wars, of peace, of shipping, and so on. These were not entirely separate issues, and neither were they entirely separate from the private sphere of the merchants and bourgeoisie whose livelihood directly depended upon such news and whose politics was in large part directed toward improving the conditions for business.

After the Revolutionary War in America, all of this changed. The ideals of a public had become more concrete; Locke's social order, outlined in his *Second Treatise on Government*, had become incorporated into the constitution of the republic of the United States. The ideal of a public good, separate from but respecting the rights of its constituents, was emerging as a real possibility and so would also be a site of political contestation. The public discourse of these changes was carried through the press which found a new political role. 'The Revolution transformed the political role of the press from the fitful public arguments and occasional controversial expressions of the colonial ear into something new: a full theater of deliberation' (Barnhurst and Nerone 2001: 45). These changes in social role were reflected in changes in the forms of the papers themselves. Barnhurst and Nerone continue that 'Calm typography, open circulation, and universal forms of address provided an ideal conduit for rational discourse, the central component of the public sphere'.

Centralization: papers become big business

Communications in the nineteenth and twentieth centuries became highly structured and showed a tendency toward centralization of ownership and control which followed the trend in large corporations toward monopolizing various sectors of production. In this concentration of ownership, the newspapers and magazines of the nineteenth century set the first patterns for mass readership in developing audiences through the presentation of news about world events in forms that would appeal to these audiences. Journalism itself became a profession, with full-time writers and editors taking on the job of producing a product. As newspaper companies grew in size and complexity, they established similar organizational schemes which were in turn reflected in their output.

Divisions of labor appeared with the construction of news increasingly specialized by its origin. As technologies of information developed and were incorporated into the news industry, departments were set up in major papers to manage the news. In particular, three divisions emerged in large, metropolitan daily papers. News and comment came via correspondence made possible by a reliable and efficient postal system, and this was managed by a correspondence editor. News came from afar through the medium of the telegraph and the monopoly wire services created by large papers and chains, managed by a wire editor. Finally, the new professional staff of reporters were guided and structured by their own editorial staff (J. Nerone 2002, personal communication). Nothing succeeds like success, and the model which emerged with the penny press became the template for creating and presenting the large daily newspapers.

This process toward monopolies of news organizations was aided by the economic conditions of the times. Economies of scale displaced smaller players from securing display advertising, and wire service cartels prevented competitors from using wire service, that is, telegraphic news. There was also a decline in the variable costs of newspapers, particularly with reductions in the price of paper, while increasing fixed costs of capital equipment, such as massive, high-speed rotary presses eliminated smaller competitors from major metropolitan markets. Even though the number of papers continued to grow throughout most of the century, more and more papers were consolidated into chains with centralized ownership. Throughout most of the nineteenth century, the numbers of newspapers multiplied, creating a rich and diverse multiplicity of voices and languages in print. The 1850 US census listed 2526 newspaper titles, and by 1880 over 11,000 papers were being published in the US. However, by the closing decade of the nineteenth century, the form of the news press had become largely standardized at least in large city markets, and it had assumed most of the characteristics that we now recognize as defining a newspaper.

As reporting and news-making were set into institutional forms, the narrative and visual forms of the newspapers and of the news itself became more normative and predictable. In a similar evolution to the diurnals of the sixteenth century, the trustworthiness of the modern newspapers became fixed to the forms that they took. A new narrative emerged with an ever growing implied contract to deliver reliable news about the events of the day as well as commentary about the political, economic, moral, and sociological importance of those events. The newspapers thus were the first creators of the 'reality of the mass media' in forming a shared background of information, beliefs, and stories around which people could live their shared private lives. Newspapers established not what was true but what was information and what was not, and so helped to generate the indicators of what was real and what was important (Luhman 2000: 36).

The sharing of a social reality of this sort leads naturally to viewing the world through the template of the medium. The news grew to be that about which people talked, and it supplied much of the manner in which people would talk about the world. Liberal economics, bourgeois models of social order and disorder, and morality stories deriving their ethics from the myths of individualism and economic freedom were among the kinds of stories that people came to expect in the news and which they tended to use as models for social action and planning. The news, as well as other emerging public discourses, helped to regularize the world around narrative and visual forms.

These papers 'also counseled readers on manners and morals. They filled the void left by the decline of ecclesiastical and governmental authorities. They told readers how to live their lives: how to behave in new or novel social situations, how to deal with ethical dilemmas, how to order their domestic arrangement, how to advance in their jobs, etc.' (1988: 157)

This change in the papers' role had great appeal as it made the papers important not merely in providing the shipping, financial, and political news: these would have little interest for the worker, the immigrant, the poor. By providing the information about how to 'get on' in the newly emerging social world, the papers moved into a void that industrialism had itself created. Veblen wrote in 1904 that 'as regards the mass of civilized mankind, the idiosyncrasies of the individual consumers are required to conform to the uniform gradations imposed upon consumable goods by the comprehensive mechanical processes of industry. "Local color", it is said, is falling into abeyance in modern life, and where it is still found, it tends to assert itself in units of the standard gauge' (1978 [1904]: 11). The 'standard gauge' was not only the measure of goods, it was also the measure of a public language. The discourse of the public must fit the dominant conditions in any culture, and the conditions of the industrialization and largely unregulated big business enterprises were reflected in the form and purposes of the mass media.

First the papers began to use a more populist writing style, making them more accessible to people with fairly undeveloped skills in reading. In close accord with a change in the writing style, newspapers changed their focus to topics more likely to appeal to their new audience: sensationalism found a home. Other developments assisted by emerging technologies included the use of illustrations in newspapers. Illustrations were first included in newspapers in 1806 in *The Times* in England with Nelson's funeral. Early images were made with engravings, often in woodblock and later on metal plates, and such illustrations were the mainstays of the weekly and monthly illustrated papers and magazines. The introduction of halftone image printing around 1880, combined with ecologies of scale, made it more cost-efficient for large daily newspapers to print photographs than for the smaller circulation weeklies to produce engravings. In addition, the new photojournalism helped to transform the communicative function of the press. The photograph was particularly well suited to the 'sceptical, matter of fact complexion' that Veblen (1978 [1904]: 329) identified as a hallmark of the new culture. As Barnhurst and Nerone have argued, news images made prior to the photo had linked the time, space, and distance inherent in the aesthetic of representation with 'the republican ethos of citizenship' while the photograph produced the 'false promise of being present, connected, and emotionally involved' (2001: 137–9). In the photographic 'reality' of the image, a new level of a discourse of truth could emerge, linked with the providers of those images, the papers.

Language, industrialization, and business

More than the technology of the press was changing. The press was now big business and bore closer resemblance to factories than to the print shops of the previous century. The products that it made, though mass produced, suited niche markets when there was money to be made, but the values of the press were on the side of business. The social fabric from which one American ideal of political participation was cut was being transformed into a patchwork quilt. The dream of a rational, public discourse to be conducted through the press was enshrined and protected in the First Amendment to the Bill of Rights, ratified in 1791. However, the idea that the public good was now a separate entity from the interests of the individual person or class was about to come into conflict with the emerging powers of industrialization. The democratic ideals arising from a fairly homogeneous community of merchants and manufacturers were challenged by the immigration into cities of Irish, Italians, Germans, Poles, Scots, and others who shared neither the religion nor the values of the middle class. While some would redeem themselves by rising in wealth and power (for example, Andrew Carnegie was a poor, immigrant Scot), the majority would remain 'the dangerous classes'.

As the major force seen to be driving these changes, industrialization appeared to many as nothing short of miraculous. Greater wealth was created and amassed during the nineteenth century than at any time in previous history. To achieve this, the factories and foundries used mass production combined with centralized control. This control, increasingly abstract and delegated from corporate heads through layers of management to the workforce, was still seen largely as an extension of the individual owner's rights to his property, that is, to that which had been transformed from a natural state to a civilized state through the owner's 'labor'. Liberal philosophy had held that the evolution of the civilized world was thus the transformation of the unimproved commons into enclosures and products (see Girvetz 1966; Halévy 1955). The individual person acquired wealth through mixing nature with the labor of his hands, and this was evident in the farmer, in the small shop, and even in the factory, so why should it not hold true throughout a dispersed corporation? Industrialization was equated with civilization in many arguments in favor of business.

However, from another point of view, the newspaper did democratize knowledge so much as it extended the mass production and mass dissemination of similar kinds of information into much larger groups of people. The eighteenth century model of leisured gentlemen reading and discussing the shipping and political news in a coffee shop gave way to the nineteenth century model of private consumption of news and entertainment which became one's knowledge of a world increasingly segmented, distant, and detached from one's own existence, though nonetheless a world in which one had to live. The newspapers did not produce model citizens organized around common ideals; rather, they helped to produce the social mechanism of a mass society, for even where papers took different political positions (pro-labor or pro-business, republican or socialist), they had very similar approaches to what constituted information as opposed to non-information. The truth might still be argued in the papers, but the greater and indisputable truth of an industrialized world could not be denied.

The Marriage of Progress, Industrialization, and Religion

Particularly in the US, centralization and control as qualities with intrinsic worth developed alongside and helped to define modern methods of organization and production. As the new physical and symbolic orders came increasingly to displace religious and other philosophical orderings, the symbolic social world in which the self was implicated changed again. The transcendent religious and mythic orderings of the world were replaced with the positivistic and teleological myths of progress, prosperity, and technology (defined now as industry). Face-to-faceness in everyday life demonstrably had little bearing on the social order and the forces that so apparently tossed about the lives of ordinary people.

Veblen had observed that within industrial culture, traditional, human-based values were undermined and replaced with the logic of the machine process:

> Within the range of this machine-guided work, and within the range of modern life so far as it is guided by the machine process, the course of things is given mechanically, impersonally, and the resultant discipline is a discipline in the handling of impersonal facts for a mechanical effect. It inculcates thinking in terms of opaque, impersonal cause and effect, to the neglect of those norms of validity that rest on usage and on the conventional standards handed down by usage. (1978 [1904]: 310)

Indeed, Veblen wrote that whatever knowledge of the world other than the machine process that a worker might have would be 'worse than useless' (1978 [1904]: 308–9). New knowledge about how to behave in the new world was required, and the newspapers and magazines rose to supply this. However, the machine process not merely changed the way that people worked but introduced changes to all other areas of life: 'The machine throws out anthropomorphic habits of thought' (1978 [1904]: 310). Indeed, the whole of the social world was altered: 'It leaves but a small proportion of the community untouched ... It falls with the most direct, intimate, and unmitigated impact upon the skilled mechanical classes, for these have no respite from its mastery, whether they are at work or at play' (1978 [1904]: 323).

The social true and social good, if not now in conflict with the familial, neighborhood, and local religious values of the individual person, were at least an alternative, and this new social order was articulated socially in the mass presses which produced weekly, monthly, and increasingly daily printed material, easily affordable, for the masses of workers and their families. Concentrated into the tenements of cities through mass migrations, the poor and working poor existed in physical conditions that had changed little since the 1840s except in the degree of crowding and degradation. In the last year of the nineteenth century, average population density in New York City was 31,000 persons per square mile. In the most densely populated section, the Jewish Tenth Ward on the lower West Side, inhabitants occupying one square mile rose to 276,672. 'Out of a population of 3,437,202 ... the tenement – which was to say the slum – population numbered 2,273,079' (Ostrander 1970: 67–8). Jacob Riis pointed out that in a single tenement in New York, over 180 persons were found to be 'boarding'.

Having long been socially identified as risks to public health, sinks of iniquity, and threats to public order, such large masses of often immigrant, and thus alien and unknown, assemblages were seen on a par with the forces of nature and thus as fitting objects of industry. They were a resource to be tapped and so tamed by the power of industry. One solution to the condition of the poor was thus to organize them within industry. The social experiment with the largely involuntary induction of millions of men into organizational forms that had been the American Civil War had just been completed when Amasa Walker, a lecturer in economics at Amhurst College, tried to take stock of the benefits and drawbacks to industrialized labor and the concomitant division of labor.

Walker observed that, although industrialized labor had a potential to enervate the minds of workers through repetition and dullness, the social benefits from industrialization far outweighed the shortcomings. The greatest benefits arose from the social associations formed in the concentration of workers in mills and factories: 'By such association workmen are brought nearer their employers, have a greater sympathy and cooperation, act intelligently and harmoniously as to their rights, and form public opinion among themselves'. He continued that

> Not only is the workman brought near his fellows and, by such contact, stimulated to industry, to acquisition, to taste; not only does such association of purposes and means afford more of the instruments of intellectual advancement – schools, lectures, churches, journals; not only does the close neighborhood of mind quicken and brighten all the faculties ... but such an association, moreover, brings the workman nearer the government and the public force; sometimes for evil but often for good. (1976 [1866]: 69)

Life within the factory system and its division of labor lifted people from barbarism, providing more goods and wealth than any individual person could extract from nature. Thus, even if the distribution of wealth was uneven and perhaps unjust (Walker stops short of this point), workers are better off than they would have been before.

In contrast with the ideals of a Jeffersonian agriculturally based society, Walker asserted that 'in the mightiest experiment of industry ever known in the world', that is, in England, the 'laboring class is almost immeasurably above the agricultural in intelligence, in independence of character, and in obedience to the law' (1976 [1866]: 71). Obedience to law, and perhaps above all obedience to order, was key, for this forged the character necessary for converting rabble into workers, and the rhythms of machines combined with the organization of factories would accomplish this end. Walker wrote: 'in the majority of cases, it will remain true that intense, spirited, persistent labor directed to one point is better than languid, nerveless, unspurred, rambling play of all the faculties. Mind, to be energetic, must not be republican. The powers must be centralized. Some must be despotic' (1976 [1866]: 70). The habits of industrial production focused and disciplined the mind and spirit of the workers. Having so benefited from their enslavement to the machine, the responsibility for self-improvement fell quite naturally to the workers themselves: 'He has other hours and other duties, ample, if reasonably used, to compensate for all the evil mental effects of his continuous toil' (1976 [1866]: 71). These are obviously the words of one who has never worked a 12 hour shift in a factory on a poor diet.

Protestant religion was already widely used in the nineteenth century to support various social causes and was already linked with secular venues and secular techniques borrowed from theater (Moore 2003: 23–4). When linked with revivalism and an idea of social good based on industrial views of how workers should behave, a popular form of social control linked to salvation could emerge.

The ideas of Walker and others helped to set the framework for the Protestant revivalism of the 1880s and 1890s which would see a merger of religion, capitalism, and the myths of social progress and evolution into a new mythology of nation, industry, and the place of the individual person within them. Many of the elements are present. In terms borrowed from the liberalism of Locke and Bentham, the individual person is responsible for acting 'rationally' in the pursuit of his or her pleasure. From the religious domain, the function of soteriology, salvation, was borrowed and transferred to the civic and the industrial areas of society. Industry and the production of goods and services, combined with the disciplining of ordinary people, would bring about the progress of humankind toward a salvation in rational, liberal order.

In the US, the religious revivalist movement of the late nineteenth and early twentieth centuries was granted very public and lucrative support by major figures in the manufacturing and finance industries. Even then, the linkage of mythic symbolism, salvation, and a docile, reliable workforce was preached in tents and churches by people such as Dwight L. Moody. Among his supporters were such angels of industry and demons of labor as George Armour, Cyrus McCormick, and J.P. Morgan. Other supporters included Marshall Field, Cornelius Vanderbilt II, and John Wanamaker. Their motivations for backing religious movements were clear: 'These men were attracted to urban revivalism as a means of instilling salutary habits of thought and conduct among the lower orders of society' (Ostrander 1970: 92–3). The most famous and ultimately influential preacher of the day was Anthony Comstock, who helped to pioneer a particular kind of social moral control in legislation.

Moody, Comstock, Henry Ward Beecher and others had their work cut out for them, and at least in rhetoric, they were equal to the task. Beecher wrote that 'No man in this land suffers from poverty, unless it be more than his fault – unless it be his *sin*.' He continued, 'if men have not enough, it is owing to the want of provident care, and foresight, and industry, and frugality, and wise saving' (cited in Ostrander 1970: 93). In Beecher's words, the values required of a reliable workforce are expressly equated with divine virtue, and the failure to achieve those values simply demonstrated a lack of moral fiber. Symbolically, the divine order had been firmly linked in such rhetoric to the industrial order. A new kind of 'visible church', that is, a church of true believers in the new order, required as well the appearance of a new kind of 'visible saint'. The signs of divine grace manifested in one were visible to other members of the 'church', as were their absence. In his *Gospel of Wealth* (1889), Andrew Carnegie described the 'talent for organization and management' as the intrinsic quality which set some men apart from others. Management had become grace and those who possessed it were truly the elect, deserving of 'great scope for the exercise of special ability'. To the extent that transcendent or spiritual values disappeared from the public discourse, religion was recrafted to legitimate the new order and to try to bring about a viability to the symbolic system of the new social order. Beecher believed that Protestant leaders could and should direct trends in culture for the greater good (Moore 2003: 59).

Industry – we would say technology – not only subdued and conquered nature and made it a servant of humanity, but was the builder and protector of civilization itself. Andrew Carnegie, in expounding his *Gospel of Wealth*, wrote that 'upon the sacredness of property civilization itself depends – the right of the laborer to his hundred dollars in the savings bank, and equally the legal right of the millionaire to his millions'. Civilization for Carnegie and others like him was *de facto* the industrialized, capitalistic, oligarchical, republic in which they lived. In an argument stunning in its tautologies, Carnegie asserted that no other social system had ever succeeded in providing mass-produced goods in such quantity as cheaply as had the industrialized Anglo-American society. Put another way, no other social system had ever before produced this social formation, and as those in power were doing quite nicely, thank you very much, everyone else must likewise benefit. Such a philosophy finds updated expression in President Kennedy's assertion that 'a rising tide lifts all boats'.

A logical extension to this position asserted that to tinker with the 'laws of accumulation and distribution' was to undermine civilization itself, and this was more than ample justification for calling out the militia to subdue by any means possible striking or protesting workers. In this simple twist, referring to a system of finances as 'laws', an idea which owed much to Herbert Spencer and Adam Smith, Carnegie and others established themselves as servants of natural processes. Thus, the industrial order is linked symbolically with the order of nature, and through this, with the divine, immutable laws of the heaven. However, rather than extending the reach of rational thought into the realm of the divine, the divine as a symbolic source is reduced to the simply material. The hierarchical peak of the symbolic system so constructed is thus not god but 'the knowledge of the world as an inventory of existential facts about all stages and as knowledge of its essential and causal contexts' (Voegelin 1987: 59). With a world view constructed upon a knowledge of the material world and its properties, 'all knowledge about divine order' is pushed 'to the edges and beyond' (1987: 59–60).

Rationally, such a system of thought could not succeed. Dissension arose at all levels of society. In addition to the organization of laborers into unions and other bodies, there were challenges to the doctrine of industrial wealth as an inherent social good. Resistance arose from economists such as Henry George, politicians such as John Peter Altgeld (Governor of Illinois), and social scientists such as Thorstein Veblen and Max Weber. Such people could not be easily dismissed as anarchists, communists, or socialists, though Altgeld and Veblen each suffered at the hands of nationalist, conservative zealots. Artists, too, rallied to protest and resist the degradation of ordinary people. Vachel Lindsay's poems 'The Leaden-Eyed' and 'Factory Windows are Always Broken' extended a populist vision of the destruction wrought by advanced capital. Sinclair Lewis' bleak visions of life on the slaughterhouse floor challenged the assertion that the poor were better off than before industrialization or that the processes were improving through which the mechanical encountered the organic (see Giedion 1970).

Clearly, many of the claims made for manufacturing and its wealth did not stand up to serious scrutiny. However, if the industrial, capitalist system could not legitimate itself as 'rational-theoretical, national-economic, or sociological' (Voegelin 1987: 62), it could succeed as a mythic system. The myth depends substantially upon a concept of the true as defined within its own symbolic system. The primary function of such a myth is to create a thought system that is inessential but self-evident. The central tenet of this system is that the current, as well as historical, evils of the world are addressable only through the continuation and extension of the current, radically collectivist, project of building toward perfection. Such a philosophy positions humankind as 'that great collective body [written about by Kant, wherein rational and enlightened beings aspire to ever-higher stages of perfection] to whose progress each man has to contribute. It is terrestrially closed; it progresses only as a whole, and the meaning of individual existence is to participate instrumentally in the collective process' (Voegelin, 1989: 61).

The laws of the system, operating as the laws of science, that is, as the truth of the universe, are, as Shotter points out, 'simply heuristic devices, useful in the discovery of the supposedly real nature of the mechanisms and objects pictured or modeled in one's theory' (1993: 151). What matters is the theory. There were, of course, other theories of how the social worked. The industrial model of the social was not the only one to capture people's attention in the nineteenth century, but it was probably the most important.

The point is that the industrial world generated its own metaphysics while denying that it had any. The 'Christian' beliefs of Moody, Comstock, and others acted to deflect metaphysics from industrialism itself; religion still functioned as if it were separate from wealth and power, but within 100 years the legitimation of religion was no longer necessary. Capitalism viewed the world in terms of balance sheets, profit and loss. Industrialism emerged as an application of this philosophy to the world of manufacturing, and by the end of the nineteenth century the Galbraiths and Taylors would apply a calculus of efficiency to every aspect of human labor and human movement in the industrial world.

The problem had come earlier, with people's confusing of the legitimation strategy of industrial technology with the essence of technology itself. Within a rational system of control, numbers, now more holy than the cabbala, became information. More importantly, the difference between data and knowledge was finally conflated into an external, obdurate truth, enforced upon the social when necessary by bayonet point but more often proven by the inarguable increase in consumption. Although this metaphysics continues to be resisted, even today, one fiery furnace would alloy the various elements of religion, industrialism, and capital into an inflexible social religion: World War II.

Vannevar Bush and the Modern Conceptualization of Information

The contemporary world and the contemporary self emerged from the industrial nineteenth century. The major elements of the social symbolic system which we inhabit today were in place in 1900. What remained to be developed were a handful of key technologies that would accelerate beyond all expectation the diminution of the individual's traditional lifeworld and the creation of a social world of instantaneous communication structured by a pervasive rationality. The key technology required to complete this change depended on the computer, and the computer required a rationale for its development and especially for its application to everyday life. In the exemplar of Vannevar Bush the rationale for data management takes the basic form that it still has today, and this rationale borrowed significantly from the combination of engineering and military discourses.

The military line in the spectrum of thought

All fields have a myth of origins, and in the case of the computer, the internet and the world wide web, the myth identifies a few key people who rise to the intellectual and social challenges of a perceived need and produce systems and products that are taken up in the entrepreneurial spirit and transformed into socially useful things. One of these is Vannevar Bush, who is credited by some as one of the founders of the computing world (see, for example, Levinson 1997: 140). This description of the processes by which social fields, such as computing, come into being does an injustice to the complex social and human processes at work. One dimension that is specifically left out is the axis of power and knowledge identified by Foucault, that is, the discourses which positioned both the inventors and the field. The particular discourses at work in the creation of both the computer and the information world grew out of the intertwined relations of what Dwight Eisenhower identified in his farewell speech as 'the military-industrial complex' and what Adams called the 'iron triangle' of military, industrial, and academic interests.

The origins of the computer are military. The Colossus computer was developed in Britain to aid in cracking German codes produced by the Enigma machine, while American research into computers was driven by the need to produce complex tables of ballistic formulae for aiming anti-aircraft guns, as well as for breaking codes. Later, the American machines were applied to solving formulae connected with the Los Alamos atom bomb research. This tendency toward military involvement continues today, with the *New York Times* reporting that most US supercomputer work is aimed at weapons design and testing while countries such as Japan tend to focus more on atmospheric modeling and other civilian uses. The same conditions were true of the machine tool industry. In 1979 Congressman Ritter observed that Japan and Germany had invested in commercial civilian rather than military machine tool systems which emphasized 'cheapness, accessibility, and simplicity in their machine designs and software systems' (Noble 1993: 120). Noble notes that as a consequence the United States became a net importer of machine tools in 1978 for the first time in over 100 years.

The influence of the military-industrial-academic complex extends beyond international competition and economics; it structures and guides each of the institutions through which it operates. Necessarily, the products of these industries, whether machine tools or students, reflect the dominant characteristics and values of the military approach to industrial development, 'characteristics which, together, constitute a system of thinking that informs, embraces, and transcends the particular technological developments themselves' (1993: 111). Noble identifies three major tendencies in the military influence on industry: an emphasis on performance (meeting military objectives), a strict sense of hierarchical command (reducing human intervention between the order and its execution), and a fetish for modern methods of capital intensive production (1993: 111–13). Within the framework of military thinking such an approach makes sense, 'but it becomes irrational in other contexts, as the military approach spills over, permeates, and diffuses through the economy' (1993: 113).

At the dawn of modern telecommunications, in the last year of World War II, 1945, two documents emerged as prophetic statements of how subsequent technologies might develop. Each article drew upon the recent developments in technology to emerge from the war, and both works pointed towards possibilities as yet unrealized in technological hardware which would introduce the most influential changes in communications history since movable type. Reading these two works ignorant of the authors' names, one would be misled as to which author became a science fiction writer. The first article appeared in a little read journal, *Wireless World*, by an largely unknown physicist, Arthur C. Clarke. This short piece, 'Extraterrestrial relays: can rocket stations give world-wide radio coverage?', put forth the idea that orbiting telecommunications satellites could be located in geosynchronous orbits above the equator, thus providing world-wide coverage. Prescient in its vision, the idea was too far-fetched, the journal too obscure, and the author too unimportant for many people to take note of it.

The second article appeared in the *Atlantic Monthly* magazine and was written by the then Director of the Office of Scientific Research and Development, Dr Vannevar Bush. The editor of the *Atlantic* in the introduction specifically drew a comparison between Emerson's essay *The American Scholar* (1837) and Bush's piece, saying that 'instruments are at hand which, if properly developed, will give man access to and command over the inherited knowledge of the ages' (Bush 1945). Alas, what the article actually proposed had little to do with knowledge, but the *Atlantic* editor was not alone in confusing knowledge with data. Dr Bush also supposed that knowledge, information, and data are largely equivalent. This misguided logic was a symptom of the age, and it continues to confuse the significance of information and data in the era of the internet. Although sometimes associated with the birth of the internet, this essay is significant not because Bush envisions the internet, as is sometimes claimed, or even the personal computer, but because he imagines the application of technologies of information storage and retrieval which seem similar to the idea of hypertext. Further, he does this in a way that reveals some fundamental shifts in the relationship of information to human beings.

Bush's concerns were superficially similar to those of Geddes (see Chapter 3): he feared that specialization was becoming increasingly necessary for progress, but at the same time he knew that researchers were increasingly isolated from their disciplines and from each other by ever more arcane publications as well as by the sheer volume of publication. Bush (1945) wrote that 'the investigator is staggered by the findings and conclusions of thousands of other workers – conclusions which he cannot find time to grasp, much less to remember, as they appear'. Geddes, too, believed that increasingly specialist thought was alienating people from their world, but his greatest concern was that narrowly rational thought fragmented people's ability to integrate knowledge into a moral and aesthetic consciousness. Bush, on the other hand, saw over-specialization as a threat to scientific and thereby social progress, not because specialization was logically or epistemologically flawed but because it made information too difficult to manage and index.

Whereas Geddes in the nineteenth century had proposed educational integration, with his Index Museum as an exemplar, as a method of bridging the gaps between specialisms, Bush proposed increasing the efficiency of storing, retrieving, and processing information. Bush's solution was an engineer's. If access, retrieval, and storage of information were the problems, technical solutions would resolve these. If man [*sic*] could 'better review his shady past and analyze more completely and objectively his present problems', the human spirit would be elevated (Bush 1945). This would enable man 'to push his experiment to its logical conclusion'. This experiment is presumably the perfection of society through scientific means. Ethical and philosophical thought are largely absent from Bush's article. Even logic is reduced to the strict formal logic of mathematics. All writing is treated as if it were random bits of information, 'the record of the race'.

Bush is proposing a system for automating some aspects of thought. Bush had considerable experience turning things over to systems. As head of the

Office of Scientific Research and Development (OSRD), Bush had overseen the coordination of scientific research with the needs of the military in the pursuit of allied victory in World War II. Following the war, he sought to extend and continue the practices of the OSRD through securing congressional and military funding for science while eliminating or minimalizing congressional oversight. This course of action brought him into direct conflict with Senator Harley Kilgore who sought to produce an organization which would, in the words of David Noble, 'ensure that science be advanced according to the principles of equity and democracy' (1984: 17). Thus, from at least 1945, Bush was advocating a kind of research and a kind of science based on the models of military research which he acquired during the intense secrecy and elitist associations of the war years.

The perceived need for a national guiding agency for research led eventually to the establishment in 1950 of the US National Science Foundation (NSF), which was not exactly what Bush had in mind. Bush wanted scientists to have control over the funding, fearing that politicians might. In arguing for scientific autonomy from public control, Bush and many other scientists made the point that science inevitably advances human interests: 'The applications of science have built man a well-supplied house, and are teaching him to live healthily therein' (Bush 1945). This claim is, as Noble observes, 'a religious one, grounded upon the fiction of an autonomous science destined by fate always to serve the public interest' (1984: 12). Thus we see the continuation of the social religion of industry. Although military and industrial controls were acceptable, Bush and others deemed governmental oversight counterproductive to the advancement of their version of pure science (see Noble 1984: 16–19). In other words, science was to be conducted with industry, and for the government, but hidden from the view of the public and the oversight of most government agencies.

The new sciences of information: 1945

Once hailed as the greatest American engineer of the twentieth century, Bush had worked with problems of the military application of mathematics and engineering since World War I. He had traveled to England to work with Robert Millikan on how to detect U-boats, and within a year of the outbreak of war in Europe in 1939 he was lobbying President Roosevelt to establish the National Defense Research Committee. This organization would be directly responsible to the President. Its purpose was to coordinate federal funding of scientific research into specific technologies: radar, atomic energy, and the proximity fuse. Bush and his colleagues were also aware that this partnership with the military could lead to massive federal funding to university-based research after the war. As Colin Burke puts it, 'the war made America's leading universities into engines for research' (1994: 85).

Bush's view of knowledge and information developed in the context of his research in the two decades between the wars. With the rise of industrial and theoretical sciences in the twentieth century, the number of journals had multiplied dramatically as the pace of technological change had accelerated. In the 40 years of the new century, aircraft, radar, polymer chemistry, and atomic physics had changed the ways of fighting wars and permeated into nearly every corner of society. Similarly, the research taking place in various countries of Europe – Germany, France, Hungary, England – was defining the sciences of physics, chemistry, and advanced mathematics. Bush had witnessed first-hand how technologies and industrial production could be applied to produce quantum leaps in the destructiveness of warfare, and he believed that research had to be guided by intelligent federal funding to keep America militarily competitive with what were still the most advanced manufacturing and scientific nations in the world.

The state of American universities was similar to the state of American libraries prior to the 1940s. Neither had a tradition of advanced, applied research, for neither had the amount of money that only governments and corporations possessed. Libraries, endowed by industrialists, philanthropists, and small amounts of state money, purchased holdings and indexed them with a view toward the needs of the citizenry, the amateur. They used the Dewey decimal index system, which was cumbersome. The real problem with Dewey, from the scientist's point of view, was that librarians and not scientists devised and standardized the index entries. 'Control had to be taken from the librarians and put into the hands of experts in the sciences' (Burke 1994: 119). Changes in subdisciplines of science and the emergence of new areas of specialization along with subsequent publication in the ever more numerous specialist journals were often reflected neither in the holdings nor in the indices of most libraries, public or university. Bush's device, the memex, was his solution to the problem. Thus, 'the ideas behind memex ... pointed to an era when the librarian and his methods would be replaced by scientists using a creative automaton' (1994: 119).

The memex device, described below, was only one solution to the problem of information management which had grown since 1918. During the inter-war years, Bush worked with a group of other scientists called the American Documentalists. Burke (1994: 100–1) notes that this group shared with Bush four basic similarities: each sought to subsidize expensive library holding and acquisitions for scientists, each proposed technical solutions to problems that proved useful in World War II, each bypassed the existing library and information organizations, and each changed their original goal of improving science to that of establishing an information industry. The idea of the memex was not a straightforward solution to a clear problem but emerged out of ideas about the general situation of knowledge. Neither was the memex built specifically for the purposes Bush advocates in his article; it was built upon a number of designs that Bush and others had worked on for 15 years in a variety of contexts. Still, it was typical for an engineer to believe that any problem could be solved with the proper design.

Engineering technocracy and the memex

The memex device derived in part from Bush's work in microfilm for the FBI. His work in data processing for code breaking and complex numeric processing would bring about the modernization of information indexing. The device would allow people to rapidly locate articles and then to construct, automatically, the fact of connections between articles along with the comments of other readers. Burke writes that 'his memex was to work like the human mind. Association among ideas rather than categories was to be its intellectual foundation' (1994: 120). A scientist at work at the memex would sit before a rather large desk-like device containing rolls of microfilm which could be accessed through an index that grew as people used it. The scientist would activate an automatic device which would record the 'ideas' he or she wished to link, and the connection would be recorded on a special part of the microfilm together with comments. The rolls then need not be shared as the indices themselves could be copied, shared and followed by colleagues. These indices would have to be physically transported, though later Bush proposes centralizing these and accessing them via telephone (see Burke 1994: 354).

The emerging technologies of microfilm, reliable mechanical mass production, and the new analogue, largely mechanical computing systems promised whole new ways in which information could be stored and accessed cheaply and in miniature. Bush envisioned that 'If the human race has produced since the invention of movable type a total record, in the form of magazines, newspapers, books, tracts, advertising blurbs, correspondence, having a volume corresponding to a billion books, the whole affair, assembled and compressed, could be lugged off in a moving van.' Certainly a fanciful insight in 1945, Bush's optimistic vision of technology has, of course, been superseded: now, DVD optical disks and high-density hard disk storage systems would considerably reduce the size of the truck needed to store a billion books.

The importance of the memex lay not in its storage system but in the method of indexing and sharing indices. The 'associative trails' could be stored and amplified technologically. These trails are the intertextual references which emerge as the process of thought draws connections, similarities and differences, between different books, articles, texts, etc. More than a simple method for improving research, Bush is pursing nothing less than the augmentation and amplification of the human processes of memory and writing, though in a very limited fashion; and as I will show below, this project was influential on the development of modern information systems.

Bush does not make many distinctions between different kinds of data and information, and from his concerns with research he finds the same problems in almost any complex social operation. Citing the example of a credit sale in a department store, Bush sees great advantage in mechanizing and automating the keeping, transmission, and storage of records. Certainly, information processing in a department store would facilitate the rapid approval and recording of credit transactions. If credit transactions could be automated, why not some aspects of scientific research?

Bush begins blurring the distinction between automation and life early in the article, specifically when he describes how a future researcher, armed with miniature cameras and recording devices – truly high-tech stuff in 1945 – moves about in his laboratory and through the world. 'His hands are free, and he is not anchored. As he moves about and observes, he photographs and comments. Time is automatically recorded to tie the two records together. If he goes into the field, he may be connected by radio to his recorder'. The acts of recording data and observations become extensions of the researcher, triggered by almost imperceptible movements.

Bush however knows that data collection is not useful science, and the precise means by which observation data are changed into science is important. His process for constructing useful knowledge is that following the gathering of data comes 'the extraction of parallel material from the existing record, and the final insertion of new material into the general body of the common record'. Again, knowledge is not linked to human activity; it is a quantum, a resource. There is a creative aspect to science and to engineering, and Bush does not propose that this can be automated. He writes that 'for mature thought there is no mechanical substitute. But creative thought and essentially repetitive thought are very different things. For the latter there are, and may be, powerful mechanical aids'. This is, in a sense, the application of the steam engine to the area of human knowledge. If a cognitive activity is repeated without creative thought, it can be mechanically augmented.

Thus machines would be linked closely to certain kinds of human activity, and this is an important point. Bush is not modeling mind; he is linking mind to a particular kind of iterative, machine-like function. This particular mental activity had only come about through industrialization and the need for advanced numeric processing, modeling, and information access. The complexities of the industrial world guarantee that no individual person or group of persons is capable of developing or even of understanding all of the complex subsystems of a complex machine or device. The Manhattan Project had demonstrated this all too clearly. Thus, one had to know the problems and solutions that other technical researchers had addressed. What, however, is germane to one's research? This question is, for Bush, the creative and intuitive question, but he misses the moral and philosophical dimensions altogether. They are simply not engineering problems.

Such a limitation of his own thought and expertise does not stop Bush from advocating an extension of his memex device and the automation of human thought to other areas of the world. He notes that

> the repetitive processes of thought are not confined, however, to matters of arithmetic and statistics. In fact, every time one combines and records facts in accordance with established logical processes, the creative aspect of thinking is concerned only with the selection of the data and the process to be employed, and the manipulation thereafter is repetitive in nature and hence a fit matter to be relegated to the machines.

Bush's model of thought is already machine-like. If creativity is concerned only with the selection of data and the process to be used in crunching the numbers, then the serendipity which enters at every stage of the research process is eliminated. Human thought and intervention are eliminated. The one aspect of research which is needed by, for example, the mathematician, is skill 'in the use of symbolic logic on a high plane, and especially if he is a man of intuitive judgment in the choice of the manipulative processes he employs. All else he should be able to turn over to his mechanism, just as confidently as he turns over the propelling of his car to the intricate mechanism under the hood.'

Manipulating large numbers is one level of complexity, but again, knowledge does not exist outside human contexts, and the sorts of models and 'findings' which one makes about the world have real consequences for real people. The more that processes are automated, the more that human activity is mechanized. The outcome is mechanized people, mechanized thought, all taking place without reference to any outside morality, philosophy, or law. Bush writes that 'whenever logical processes of thought are employed – that is, whenever thought for a time runs along an accepted groove – there is an opportunity for the machine'. The iterative function is key. Everything which can be automated should be. Freedom from all of the tasks of life which might reliably be transferred to machines would provide people with the time and the means to devote their attention to acts of intuitive choice and higher thought.

Even the moral training of students can be automated through the judicial institution of logic machines.

> Formal logic used to be a keen instrument in the hands of the teacher in his trying of students' souls. It is readily possible to construct a machine which will manipulate premises in accordance with formal logic, simply by the clever use of relay circuits. Put a set of premises into such a device and turn the crank, and it will readily pass out conclusion after conclusion, all in accordance with logical law, and with no more slips than would be expected of a keyboard adding machine.

Leaving aside the issue that Bush is now pronouncing on educational philosophy, more than formal logic is required for thought and research, and more than logical laws are necessary for the demonstration of any qualitative proposition. Bush pushes too far the connection between his mechanism of associations and human thought. In the end, he is not indexing information, he is proposing something like an automated system of generative semantics. His assumption is that the creation of indexes in the machine stands for the processes of human thought and that the indexes themselves (in conjunction with the records they indicate) thus maintain a one-to-one relationship with knowledge. His superficial surface language, the index system, is presumed to directly convey the deep structure of thought and experience.

Bush's philosophical context

A key to Bush's thinking is found in his assumption that technology and industrial production *are* civilization. Parallel to the position put forward by Carnegie and others, Bush's understanding of civilization was technical, rational, and quasi-religious. In his 1949 book *Modern Arms and Free Men*, Bush writes that there are two 'controlling motivations that have held [men] together. One is fear, utilized in the elaboration of systems of discipline and taboos. The other is the confidence of one man in another, confidence in his integrity, confidence that he is governed by a moral code transcending expediency' (1949: 7). This moral code comprises 'a system based on the dignity of man, built on good will' (1949: 8). His thesis in this book is that this vague humanism and mutual trust are well suited to 'dealing with the intricate maze of affairs that the applications of science have so greatly elaborated'. Yet Bush himself understood that technology had transformed the world from what it had been before and that the 'application of science in controlling nature ... has also modified the underlying philosophy with which men approach the problems of their organization and government and every other aspect of their existence'.

Science itself is not the source of the good for Bush, and he acknowledges that science arms both the villain and the hero. However, against the 'rule of tooth and claw' which was the past, he posits a future world of 'self-governing peoples, creating health and prosperity in their midst ... until finally there emerges one world governed by a system truly responsive to the enlightened will of the whole people' (1949: 172). This health and prosperity are the products of scientific technology, and the enlightened will of self-governing people emerges out of their access to scientific and historical information. In other words, his system works so long as everyone is playing the same game, and that game is a highly technologized version of Big Science. The redeeming culture of Matthew Arnold is now transformed into access to information.

Even the *polis* of this new world, Bush's 'self-governing people', are not the great masses of ordinary folk but a natural aristocracy that would govern the public opinion and the direction of pure research. Zachary notes that Bush believed that it was the duty of a minority of American citizens to 'establish the climate of opinion that will determine the action of even the great men in place of power' (1997: 353). Just as Carnegie believed that management was an inherent virtue possessed by some which entitled them to greater freedom of action, Bush's arguments put forward an elite of engineers and scientists. The idea was not his; Walter Lippmann had argued in 1922 (1965 [1922]) that society was too complex to be run in the old mold of democratic participation. Experts alone possessed the knowledge and understanding of the industrial world's complexity, and they should make the important decisions. The role of the press was to inform the citizens of what the experts were doing and to help gain their assent.

Bush's legitimation strategy and the role of the military

At the end of World War II, engineering and manufacturing had developed the means to move millions of people and incomprehensible amounts of machinery across oceans. It had brought about the advancement of the aircraft, the submarine, the rocket, and finally, that greatest of achievements, the atomic bomb. But by the middle of the twentieth century, engineering had become something quite different, and this came about particularly through the increased mutual reliance which engineering and the modern military had upon each other. While recognizing the bravery of the allied soldiers, sailors, and aircrews, one must concede that the allies did not defeat their enemies through superior soldiering but through superior engineering and manufacturing. People had been able to use the application of knowledge in systematic ways which merged knowledge with other natural resources.

For Bush, knowledge was another kind of natural resource, but it was of the kind that is manufactured. The inclusion of applied knowledge within nature in this way is another bit of semantic slippage. Bush's reasoning ran that *government financing* is necessary to provide an adequate level of *basic research*, which is necessary to provide the scientific foundations for *advanced technology*, which in turn accounts for a large part of *economic growth* (Niskanen 1997: 83). The major factors which hindered this development were lack of funding and the amount of specialist information, which was too poorly organized and indexed to be of maximum use to the scientists. Bush witnessed what he saw as the solution to the funding problem during World War II. As director of the Office of Scientific Research and Development, he directed Oppenheimer's research at Las Alamos and knew what was possible with virtually unlimited federal funding.

However, rather than having developed the American bases for continued technical, scientific and industrial evolution, the war had, in Bush's view, bankrupted 'the intellectual banks of continental Europe, on which we have formerly borrowed' (in Mowery 1997: 26). Much as German missile scientists, aircraft designers, and nuclear physicists had been eagerly sought-after prizes at the end of the war, knowledge itself appeared to be a resource and a commodity which the US had largely on loan from those countries and cultures that had developed it. This conclusion leads Bush to advocate in 1945 for the federal funding of basic research only, which he defines as looking for fundamental knowledge without being 'conscious to specific human needs' (1997: 26).

This deliberate distancing from specific human needs, and from the world of human beings in general, severs scientific and engineering values from the cultural and social. Problems are taken up because they are technically 'sweet', that is, intrinsically interesting to the researcher, or because they are specifically directed by the funding agencies. Thus, either the structure of knowledge or the structure of political power dictates the directions of research and development. Noble writes that 'the viability of a design is not simply a technical or even economic evaluation but rather a political one. A technology is deemed viable if it conforms to existing relations of power' (1993: 63).

In this case, the technology with which we are interested is not hardware but knowledge and information themselves. The relationship of *information* to power was beginning to displace the relationship of *knowledge* to power, and this was made possible because information had displaced knowledge in the understanding of certain people.

If engineers were ill-equipped to distinguish the subtleties of knowledge and information, neither could guidance in this problem come from the universities of the day. The major universities had too much at stake in obtaining and holding onto federal and corporate funding, and the smaller universities, the land-grant colleges, the normal schools and teacher colleges had only a tenuous tradition of intellectual leadership and one that was not widely heeded. Not until the twentieth century's marriage of social sciences and production in advertising, efficiency, and social control were the social sciences taken seriously in the United States. Even large institutions often lacked the leadership to influence important debates. In the 1930s Abraham Flexnor, Director of Advanced Studies at Princeton, observed that

> The problem of America is not 'Main Street'; there are Main Streets in all countries. The hopelessness of America lies in the inability and unwillingness of those occupying seats of intelligence to distinguish between genuine culture and superficial veneer, in the lowering of institutions which should exemplify intellectual distinctions to the level of the vendors of patent medicines ... Babbitry in the presidency of great universities is an exclusively – as it is widespread – American phenomenon. (cited in Ostrander 1970: 146)

Arguably, the climate for university influence on contemporary thought has become even more chilled since Bush's day, with an increased reliance upon publications, research output, and the securing of government or industry grant money.

The Information World

Nineteenth century industrialization created a world in which people needed to be massed together to perform their functions for the machines and factories. The industrial process displaced systems of thought based upon a traditional or religious basis and introduced its own metaphysics and habits of thinking. In transforming industrial civilization into nature, that is, in making the assumption that the products of technology *are* the world, an 'inner-worldly' religion is created. God may intervene in nature, but the divine hand is unwelcome in the functioning of the machine. The machine, whether social or physical, must operate according to the original intention of the designer. The unintended and the unexpected, which once constituted grace, have no place (see Dupuy 1980).

The collectivity about which Voegelin wrote is 'now developed further into the opinion that only that is true which promotes the existence of the organically closed, inner-worldly national community' (1989: 62). The laws of truth must necessarily correspond to the successful functioning of the machine at all levels of the social. If these laws of truth can be automated, as Bush proposed doing with formal logic, so much the better. But what of the people within such a system? Obviously, the self which is well suited to functioning as a part of the machine will have an advantage. The great advantage, as I will show in the next chapter, is that individual moral and social responsibility for much of life are taken away and attributed to one or another aspect of the system.

Voegelin is clear about where this sort of symbolic system leads. He writes that 'when the individual has assumed the attitude of inner-worldly religiosity, he accepts this position; he views himself as a tool, as a "Hegelian" machine-part working in the overall whole, and voluntarily submits himself to the technical means with which he is integrated into the collective organization' (1989: 64). Whatever knowledge about the world which a person creates within this way of thinking leads only toward the construction of yet more techniques for strengthening and extending that world and its symbolic system. It is the tendency of technology, Ellul (1980) reminded us, to augment itself. As the symbolic system closes upon itself, and as individual people within the symbolic system adopt their orientation as a part of it, the self-legitimation of the system reaches its completion. 'All operationally closed systems have to generate their own indicators of reality at the level of their own operations; they have no other alternative' (Luhman 2000: 89).

The nineteenth century industrialists created Weber's 'iron cage' of rationality, but Bush sought, and others continue to seek, to automate the functioning of people within it. Rather than freeing people to perform the higher, nobler tasks of creative thought, such automation merely binds people more tightly to the mechanized processes of thinking and living. So it is that we lose sight of the real relationship of technology and thought and may easily slip into one or another kind of determinism and believe that technology makes culture. However, the myth of the machine world is built upon the legerdemain that it is the natural world and is thus a reflection of a higher order, either divine or scientific. Yet, David Nye reminds us that 'human beings, not machines, are the agents of change, as men and women introduce new systems of machines that alter their lifeworld' (1997: 180).

The letter-writing individual of the eighteenth century learned to construct a linguistic social self in the imagined world of merchants and minor industrialists. The mass newspaper reader of the nineteenth century was presented with a social self and a reformed public sphere already largely constructed in the world of tenements and factories. The self was propagated through the language, content, and forms that existed in the newspapers as well as in the ideals of a society which only needed individuals at the top of the hierarchy; below that, individualism was a most convenient hook for the emerging quasi-religions of mass marketing, mass psychology, and modern nationalism. Little changed in the twentieth century except for a growing awareness that the *de facto* state religion contained too many contradictions. Urged to create individual selves in one group of beliefs, people found themselves increasingly constrained to the collectivity in every aspect of life.

The automation of the individual finally closes the feedback loop. With the emergence of 'ubiquitous computing' in the late twentieth century, people could contribute to the generation of an 'unceasing flow of information, which becomes the only validated reality' (Nye 1997: 170). We have come close to 'the ideal of the system', that is, 'to achieve a perfect fit between experience and the continuously generated text' (1997: 172). This text is positioned within the 'reality' of language and discourse already generated in the mass media and is sanctioned as the one central truth of the culture which cannot be challenged: each of us is a part of the system.

SEVEN

Information and Social Order: Pornography and the Public

We are passing at present, despite certain appearances and presumptions, through an age of terrific un-culture. Never perhaps has the ordinary man been so far below his times and what they demand of him. Never has the civilized world so abounded in falsified, cheated lives. Almost nobody is poised squarely upon his proper and authentic place in life. (Ortega y Gasset 1966: 74)

The advent of computing technology as a ubiquitous part of everyday life – and this was an express aim of some early designers – fits well with the other tendencies of industrial society toward specific patterns of regularity, routinization, and centralized control. Simultaneously and in various ways, it also disarticulates many aspects of the old, shared spaces from the individual people. In this sense, the growth of digital technologies follows the patterns of industrialization both in its organization and in its effects upon the social.

After an initial period during which the personal computer, internet, and world wide web were celebrated as liberating technologies that democratized information, created new communities, and opened the world of information to all with the money and interest, they began to demonstrate that their primary purpose was not a straightforward liberation but a kind of linkage of people to systems in new ways combined with a modernization of poverty. The personal computer and the internet which followed were not unformed clay out of which people could make what they wished. The very characteristics of these systems transformed the ways in which communication was used and so also changed the rules around which people's selves would be constructed. It was not, I emphasize, the technology of digital communications which alone changed the social. Rather, the conditions already existing in the social domain structured the forms in which digital communications would appear and the ways in which they would be used. However, these forms were new, and a considerable part of the contemporary muddled thinking about information, about the effects of information, and about the social role of language in general, derive from a confusion about the forms of language and the characteristics of the systems in which language appears.

The contemporary situation parallels the conditions that arose in the nineteenth century as the 'bookishness', literacy, and orientation to images that were made possible by the mass production and distribution of printed materials became a significant part of the consciousness and social identity of both the bourgeoisie and the working class. At precisely this moment, the perceived social need arose which required that the masses be symbolically contained within culture and within the social, and such containment could only take place if both the social and culture were redefined. In order to be that which was created and catered to in the manufacturing and mass production processes, the social had to become something more nebulous and abstract than the imagined political sphere which had served as the archetype for the formation of the American republic, and culture had to be more reliably pedagogic than was required for the edification of self-governing democratic citizens. The introduction of much wider (though not yet universal) suffrage in the United Kingdom and the United States brought numbers of previously excluded persons into the political and hence public sphere at just the time that these persons were coming to know themselves as members of a class who were united through their participation in mass-produced symbolic forms furnished by newspapers and magazines.

Even as it came into being in the educational and reform movements of the nineteenth century in England, Australia, and the United States, the implications of such an operant definition of the social world, that is, a definition which effectively conflated culture with information, were poorly understood, and this ignorance of the changed relationship between the individual person, the world, and language continues to this day. The root of this splitting extends into the conception of the individual person as atomistic and egocentric, an isolated speck of consciousness adrift in a world of language and meaning. Such a condition necessarily positions consciousness toward culture in an instrumental way rather than as something which is constituted within culture. This conception also foregrounds the knowledge that consciousness has of itself in the world as the measure of one's happiness and success. The individual self thus stands as a counterpoise to the social, a contrast and distinction to it. With this model of psychology, the 'individual' self which elaborated in the late eighteenth and early nineteenth centuries was well positioned to develop into the segmentalized, fragmented self of the twentieth century.

The presupposition underlying this split or rupture in the experience of people suggests that a world exists or has been created, named 'culture' or 'society', which is separable and distinguishable from the world of lived experience. Initially this world was the social domain, the domain of culture. Later, the 'real' world would become information itself, a topic I explore in the next chapter. However, the characteristics of this created social world are crucial to understanding how this alternative world and the selves predicated upon it exist in the world.

The Alternate World

This 'coexistent world' need not appear entire or all at once, but may become perceived here and there, in dribs and drabs, as a natural consequence and sequela of the segmentation of experience, the alienation of affect and empathy, and the other attributes of the modern self discussed earlier. The alternate world appears as itself when it first begins to take on the coherence and semiotic completeness to offer alternative forms for the world, complete with explanations, values, and meanings that come from outside the local. The epistemological history of this bifurcation extends at least as far back as early liberal philosophy and its distinction between 'the state of nature' and the state of civilized persons. In this early separation of the 'natural' or personal from the constructed world of society, the necessity of two mutually exclusive domains of possible experience is created: one grounded in the personal and the other in the social. Rousseau, Hobbes, Locke, and others identified such a split and maintained that some individual rights were necessarily conceded to society or civilization in return for the protections that the social or the state would provide.

Liberal philosophy in the words of Hume, Bentham, and Mill framed the social problem of the newly constituted public as a need to control and contain the energies of the now urbanized masses. The conception of the individual person as an isolated point of egoistic desires created the concomitant question of how, from a social, scientific, engineering point of view, these individuals should be organized and governed. While each person might follow his or her own desires for happiness and gratification, there arose the question as to how these individual desires might be harmonized with the general interests of society. Liberal philosophers held that this harmonizing function was the duty of the legislator, and Halévy (1955) terms this process 'the artificial identification of interests. This idea, held by writers such as Hume, maintained that '*every man should*, on principle, *be held a knave*, and once this principle had been laid down ... the art of politics consists of governing individuals through their own interests ... such that in spite of their avarices, they shall co-operate for the public good' (1955: 17). Such a notion reflected the changing definition of 'civilization' (observed by Boswell) through the mid to late eighteenth century from a process to a state of social order and refinement (Williams 1983: 57).

The problem was, how could such a control be exerted over the minds and desires of the masses? Clearly, some changes in conceptual categories of the social were required, and these would lead to changes in numerous, far-reaching ideas about culture, information and the social. In particular, in the late nineteenth century culture itself was reified into a conveyor of ideals and values which could produce an elevating and ameliorating effect upon the masses. At the same time, whatever these same masses practiced in their daily lives, sang, wrote, read, or played, was, by definition, not culture.

This use of the idea of 'culture' would have been inconceivable prior to that major shift in the function of language which arose with the mass production of language. Although Nebrija and others had conceived of the use of an official, unified language as a way of unifying kingdoms and nations as early as the late fifteenth century, the deliberate manipulation of the symbols and semiotics of a culture for didactic purposes was a new idea. In the mid seventeenth century, John Milton had ridiculed such a centralized approach to social control, in the form of censorship, in the *Areopagitica* (1644). Writing from within a world which was still largely lived in the vernacular, local experiences of people, Milton did not see how a centralized control of all of culture could be instituted.

> For if they fell upon one kind of stricnesse, unlesse their care were equall to regulat all other things of like aptnes to corrupt the mind, that single endeavour they knew would be but a fond labour: to shut and fortifie one gate against corruption, and be necessitated to leave other round about wide open. If we think to regulat Printing, thereby to recifie manners, we must regulat all recreations and pastimes, all that is delightful to man. (Milton, 1644)

While books and pamphlets might serve as vehicles for transferring even dangerous ideas, Milton held that each person had not only the right but the necessity of choice. More to the point here, Milton could not conceive of using all the component forms of culture as if they were parts of a whole. Culture was not yet a system of interrelated yet separable practices. Culture did not yet appear to his thought as a noun denoting a whole.

A second problem arose with the reification of 'culture' into values, a problem which seemed largely to have eluded the libertarian and utilitarian philosophers. The nineteenth century had seen the collapse of other previously existing, and apparently extrinsic, hierarchies of value and order that had lent stability to the social and the public as well as providing points of entry for individual persons into these domains. Religion, having lost much of its traditional hold to the new symbolic and physical forces of steam, electricity, mass production, etc., found expression in the service of the social order. The change had been a long time coming and had its heralds in the philosophy of Nietzsche and in the aesthetics of Baudelaire as well as in various forms of Romantic art, but nowhere was the change more apparent, more palpable, and more immediately real than in the quotidian lessons taught by the physical world which was daily being transformed around people. Streetcars, railroads, factory production, as well as the burgeoning mass media existed in at least three modes simultaneously: as physically real things, as symbols, and as constellations of information which created and sustained them.

At the beginning of the twentieth century, Henry Adams famously noted at least two aspects of this change, cast in his words as a contrast between the old world and the new, between Europe and America, and he was not alone in drawing this distinction between 'two kingdoms of force which had nothing in common but attraction' (1961 [1918]: 383). Adams contrasted the power of the Virgin – imaginative, symbolic, and linked to the mysterious and profound power of reproduction – with the simply mechanical power of the dynamo, the new force for the production of power. Adams saw this change as a kind of a loss, a severing of the ties that linked people with their historical heritage and with the symbolic expressions of being human. He wrote:

> any one brought up among the puritans knew that sex was sin. In any previous age, sex was strength. Neither art nor beauty was needed. Every one, even among Puritans, knew that neither Diana of the Ephesians nor any of the Oriental goddesses was worshipped for her beauty. She was goddess because of her force; she was the animated dynamo; she was reproduction. (1961 [1918]: 384)

In contrast, the new symbolic order not only had embraced another sense of the world, but could not know in its lived experience what had gone before:

> All this was to American thought as though it had never existed. The true American knew something of the facts, but nothing of the feelings; he read the letter, but he never felt the law. (1961 [1918]: 384)

Indeed, a new law was being elaborated, a law built around industrial production in every area of life. Long-standing ethnic, religious, and symbolic structurings of the social would continue to exist, but modernity required new ways of thinking about and structuring the social order.

Adams conceived of the new world in its symbolic and physical manifestations, but it was in the newly emerging realms of public education, psychology, and later advertising and public relations that the neglected domain, that of information as the world, would become apparent. Among the first writers to treat culture itself as information was Matthew Arnold.

Matthew Arnold: Culture as Virtue

At a moment of great social transition, Arnold in *Culture and Anarchy* (1969 [1869]) put forward a series of arguments against the rule of the aristocracy and for the rule of the state governed around the principles which he saw ennobled in culture. He upbraids the aristocracy for being out of touch with the lives of ordinary people, but he does not see the common working class as refined enough to govern themselves. His arguments are at times racist, particularly against the Irish, and at bottom ethnocentrically liberalist. He is not arguing for a universal application of cultural laws, but for their application in England for the English. A part of the context of this work was the ongoing issue of franchise and empowerment framed by the Reform Acts of 1832 and 1867. Between the passing of the first and the second, much more extensive Act under Disraeli, large-scale demonstrations of workers demanding rights took place in London and elsewhere. This 'populace' manifested itself as 'that vast portion, lastly, of the working class which, raw and half-developed, has long lain half-hidden amidst its poverty and squalor and is now issuing from its hiding-place to assert an Englishman's heaven-born privilege of doing as he likes and is beginning to perplex us by marching where it likes, meeting where it likes, bawling what it likes, breaking what it likes' (Arnold 1969 [1869]: 105).

To some, such as Carlyle, it seemed that an imminent fall into barbarism was at hand. Carlyle's own pamphlet 'Shooting Niagara: and after?' was published in *Macmillan's Magazine* in August 1867 and was deeply pessimistic about the possibilities of producing a unified nation out of the diverse social forces then competing for attention and representation in the social and political realms. The political and philosophical projects of both Carlyle and Arnold, as well as others, thus took place in a period largely defined by the problem of bringing ordinary people, especially the newly emerging working class, into some relationship and rights of participation with the social processes and institutions which were both the English government and the culture of those who had framed it.

The question, of course, was how these unwashed masses should be brought to right thinking and correct action. Arnold rejects the possibility of innate human goodness, citing the 'obvious faults of our animality' (1969 [1869]: 55). Neither does Arnold believe that the mass media of the time will promote the integration of people into the social. Newspapers themselves are the main promoters of the notion that people 'without the labour of perverting ourselves by custom or example to relish right reason, but by continuing all of us to follow freely our natural taste for the bathos, we shall, by the mercy of Providence, and by a kind of natural tendency of things, come in due time to relish and follow right reason' (1969 [1869]: 120). Clearly, the great threat to England was the 'unchecked and unguided individual action' (1969 [1869]: 127). The right to 'do as one wants' was in conflict with the desire of the state and of those enfranchised as power-holders in the state to protect themselves from change.

In this instance, information as the transmission of cultural messages and values was expressly politicized. While mass marches and demonstrations certainly gave impetus to the impulse of Arnold and others to find ways of disciplining the working class into the values and ideals of formal English culture, it was not so much a direct threat of social collapse or imminent civil chaos which motivated the debate. Rather, the express need to politicize culture as a discourse lay behind this particular expression of liberalism. While cultural works had always had a potential political or religious dimension to them which could be challenged, judged, and sometimes used as a basis for judging the author or even for destroying the work itself, culture had not previously been argued as an integrated, comprehensive framework for the formation of people's values and ideas and for the guidance of their action. Indeed, one risk we run in reading Arnold's writing sociologically is that we miss the ritual component of his activity in defining the word 'culture' in a new constellation of contexts. Williams notes that Arnold conflates the meaning of culture as 'a general process of intellectual, spiritual and aesthetic development' with the meaning of 'the works and practices of intellectual and especially artistic activity' (1983: 90). Further, this blurring of two denotations contributes to the continued pejoration of the word 'culture' to the present time.

Arnold succeeded in fixing for the Anglo-American world the notion that culture is a medium for the transmission of ideals. This is a turning point in the history of communications, for if a medium could in itself be judged as morally acceptable, another medium could be condemned for being unacceptable. Culture, in Arnold's formulation, becomes a social process into which individual persons are introduced and from contact with which they are transformed. Arnold, noticing people outside his social domain, sought to find a way to contain them within the spider web of an acceptable form of culture.

Arnold was, of course, not alone in this approach. Various philosophies for educating the workers and the poor were tried out in the nineteenth century. Some, such as public education – a project that Arnold was deeply involved in – sought to provide basic skills in reading, writing, mathematics, and civic responsibility. The liberal arts were reserved, largely, for the private schools of the wealthy. In some instances, workers themselves took the responsibility to provide some enhancement of their knowledge, forming societies, hosting lectures, and arranging education. In other cases industrialists funded schools for the children of their workers. The interest here was not, of course, the liberation of minds or the preparation of free-thinking people but the construction of workers with the appropriate attitudes, values, and limited industrial skills to operate in a machine environment. The ideals of republican virtue were, in fact, anathema to such programs. Gertrude Beeks, an industrial educator, warned that '"the so-called democratic ideas should be avoided" in such programs because it poses a threat to order in the factory' (Jansen 1988: 159). Thus, the long-term effect of using culture and education as substantive forms was not the elevation of the masses but the reduction of knowledge to a commonplace which could be taught to anyone.

Unresolved Contradictions in Modern Culture

Such examples of the paradox of treating information and education as culture illustrate the tension between the machine age and many of the ideas which legitimated the social order of the day. The rights articulated by Carnegie and others were grounded in a natural rights view of property which, as Veblen observed, was 'a conventional, anthropomorphic fact having an institutional validity, rather than a matter-of-fact validity' (1978 [1904]: 318). In other words, the legitimation of wealth as theology was based on a philosophy which ran contrary to both the logic of the machine age and the experience of the working classes. This contradiction in social thinking and representation led to various outbreaks of social violence and industrial actions along with the predictable repressive reactions of the state in the service of business. The Pullman strike, the numerous mining, railroad, and steel mill strikes, and other forms of protest continued though in diminishing frequency and disruption into the Reagan and Thatcher regimes in the US and England.

Arnold and other social reformers had been unable to bring about a change in the consciousness and cultural position of the masses of poor and workers for two reasons. First, the forces of industry and business themselves controlled much of the public discourse. If anything contrary was taught in schools or lectures it was likely to appear as another example of the uselessness of education rather than a refutation of the social order. The physical forms of the social world – the factories, buildings, wealth, political influence, and so on – were the concrete world in which people lived, and as Marx and others noted, these conditions altered as well the relationships that people had to each other. The affective and historical linkages between individual persons and between groups were either eroded by these changes or replaced. The second cause of the reformers' failure was the absence of a concerted, well-organized, and professionally managed intervention in all aspects of language. To be accurate, such an intervention did occur from at least the 1920s on, but it further strengthened the symbolic position of business and industry.

The rationalization of information changed everything. Throughout the twentieth century, a small number of communication technologies were deployed which used the old forms of entertainment and news provision to construct a social language, indeed a social sphere, which differed from all that had gone before. The narrative and aesthetic forms of art continued to be used, but the format in which the information appeared had altered. The press, radio, the movies, and later television all benefited from the appearance of being official, socially sanctioned, and therefore somehow more reliable and real than the everyday world of rumors, stories, and vernacular narratives. Nothing really happened until it appeared in one form or another of the official social language. Information became *de facto* truth. Further, this was a truth which was not imposed from above, from the seats of power, but which circulated through all aspects of the social and of the private as well.

In Britain, which had a more developed sense of a role for government in social responsibility, the Arnoldian project of social improvement through culture found institutional form in the policies of the British Broadcasting Corporation (BBC). Arnold's project inspired Reith to work toward establishing 'the BBC as an institution for cultural enlightenment, and for political education also, with the task of enabling a newly enfranchised general public to exercise their citizenship rights responsibly instead of allowing their hearts and mind to be captured by the evil forces of either Bolshevism or Fascism' (McGuigan 1996: 56). In order to accomplish this task, the private corporation which had been the original chartered form of the BBC was acquired by the government in 1927. In the United States, the market was left to resolve such issues with little governmental interference beyond working to ensure that corporations acted with at least a nod toward the public good. Despite limited government influence in the developing structure of commercial broadcast media, the mass media continued nonetheless to reflect and create the values of an industrial society.

Even when appearing oppositional, mass media functioned as 'official' sources of information and social influence and contributed to the normalization and naturalization of specific ideas of culture. This process continues today in talk radio and 'vox pop' segments, allowing an expression of democratic discontent within forms that contain dissent and redirect it toward the culture-hallowed bugbears of the time: communism, socialism, terrorism, etc. In particular, the commodification of culture as 'mass culture' contributed greatly to the creation of a mass identity that could transform older, traditional values and beliefs into those better aligned with the needs of an industrialized world. Popular newspapers and magazines preceded cinema as the couriers of the new values. Richard Hoggart (1957) was among the first to examine critically the way in which popular culture transformed the existing world of the working class. Key among the distinctions he notes is the bifurcation of the world into an 'us and them,' a skepticism toward politics and political participation (1957: 102), a concretization of the local world of family and neighborhood in distinction to the 'shadow of the giant abstractions' (1957: 104), and a focus on the immediate. He writes, 'If we want to capture something of the essence of working-class life ... we must say that it is the "dense and concrete life", a life whose main stress is on the intimate, the sensory, the detailed, and the personal' (1957: 104).

The sense of having a life apart from the lives of the bourgeois, that is, a life with few opportunities for change and self-determination, as well as the sense that life is grounded in the daily grind, have traditionally been reinforced by magazines, newspapers, and other publications aimed specifically at the working class and the masses of people who had become politically noticeable with their migrations into the cities. While some publications catered to the 'old' values, the pressures of the market and the pressures of 'progress' guaranteed the emergence and ultimate success of publications that would prove leveling and fatuous in 'a further instance of a possible interplay between material improvement and cultural loss' (1957: 343). Hoggart noted that 'the older forms of class culture are in danger of being replaced by a poorer kind of classless, or ... "faceless" culture' (1957: 343). The litany of writings that address the vulgarity, sameness, and cliché-ridden style of popular mass media – and the trend accelerates with the growing centralization of ownership and control of media – renders Hoggart's words almost banal, but these trends were not so often noted in Britain and America in the decade immediately following World War II.

Thus, a moral and epistemological field was engineered and mass manufactured. Words and meanings increasingly originated not with people but with corporations, businesses, and professionals, and the information which individual people could put into circulation was already predetermined in form and largely in content. The public critical language which had seemed so intriguingly close at hand in the late eighteenth century never had developed. Simultaneously, the vernacular languages and traditions which had fostered identity and values grounded in tradition and binding together communities were devalued and replaced by the voice of business and industry.

The transformation of the public into the mass

In several senses, 'the public' in the modern usage elaborated in Anglo-American cultures has always been a business. The bourgeois publics which people sought to bring into being in their relations with others were primarily established around the idea of exchange, that is, creating relationships that would organize social groups for the mutual financial benefit of their members. It was never clear, even to John Locke or Adam Smith, what the profound implications of a society so organized would be for the individual persons within it. They could not imagine how pervasive and extensive the influence of business and manufacturing would become. Since the eighteenth century, the emerging bourgeoisie had tried to link aspects of life such as breeding and affect to the project of creating the public and generating personal wealth. However, in the long run, sexuality and emotions, and even psychology, were more easily structured and managed, and more lucratively deployed, as products in the marketplace. What could not be taught in the public schools and lectures could be sold in the shops, newspapers, magazines, and in the remainder of the public spaces, the media. The matter of the public for business was to extend the mercantile and commodifying activities to all aspects of life. In this way, the public of classical libertarian writing and thought was transformed into the mass target of mechanized publishing. Jansen writes that:

> The nineteenth century press also played a critical role in articulating the industrial reconstruction of American social realities and in selling the new order to the people ... the penny presses acted as guardians of the moral authority of industrialism. The penny papers ... also counseled readers on manners and morals. They filled the void left by the decline of ecclesiastical and governmental authorities. They told readers how to live their lives: how to behave in new or novel social situations, how to deal with ethical dilemmas, how to order their domestic arrangement, how to advance in their jobs, etc. (1988: 157)

Thus, rather than educating people about how they might advance their lot from working class to middle class, the media served more commonly to help them adjust to their position within the social order.

The antagonisms between the ruling class and the newly formed masses effectively excluded any thought of allowing the unwashed to participate in the public. Debates and some changes to expand voting privileges kept alive the idea of incorporating the working class into the public, even though, increasingly, the public sphere excluded participation by people on the basis of class, gender, ethnicity, and religion. Decision-making in government and in the social realm was confined to a more and more exclusive club of power-holders. While an occasional working-class person might achieve an advanced education or even rise to a position of power within a company, this served to promote the myth that the way was open to everyone, that the same rules of egalitarianism prevailed. The truth was that most working-class people in the late nineteenth century felt themselves estranged from politics and culture (see Hoggart 1957: 272ff).

While not comprising the whole of the social domain, mass media conveyed both a model of the underlying structure of the modern world and a mediated experience of it. This experience, derived from the machine ethos, was increasingly flattened and homogeneous. Veblen wrote that:

> As regards the mass of civilized mankind, the idiosyncrasies of the individual consumers are required to conform to the uniform gradations imposed upon consumable goods by the comprehensive mechanical processes of industry. 'Local color', it is said, is falling into abeyance in modern life, and where it is still found it tends to assert itself in units of the standard gauge. (1978 [1904]: 11)

Giddens (1991: 26–7) identifies two basic features of this mediation of life: a collage effect of juxtaposed information in which the 'world of place has largely evaporated' and an intrusion of distant events into everyday consciousness. At the level of the self, these forms of experience are fragmenting or 'disaggregating'. Yet in the context of a mass society of people with access to more or less the same information in the same forms and of people who increasingly had to privilege these forms of information, this mediation of experience also produced certain unities of thought and values.

Another way of viewing the changes in the public and social spheres in the nineteenth and early twentieth centuries might present the public and the social spheres as increasingly distinct. The public remained the culture-hallowed domain of politics although the politics conducted there increasingly reflected the alienation of most voters from the issues and the processes of addressing them. Politics appeared more and more as the right of people to assent to decisions already made for them. The social sphere, however, now disarticulated from politics, became the site where politics and the social order were legitimated and enforced but seldom negotiated.

There are many ways in which this substitution of the social realm for the idea of the public might be traced. Émile Durkheim observed as early as the 1930s that the social conditions which had established rules of human interaction and conduct had radically altered as a consequence of the rise in machine processes. He believed that in undergoing the change from a 'mechanical solidarity' to an 'organic solidarity' people were systematically losing their connection to the social collectivity. The anomie which would develop from the loss of the traditional social would, in his view, lead to disillusionment and suicide as well as 'unrestricted and uncontained' emotions and appetites (Giddens 1972: 133). Veblen suggested that the machine world itself contributed to the erosion of 'the ancient norms of Western Christendom', and he remarked on their replacement with new forms. He wrote that, 'In the nature of the case, the cultural growth dominated by the machine industry is of a sceptical, matter-of-fact complexion, materialistic, unmoral, unpatriotic, undevout' (1978 [1904]: 372).

The social collectivity was also strengthened, though not around either the eighteenth century ideal of the public or the classical ideals of a *polis*. The common ground for the social in which people could participate was the reduction of all needs to those which could be expressed in the mediated experience of the social itself. Through various forms of objectification, the social extended itself into the personal and the private while simultaneously extending the concerns of consciousness outwards into regularized and standardized information. The self is thus fragmented through its implication in social processes which are deterritorializing (arising from the loss of connection of language to place) and atemporal (arising from the near simultaneity of information and the loss of connection to historical narratives). 'So far as the self is concerned, the problem of unification concerns protecting and reconstructing the narrative of self-identity in the face of massive intensional and extensional changes which modernity sets into being' (Giddens 1991: 189).

The mass media generated – and continue to generate – commonalities of experience and language, but these very commonalities and shared perspectives as well as shared definitions undermine the possibilities for a shared public space. The immediacy of media and their concerns with timeliness, reflecting the values of commodification and commercialization, shorten the span of time with which society is concerned. Concern with understanding one's place in the immediate world displaces concern with longer periods of time, just as excessive concern with self displaces thinking about cooperative ventures with others. Narrowly functionalistic or hedonistic concerns cripple the possibility of thought or planning which might transcend the immediate. Yet, as Arendt noted, 'If the world is to contain a public space, it cannot be erected for one generation and planned for the living only; it must transcend the life-span of mortal men' (1958: 55). Thus the public space in this formulation must engender a place which is communal and transcendent both of the present and of the individual person.

However, the public in this usage of the world must also be capable of accommodating many perspectives. Without a participation in a shared reality which emerges from multiple perspectives and subjectivities, the people cannot come together and neither can the self be unified. Instead, multiple selves operate in various discursive formations and frame various subjective experiences within the world, and these selves do not necessarily inform each other, nor must they have any congress with each other. People elaborate their selves in various public and private domains, but as these domains are themselves disarticulated one from another, there is no necessary moral, experiential, narrative, or epistemic connection between them. Selves can operate in diverse realms, in multiple formulations. One may have one self in a particular setting and another self when implicated in other activities.

Two of the major realms in which the contemporary self is implicated are the social, governed by commodity exchange, and the private. In the philosophy of Hannah Arendt, 'the rise of the social ... means the institutional differentiation of modern societies into the narrowly political realm on the one hand and the economic market and family on the other' (Benhabib 1992: 90). Society then becomes the 'realm of social interaction which interposes itself between the "household" on the one hand and the political state on the other' with the consequence that individuals can no longer act within the public space of politics but are reduced to 'economic producers, consumers, and urban city dwellers' (1992: 90). In such a world, the conditions in which the individual person articulates a self are neither the conditions of a community of people doing things together nor the conditions of a directed and ordered world. Rather, the industrial (or postindustrial) self is implicated primarily in activities of production, consumption, and alienated social existence.

Within this social world, all relationships are reducible to commodity exchanges, but the definition of the word 'commodity' has broadened considerably. Not only people but all of life is commodifiable: food, work, sex, love, friendship, and so on. It is not that individual people generally directly take on the buying and selling of these services, although many do; rather, the representation and meaning of these previously inalienable and basic human activities become inextricably bound up with their appearance in the marketplace. Activities such as measuring out quantities of food for purchase, which had once been done by the shop owner, from about the 1880s on became simply the buying of packaged products which in turn were given brand names to counteract the alienation of the process (see Klein 2002: 6). By the end of the twentieth century, traditionally stable and time-hallowed ideas such as 'nation' had been simplified into 'branded' products. 'Brand states will compete not only among themselves but also with the superbrands such as the EU, CNN, Microsoft, and the Roman Catholic Church ... The state, in short, will have to become the State®' (van Ham 2001: 6).

The language of the social, which defines most of what people do together, increasingly became the language of commerce. Whatever remained of the old values and traditions became increasingly quaint and exiled either to the commercial domain of tourism (another modern invention) or to the 'personal' or private sphere of existence. For a while, the nuclear family was presented as an ideal type of a form of private existence which embodied the values of the broader society: patriarchy, consumerism, attenuated sexuality, well-regulated lives, and so on. However, the nuclear family, constructed around the exercise of strength and deference in fairly fixed relationships, offered 'only the prolongation and multiplication of one's own position' (Arendt 1958: 57). Arendt continues that 'Subjectivity and privacy can be prolonged and multiplied in a family'; however, the self cannot be extended and elaborated in this setting. This is precisely because the family, as the space of privacy, does not allow one to appear in public doing things with others. The self in the private world is closed off from the public, and the hue and cry about the loss of traditional family values reveals precisely the extent to which this mythic construction has become in danger of exposure as a fraud and of subsequent complete collapse.

The Social Confinement of Sexuality in the Creation of the Filmic Public

In addition to taking on the weight of subjectivity and privacy, the family also became the sole permissible site in which to act out libido and sexuality. There had long been a trend in Anglo-American society to create a public sphere which comported well with the needs of capital. The public was to be a sober, non-sexual place. Through the eighteenth century the coffee house had displaced the public house, and shortly after, the private reading in one's home began to displace the public theater and the carnival. Stallybrass and White note that 'the emergence of the public sphere required that its spaces of discourse be delibidinized in the interest of serious, productive and rational intercourse' (1984: 97). However, that libido had to go somewhere. The old adage, *naturam expellas furca tamen usque recurrit,* has some currency. The orientation of the working classes, and especially of children, to the sober, moral values required of a well-ordered, industrial society ultimately led to new expressions of sexuality.

The re-entry of sexuality into the public was through a new medium which also defined the twentieth century as the first primarily imagistic period in human history. The 'Golden Age' of cinema, the first 30 years of the twentieth century, was also the great era of scarcely veiled allusions to the sexuality possible only in private. Valentino's 'Sheik' was such a powerful character for his audiences in part because it was one of the very few public representations of sexuality available. Other films and other actors of both genders challenged the myths of the middle class, churchgoing, nuclear family in dramatic forms, though never approaching the degree of liberty in showing nudity or sex as does the modern cinema. Nonetheless, the re-emergence of even such a highly attenuated sexuality in the public sphere threatened to unravel the whole fabric, at least in the minds of some. Faced with a growing threat of legislation and censorship, in 1930 the two largest film production and distribution agencies in the US adopted The Motion Picture Production Code. It was, however, another four years before 'a cabal of religious, civic, and industry groups coerced the studios into expanding and enforcing it' (Morris 1996).

In its preamble the 1930 code states:

Motion picture producers recognize the high trust and confidence which have been placed in them by the people of the world and which have made motion pictures a universal form of entertainment.

They recognize their responsibility to the public because of this trust and because entertainment and art are important influences in the life of a nation.

Hence, though regarding motion pictures primarily as entertainment without any explicit purpose of teaching or propaganda, they know that the motion picture within its own field of entertainment may be directly responsible for spiritual or moral progress, for higher types of social life, and for much correct thinking.

The 'Hayes code' enforced not only, and perhaps not even primarily, sexuality but spoke to a range of 'socially unapproved' behaviors that the predominantly working class audiences should not be encouraged to emulate: 'No picture shall be produced that will lower the moral standards of those who see it.' Already assuming the conclusions that the largely conservative Payne Fund studies would arrive at (see Denzin 1992: 100–12; 1995: 18–21), the authors of the code excluded the representation of 'white slavery', drug trafficking, 'sex perversion', full nudity, miscegenation, and other practices in addition to 'excessive and lustful kissing, lustful embraces, suggestive postures and gestures'. Thus, not only specific acts, or allusions to acts, were forbidden, but also entire domains of society: prostitution, white slavery, and drug dealing were simply not explored or represented. As such, in this new 'cinematic' and spectacular public, the theater audience, these activities had no public face, no representation in the dominant narrative discourse of the day.

The UK and the BBFC

The English courts had established the implied damage from the effects of obscene materials in 1868 with the case of *Regina* v. *Hicklin*. The decision established a test to determine 'whether the tendency of the matter charged as obscene is to deprave and corrupt those whose minds are open to such immoral influences and into whose hands a publication of this sort might fall'. The decision and the subsequent test which emerged from it hinged on an unproven and perhaps non-existent effect of media upon the most susceptible person in society. Legal scholars have long recognized the many difficulties implied in this ruling, and one issue stood out:

> Perhaps the most troublesome portion of the *Hicklin* rule ... was the statement that a book was obscene if it suggested 'thoughts of a most impure and libidinous character'. This judicial preoccupation with thoughts induced by the reading of literature – with no requirement that the antisocial actions be tied to the reading matter – has continued to this time. (Teeter et al. 1989: 333)

Expressly, then, the interior experience of a person, his or her thoughts, desires, etc., was recognized as an appropriate site for the intervention of legislation and a policing of morality. The boundary of public and private became even less clear, and the implied effect of some experience of culture – whether in writing or in images – could be assumed with no test in reality. This is more than a simple exercise of the power to tell others what they may or may not read. The *Hicklin* test and similar subsequent decisions in both the UK and the US established that no private space of thought or desire existed because it had been induced by culture. Further, it drove those desires now labeled as deviant by the acts of policing even further from the public sphere. Sexuality, having been banished from the public sphere, was now driven even from the intersection of the public and private.

Having produced the prevailing definition of obscenity, the British also developed their own regulatory body for cinema in 1912, two full decades before the US. In response to a growing local regulation and censorship of films, the British Board of Film Censors was formed. Although a non-profit, non-governmental body, the Board, later renamed the British Board of Film Classification, quickly showed its intention in upholding more than middle-class sexual mores. The Board achieved its full form under the guidance of T.P. O'Connor who became President in 1916. He spoke before the National Council of Public Morals about his goals and objectives in forming public morals and about his views of the working class. This speech was quoted in the *Western Daily Mail* on Saturday 1 May 1926.

O'Connor acknowledged that cinema was a powerful social force, even suggesting that every school should have a cinema attached to it. What would be shown in these cinemas was clear; it would be morally and socially edifying. O'Connor is quoted as saying, 'I don't accept the proposition that the taste of the masses is necessarily high'. This assumption is made the more interesting for O'Connor citing his own experience in sensational journalism as the source of this personal knowledge. He explains that, 'In the press, divorce proceedings and crime are a very potent factor in the increase of circulations'. This quantitative measure of the quality of culture leads then to the dismissal of the masses. 'There is nothing that interests the common mind so much as a story of crime. We must take into account weakness and bad taste and not expect too much'. Because people like film and newspapers and use these to form publics of discussion and interest, they are weak and lacking refined aesthetic sensibilities.

Among the items that the BBFC thought inappropriate for audiences were the usual 'indelicate sexual situations', 'scenes laid in disorderly houses', and scenes dealing with 'white slavery'. However, the BBFC went much further in its service to the state during wartime; it also excluded films dealing with 'relations of capital and labour', 'realistic horrors of warfare', and 'subjects dealing with India, in which British Officers are seen in an odious light, and otherwise attempting to suggest the disloyalty of Native States or bringing into disrepute British prestige in the Empire'. Clearly, this link between the need to limit exposure to sexual material and the need to ensure proper political subjectivities had converged into one public institution and its plan for action. Realism and the use of cinema for serious social commentary in precisely the visual and narrative forms that cinema transmits well were censored. The ostensible aim was the imposition of a nationally consistent standard rather than the confusing and expensive proliferation of local standards. The development of a new techno-logy seemed to beg the creation of national standards boards in both the US and the UK. The organization of matters of morals in a technological society followed the organization of every other form of information and manufacture in the centralization of ownership and control.

This centralization continues to present itself as an argument for national standards and legislation, but the underlying agenda of controlling the unsa-vory and excluded members of society remains. The fear and distrust of the masses continues to the present day, demonstrating that for many leading the censorship crusade the issue is not pornography *per se* but the fact that it was being made available to everyone at affordable prices. Pornography was seldom a legal or political issue until it found its way to the poor. This was an express issue in the later debate about the alleged obscenity of D.H. Lawrence's *Lady Chatterley's Lover* and the famous statement to the jury by the prosecutor, Mervyn Griffith-Jones: 'Ask yourselves the question: would you approve of your young sons, young daughters – because girls can read as well as boys – reading this book. Is it a book that you would have lying around the house? Is it a book you would wish your wife or servants to read?' (quoted in Travis 2000). Expressly gendered as a practice, reading certain sexually oriented materials threatened to undermine the moral balance of private and public, upper and lower class.

The sexual, gendered, private space created by the understanding of culture as something having moral and psychological effects on people was thus not ignored or denied. Rather the thoughts and feelings of people, as an intersection of the public and the private, were recapitulated in new forms which fit closely with the views of family, sex, politics, and a society that expressed an emerging ideology about life in the modern, urban, industrial society. It was to be expected that only a modern medium, the cinema, would serve as the site where the education of the practices for social control, cast in narrative as moral lessons, would be enacted. The cinema combined the technologies of industrial society and the lessons necessary for its functioning in a set of social and aesthetic practices. These practices, learned and internalized by moviegoers, created new publics whose organization was not the news but entertainment. As such, this new public was different from what had gone before in that its end was not the provision of a forum for informed debate about politics and the world but the creation of a deliberate and secondary reality.

The movie screen, although viewed in an ostensibly public place, was in fact a voyeuristic look at a private domain that reflected not the reality of possible sexuality but the imagined excesses of it which had to be eliminated, policed, and controlled. At first this process occurred through the social agencies of legislation, police forces, and production codes, but the end result was the production of people who had internalized the policing functions in their understanding of the cinematic process itself. Cinema viewers, through the processes of participating in the industrial projects of cinema, were taught to see in particular ways and to experience particular subjectivities based on those ways of seeing. Denzin writes that:

> The cinematic imagination mediates ... complex, intersecting visual cultures, constantly attempting to make sense of two versions of reality: the cinematic and the everyday. But a paradox is created, for the everyday is now defined by the cinematic. The two can no longer be separated. A single epistemological regime governs both visual fields. Cinema not only created the spectator in its own eye; it created what the eye of the spectator would see. It then subjected that eye and its vision to the unrelenting criteria of realism and the realistic image of reality given in the camera's image. (1995: 34)

The cinematic thus colonized perception, subjectivity, and the social. Virilio (1994) refers to this process as the creation of 'stereo realities'. Simultaneously the cinematic allowed the power and the agencies of power to extend their influence into the consciousness of ordinary people in everyday life. The cinema brought to fruition the imagined technologies of control and brought the extension of public interests into the inner recesses of thought and desire.

As the cinema, and later television, helped to create the thoroughgoing intrusion of the spectacular society and so finally achieved the degree of social control dreamed of by early reformers, there was a resurgence of public interest in purchasing and consuming a range of articles having to do with sex. These appeared most recently in the period of relaxed sexual mores beginning in the mid to late twentieth century. Markets began to take shape through publications such as *Playboy* and the increasingly blatant use of sex in entertainment, in advertising, and in much of popular culture. The social reformist impulse toward control had come to fit well with the utilitarian and capitalistic philosophies. What could not yet be reconciled was the moralizing, conservative bourgeois repression of sexuality in the public.

There was, then, a paradox regarding the place of pornography in the scheme. While there were sporadic attempts to control and limit pornography, pornography as a genre and aesthetic system could not exist in its most obvious, blatant, and fullest form until it could fit within the existing social order. To be precise, there had to be a lucrative supply of hyper-sexual images and words (the capitalist condition) delivered to the isolated, hedonistic egoist (the libertarian condition) in the private sphere in such a way that there was no violation of the ostensibly delibidinized public domain. No matter the local legality of pornography, many people would simply not access it unless they could acquire it in secrecy, outside the moralizing gaze of the public. There might be occasional approved social uses such as at bachelor parties where the viewing of pornography or purchasing the talents of a stripper constituted some part of the rites of passage. Still, enough opprobrium attached to regular acquisition of pornography to limit people's seeking it out. While VHS tapes provided one technology for fulfilling this condition, to acquire them meant either going out into public or using a quasi-public supply system such as the post. Only the anonymity of supply could guarantee the success of the system, and this was precisely what the internet provided.

The electronic public

Curiously, the internet is not a public place in any traditional sense. Almost everyone online is in a private or semi-private space, either at home or at a worksite. The public that exists online occupies no place, has no physical characteristics, and cannot see into the private spaces from which each of the ostensibly present participants peers. Gender, class, race, ethnicity and all the other markers of social difference and identity appear only as one chooses to put them forward, and even then, there is no evidence other than one's word that these characteristics are what one has said. As such, there is a great deal of play, experimentation, and sometimes duplicity (Turkle 1995; 1998).

The shifting of gender and online role-playing activities are possible because a component of the self, that which is not revealed in the communication, remains split off, in the private sphere, but it is co-present in the consciousness of the person online. The electronic self, that which is created through the mediation of electronics communication technologies, is primarily a private self, communicating with one other person. Even when communicating with a group, as in an MUD, the online self is still alone in its physical space. Consciousness of activities involving others is thus split, or to use Robert Jay Lifton's term, doubled.

Neither are chatrooms and MUDs the only place where consciousness is doubled or split. Participation in such online activities may displace parts of life occurring in the physically present world, but other sorts of online activities such as websurfing also allow the individual person to engage in mediated relations with online content. Many studies have noted that increased time online results in a reduction of time spent with family and friends, and this often becomes a source of contention within families as the private self, the online self, consumes more time and interest (Nie and Erbing 2000). This is especially the case with online pornography consumption and use. Thus, self and desire may emerge from somewhere even more private than the family or one's marital partner. This bastion of personal privacy is the self online.

Pornography Online: the Promise of Individual Freedom and the Threat of Social Control

The initial promise of the home computer was to organize the management of the household along the same lines as a business or corporation. This impulse was congruent with the aims of industrial modernism in general: the pursuit of efficiency, narrowly defined through applied technology. The IBM Personal Computer, launched in 1980, was useful for little else. It was a glorified typewriter, filing cabinet, and calculator, but it was also the nose of the camel under the tent. In itself a fairly limited machine, the PC at first did not address the great promise of personal computing that lay in the linking together of different machines in different locations. An infrastructure for doing this, the Arpanet, had been developed in the 1970s, and through various incarnations (for example, Bitnet) the basic idea of digital data transfer using a distributed packet switching network was developed. With the introduction of a graphical user interface (a GUI, pronounced 'gooey') the arcane command line operation of the old internet and Unix-based machines was replaced with a much more 'user-friendly,' that is, commercially viable, way of accessing information online.

Various technological improvements to the basic system were required, particularly in the speed of transmission (bandwidth) and the ability to display and manipulate images (graphics capabilities). Generally referred to as multimedia, this convergence of technologies turned the PC into something possessing the characteristics of several home devices. The television, the VCR, the camera, all merged into this new device. And the uses of this new system changed as well. No longer a device just for managing home finances and writing student papers, the PC was connected to a body of information which was growing at rates no one could accurately measure. Terabytes of information were flowing between individual users and between them and mainframe systems. And from the very beginning, there was pornography. It developed online in Usenet newsgroups in the form of uuencoded e-mail postings, and with the development of GUIs and fast modems it became a staple of the online world.

Only reluctantly admitted, pornography has provided the economic basis for much of the web's existence and has a secure hold in cable, satellite, and broadband services including cable TV to the home and to motels (Egan 2000). It has funded the development and deployment of technologies such as secure online transactions and streaming video. Despite its contributions to the popularity of the internet and its undoubted success in helping millions to learn basic information technology skills, pornography has spawned counter-arguments and condemnations as well as attempts at legislative control of its online ubiquity. There is always the question of what constitutes pornography, and this has been debated in law, preached from pulpits, and tested in publications of various materials. Largely, pornography is a matter of degree. There is some point at which a woman seeking a picture of a vagina, for the most understandable reason of having a point of comparison, has recourse to either the line drawings on a tampon box or something called pornography.[6]

In one sense, there is nothing new to this. Changes in the amount and type of information that people may receive have always triggered concerns and reactions from those who fear for the endurance of the existing social order. From Socrates' deep suspicion of writing to the English Roundheads' desire to morally improve their people with censorship, from Jane Addams' fear that movies would corrupt young people, to Senator Exon in America, Senator Harradine in Australia, and William Hague in England, with the appearance of each new technology of communication the same concerns surface over and again. Conservatives and persons in positions of privilege try to maintain existing forms of communication along familiar lines while limiting new forms of communication to themselves, to government, or to others in power. The transformation of the mechanisms of human language and social memory brings forth concerns that border on the xenophobic. As familiar as the singsong taunts of the schoolyard, the rhetoric of fear and displaced anxiety increases proportionally to the size of the apparent change and the limits of the state and the social to control it. The battles to control information in the face of technology's redistribution of information become the sites of activity at which politics is defined in the current age.

As with much new that appears in the social world, each new medium of communication must be established within the framework of social meanings. So too, the habits of using each medium and the effects of these habits on people's thoughts, identity, and interactions with each other changed across time and differed from what had gone before. These, too, must be made understandable: a part of the social order. The book introduced a 'dangerous proliferation of signification' (Foucault 1984), a democratizing of information and knowledge which was finally controlled by laws of intellectual property, the establishment of the author function, and the creation of various social groups which defined themselves in the kinds of literatures they read. The internet and other digital communication systems similarly present a new set of threats to the social order. While not a wholly new medium, borrowing on the previous histories of text, images, and music, the digital technologies nonetheless are most threatening because the pre-existent restraints on the varieties of information and most importantly on the meaning of information have been outstripped.

The challenge from a social point of view is that anyone can get access to anything, and possess and use this information in new ways, and few of the social controls, whether moral, economic, or legal, are applicable or capable of being applied. Traditionally, problems of slippage in the control of information are addressed as problems of morality (the corruption of children) or as problems of property (copyright, intellectual property), and in either case, the legal establishment is commonly invoked to bring these matters to heel.

Faced with this uncertainty and slippage of the coherence of the symbolic social world, various people representing the threatened institutions invoke a range of metaphors to attempt to contain and control the new communication processes. Some speakers employ economic metaphors, referring to information as a commodity subject to tariffs, taxes, and corporatization. Other speakers will directly address the new uses of information as a moral concern. Inevitably, in cultures with an Anglo-European heritage, morality and property form a dichotomy of problems which arise together, though they are seldom seen to be linked. Most commonly, these two positions are collapsed into a single argument where economics and morality occupy related, though not quite interchangeable, positions.

In general, those situated within conservative discourses and the attendant institutions tend to attach the most extreme examples of a failing social control of signification and meaning to moral issues, while taking progressive stands toward economic or government issues. The opposite also appears true: speakers associated with liberalistic or libertarian discourses will attach the greatest threat to economic control of the new medium while seeking to protect the sphere of the individual's use of it. In recent years, we have witnessed several examples of this bipolarization of rhetoric around the new digital technologies. In the contemporary case, the two poles of debate are marked at one end as cyberporn deviance and at the other end as totalitarian policing of thought and desire.

Pornography and children: the conservative pole

The greatest and most commonly enunciated argument against new forms of information concerns the threat to children that the new information or new delivery forms provide. In terms of the liberal discourse, the issue is between the individual's right to read or watch what one chooses in conflict with the social need to maintain standards of morality and propriety.

Children's moral education thus comes symbolically to represent one extreme pole, that is, one perceived challenge to the order of the social. Predictably, in the contemporary case, the issue is the sexual education of children. What sexual materials do we wish children to have, and at what ages is this material appropriate? Underlying this idea is some vague media effects theory, which is never enunciated but generally assumes either that children will want to mimic the behavior that they see in pornography (especially homosexual and fetish behavior) or that their 'innocence' will be taken from them by viewing these materials. This last argument is especially interesting given the intense pressures that advertising and manufacturing place on the sexualization of the young.

Some countries, such as Canada, have vacillated between holding that their existing legislation is sufficient to cover issues arising from the new media and recognizing various social pressures to develop new laws. Others such as Singapore have introduced laws to limit the publishing and in some cases the possession or consumption of certain kinds of banned materials. The United States has had several attempts at passing comprehensive legislation regarding online content, but to date has largely applied existing state and federal laws. Although several countries have imposed some form of censorship on internet content, few have been as draconian or as criticized as the Australians. Of interest here is not the legislation *per se* but the language used in the debate about the bill and in its presentation.

In 2000, Australia instituted its new internet censorship legislation, The Broadcasting Services Amendment (Online Services) Bill. This particular amendment to existing law grew out of a government movement which began to be publicly voiced as early as 1994. In November 1995 the Senate Select Committee on Community Standards Relevant to the Supply of Services Utilising Electronic Technologies released its report laying the foundations and defining the terms for much subsequent debate and legislative action. In her remarks upon tabling the document, the Chairperson of the Committee noted the following:

> What the Committee found was that material which would be refused classification in any other medium, such as in publications, films and computer games, can be found on-line. The Committee heard of there being depictions on-line of child pornography and bestiality which are banned imports into Australia under customs controls and are refused classification if presented to the Office of Film and

Literature Classification. Witnesses stressed to the Committee that such material represents only a very small part of the total volume of material available on-line. However, the Committee takes the view that in the maintenance and protection of community standards action should be taken to ensure that otherwise refused or restricted material should not be available to children on-line. (Report on Regulation of Computer On-Line Services Part 2, 1995)

The Australian government's approach to controlling information requires that information be examined and classified, that is, located within a hierarchy of values, topics, and presumed readerships, before it can be released to the public. Two noteworthy observations must be drawn from this paragraph: it places an emphasis on the availability of obscene or pornographic material to children, an emphasis that continues throughout the report; and information is discussed as if it is a substance, something which is imported like any manufactured good. Two different arguments are clearly nascent in this approach to information. First, one must treat information as a commodity which is bounded by economic discourses and regulated in ways similar to other commodities. Second, a moral argument about the control of content and community standards is being made. Both of these arguments, though well worn even by 1995, carry with them a number of unexamined presuppositions which can only arise through a view of information particular to the late industrial age.

The *Hicklin* test, described above, had already been superseded in law by various rulings in the US Supreme Court. Cases such as *Roth*, *Ginsburg*, and *Miller* had produced more detailed tests for what constituted a threat to the public good. Still, the use of children as the signifiers of a moral imperative for censorship recurs frequently in the public and political rhetoric of control, and examples range from Tipper Gore's campaign to label CD recordings in the US to the (now repealed) Communications Decency Act. The appearance of the internet raised these imperatives to new levels. The combination of a new communication technology, nearly unlimited access to previously difficult to obtain sexual materials (both pornographic and otherwise), and the historical argument of a threat to the morality of children proved irresistible.

The 3 July 1995 *Time* magazine issue had as its cover story a report which raised an alarm about cyberporn. The cover picture featured a doctored photo of a child, horrified, staring over a keyboard and into the space of the person viewing the magazine. The article is about cyberporn, but in having the child stare outward into the viewer's space, we are expressly drawn into the immoral sphere of pornography. We are what lies beyond the screen, the image that horrifies the child. The article, written by Elmer De-Witt, is largely built around a hotly contested study conducted by Martin Rimm at Carnegie–Mellon. Rimm conducted statistical analysis on BBS and Usenet newsgroups whose content was pornographic images. Widely cited and with the imprimatur of authoritativeness that publication in a major news magazine carries, the article contributed to the accepted truth that the internet was awash in pornography and hence the children are at risk.

In the US the most important pornography legislation of recent years was the Communications Decency Act. Also known as the Exon bill, this was an amendment to the Telecommunications Act of 1996 which stated:

> Whoever – (1) in interstate or foreign communications knowingly – (A) uses an interactive computer service to send to a specific person or persons under 18 years of age, or (B) uses any interactive computer service to display in a manner available to a person under 18 years of age, any comment, request, suggestion, proposal, image, or other communication that, in context, depicts or describes, in terms patently offensive as measured by contemporary community standards, sexual or excretory activities or organs, regardless of whether the user of such service placed the call or initiated the communication; or knowingly permits any telecommunications facility under such person's control to be used for an activity prohibited by paragraph (1) with the intent that it be used for such activity, shall be fined under Title 18, or imprisoned not more than two years, or both. (47 USCA §223(d) Supp. 1997)

Overturned by the US Supreme Court for its unconstitutional vagueness in several areas, the bill had attracted the ire of anti-censorship groups throughout the United States. Senator Exon had explained his reasons for wanting to enact the bill in language remarkably similar to that proposed by the Australian Select Committee. Senator Exon said:

> Mr President, a few days ago I had a remarkable demonstration, in more detail than I had even fully known, of what is readily available to any child with the very basic Internet access. I want to repeat that, Mr President: Of what is readily available to any child with the basic Internet access. It is not an exaggeration to say that the worst, most vile, most perverse pornography is only a few click-click-clicks away from any child on the Internet. (Exon 1995)

Again, one encounters in the Senator's words the argument that children must be protected from the evils of pornography. The reason for the need for this protection is never given; neither is the nature of the threat. Indeed, the need to protect children from pornography is almost completely taken for granted within the prevailing discourses of morality. No explanation is required, and little evidence other than the anecdotal is presented of the frequency, medium, or type of the pornography encountered, thus neatly eliding a discussion of both morality and media effects. From the standpoints of a discourse analytic approach, a symbolic interactionist approach, or even a depth psychology view, something important is circulating regarding the sexual presentation of children, but the issue is not explored in public discourse. Some issue regarding the sexualization of children is being raised, but the precise nature of this is not explored. Certainly, the numbers of children sexually assaulted in nearly every country of the world and the increasing representation, primarily of girls, as sexually mature objects of desire in advertising, beauty pageants, and the like are cause for concern and grounds for a serious social debate. Yet this discussion remains marginalized as a 'feminist' issue and seldom appears in the mainstream press.

One could speak here of Foucault's repressive hypothesis, noting that Western nations are speaking fluently about the sexualization of children, just as the Victorians spoke so often about sexualization in general. In the current case, one outcome of limiting the discussion to pornography is that it completely obviates the need to examine any of the deeper issues. In focusing solely on protecting children from exposure to pornography, one addresses the issue without examining such deeply threatening topics as men's lack of responsibility as the overwhelming perpetrators of sexual violence against children or the generalized commodification of identity as sexual function.

Censorship as politics

Pornography was always that which was intended to be hidden and permitted only to adults. Further, it was never a social problem warranting legal action until it began to spread to the lower classes. Jansen notes that 'bourgeois aesthetics could tolerate erotic pictures in museums but not on postcards' (1988: 159). Literacy and cheaper printing made pornography available, but the internet truly democratized access to this forbidden material. In making pornography available, it also made other forms of information available as well. The recipe for manufacturing explosives from diesel fuel and ammonium nitrate fertilizer, widely published in farming magazines and other sources easily available at the local library, became a justification for moral panic when it appeared on the internet. As pornography had been the first material to be banned in modern society, it easily became the model for the limitation of other forms of information.

The telltale marks of overweaning power appear clearly here. All that is discussed is the 'evil' of the material and the fact of social 'harm' that it might bring about. The broader questions of what precise harm might result or of the morality of the material are never raised. Rather than a discussion of issues, one finds a silence about all but the dominant point, the first mark of severely limited thought. There is endless discussion of, for example, the need to control and protect children that surpasses even the moral assuredness of anti-communist crusaders in the 1950s. Such an assumption of correctness, and of the need to establish moral correctness for others, marks the argument as clearly totalitarian, though masked as a sort of benevolent paternalism. Many 'cyber liberty' defenders have argued this point: masquerading as a protection for children, another agenda for control of public information is being waged.

Irene Graham (1999), writing of censorship in Australia, notes that 'the vast majority' of films classified as R in the Australian system (to be viewed only by adults) 'are so classified because they deal with social and political issues'. These issues include crime, corruption, marital problems, drug use, racism, religious issues, and others. Building an argument based on the numbers and kinds of information classified R, Graham concludes that 'This legislation is about blocking the free flow of adult discourse on social and political issues'. She cites passages from Howard Rheingold's (1996) article *Democracy Is About Communication* to argue the case that the central issue of censorship is the power to control public expression and discourse. Graham is not alone. Many organizations such as the Electronic Freedom Foundation and Electronic Privacy Information Center have advanced arguments similar to Graham's. Overwhelmingly, they pursue the point that reliable and uncensored information is essential to the functioning of a democratic public, and that government attempts to control or monitor electronic information, whether in e-mails, websites, or other forms, constitute tyranny by stealth. Having been presented with the internet and with the decentralized structure of information distribution, many people are reluctant to give it up. Curiously, once people have embraced the distributed, decentralized structure of the internet, they immediately set about creating centralized structures in the forms of online communities, chatgroups, and the like.

In response to the statements of people such as Brian Harradine (a Tasmanian MP and sponsor of much anti-pornography legislation) or Senator Exon, one encounters a counter-argument that the pornography 'hysteria' is simply a fabrication of conservative pundits and mass media hungry for a sensationalist story. For example, numerous webpages, often cross-referenced, exist which refute the evidence of the 'Rimm study', the work behind the *Time* article. These counter-arguments range from *ad hominem* attacks on the author to serious analyses and critiques of the statistical and sampling methods as well as of the conclusions drawn. However, these websites generally maintain a stance of defending online activity against government control. Thus, a libertarian argument, often making explicit reference to Thomas Jefferson's letters and philosophy, arises in opposition to the economic and governmental arguments to limit the proliferation of ideas and meanings. Truly the notion of the public has been lost to contemporary politics in the US, Australia, and other supposedly liberal societies.

My point here is not to prove or disprove a particular position about the effects of pornographic images on children or anyone else. Rather, I intend only to highlight the extent to which the argument moves through a number of historically identifiable theories of media effects. However, even the existence of the argument about the censorship and control of information is in itself a limiting of discourse and identity and hence a form of control. Mark Poster (1995) writes that:

> modern theory's insistence on the freedom of the subject, its compulsive, repetitive inscription into discourse of the sign of the resisting agent, functions to restrict the shape of identity to its modern form, an ideological and legitimizing gesture of its own position rather than a step toward emancipation.

In other words, the existence of discourses of governmental control will lead some to resist these in oppositional ways, and in so doing, they assume a position already established within the liberal political world view that legitimizes the position of the censors through the act of an apparent public discussion and that silences the opposition as having had its say. What is preserved is the sign of democratic processes; what is obscured is the real function of power to position identity and language within the signifying process.

Recently, however, pornography has dropped away as a prevailing social concern, and a wholly new set of concerns has surfaced that make clear the interests of state and corporate power in limiting access to information and supervising the conversations and correspondences of ordinary people. Since 11 September 2001, governmental attempts to exercise control over information have greatly expanded in the United States, under initiatives put forward by the FBI and other intelligence agencies and supported by the Attorney General, John Ashcroft. The USA PATRIOT Act was passed with no debate and without even being read by many legislators, and it gave sweeping powers to the police as well as federal agencies. The use of the 'Carnivore' internet monitoring system was instituted and the covert gathering of a range of information about US citizens and others, without judicial oversight, was permitted. A subsequent act, sometimes called Patriot Act II, is even more sweeping and would seriously challenge several amendments to the US constitution, notably the First, Fourth, and Fifth Amendments which provide for freedom of speech, due process of law, and the right against self-incrimination in trial.

Using the threat of 'terrorism', an activity or series of activities so loosely defined as to include nearly any activity, association, or crime, the intelligence community finally dropped the illusion that monitoring and, more importantly, the careful 'spin' of information were not a priority for social control. All forms of dissent and debate suddenly have become suspect and subject to surreptitious inspection. These agencies possess a power undreamed of by Matthew Arnold and the social reformers of the nineteenth century. Also dropped is the illusion of improving the masses or the working class in order to allow their participation in the public. What remains is the simple policing of a cinematic, second-order reality of mass media representation and discourses such that any organized and coherent idea of opposition becomes unvoiceable in the mainstream of public discourse and hence appears as irrational and unreasonable. The point has finally been reached that, armed with the power of the computer, the collective entities of the state and the social world are managed as information construction and flow. In such a system, as Eric Voegelin demonstrated, 'the meaning of individual existence is to participate instrumentally in the collective progress' (1989: 61). That such a 'radically collectivist' project should masquerade as the defense of individual rights and liberties, particularly the rights of free expression, only illustrates the extent to which the ideas of the public and of democratic participation in the ongoing conversation of self-governance have already atrophied to the point of paralysis.

EIGHT

The Metaphysics of Information

The aversion towards the words culture and administration – an aversion by no means free of barbarism and overshadowed by the urge to release the safety catch on the revolver – must not conceal that a certain truth is involved in it. (Theodor Adorno 1991: 108)

The extension of electronic and especially digital communications to all areas of life in the Anglo-European world has created a social domain that is much more unified than those which preceded it. This unity has been brought about through two aspects of the same development. Information as a substantive thing now provides both the object of the unified social gaze and the subjective experience of it. Each is pregiven and overdetermined through the same social reliance on a belief in a particular kind of reality of information. This unification of information and the world as one thing permits, and perhaps demands, the falsification of each. If there is no world outside language and the descriptions of it, there can be no test of the reality of statements and beliefs. Consequences likewise become separated from actions. The unification takes place in the social domain as well as in the consciousness and selves of people whose interactions with the world are increasingly mediated through their use of 'information technologies'.

Since Condorcet proposed creating a universal scientific language of statistical measures that could be translated without loss into every language and every vernacular (Mattelart 1996: 44), Western societies have enacted one or another set of techniques to bring about the unification of a 'true' view of society, that is, a view that comports with the dominant language of power. Census taking, demographic measurements, and the keeping of police reports and records – all of which became socially important first in the eighteenth century – marked the beginning of the shared social reality of information. While statistics are hierarchical in their application – those compiling the information have a view denied to the objects of their study and to many of the consumers of the study – the simultaneous rise of mass media and of the representational identity of both the middle class and the working class created an ostensibly democratic view of information from the standpoint of the individual person located within these milieux. Information, news, scientific truths – each emerged within discourses that promised objective and sharable words, values, and symbols.

The control of both the hierarchical view and the democratic view highlights two parts of the same expression of power: the power to define the reality of the social. Commonly, the explanation of the hierarchical view, that is of the statistics, scientific studies, social trends and tendencies, and so on, has been a site of contention: what do the trends mean, what is the significance of particular numbers? What is often overlooked is the way in which these numbers, together with their interpretations, have come to stand in the place of the real world. Such numbers and their meanings are not neutral, of course. They reflect the values of those persons and organizations that compile and interpret them. However, the existence of such information and the value of its interpretation in particular cultural situations highlights the characteristic of such societies to translate their values into numbers. The characteristics of its dominant social gaze say much about a society.

Certainly, both the spreading influence of machine values of routinization and mass production and the commodification of all aspects of life under contemporary capital have played a part in the production of the information societies. Additionally, the meshing of technology, the military, and finance with government have greatly contributed to shaping the current situation. As US President Eisenhower noted in his 1961 farewell address:

> This conjunction of an immense military establishment and a large arms industry is new in the American experience. The total influence – economic, political, even spiritual – is felt in every city, every state house, every office of the Federal government. We recognize the imperative need for this development. Yet we must not fail to comprehend its grave implications. Our toil, resources and livelihood are all involved; so is the very structure of our society.

Eisenhower understood that the aims of the military, the aims of the armaments industry and the needs of a civil and democratic society were fundamentally in conflict; however, he believed that the political institutions and vigilant individuals could counteract the influence of the military-industrial complex.

Since Eisenhower's day, however, the inherent social conflict located within a military-industrial state has been obscured. The contradictions apparent in the processes and institutions of the current situation are masked, and one of the greatest of these contradictions is revealed in the common belief that the current social structure represents society as a whole while at the same time representing the interests of a ruling elite of the wealthy and the military. Such unresolved contradictions within a society require management to prevent their breaking out into consciousness and conflict. In this case, militarism melds with a jingoistic patriotism, usually argued as necessary because of some external threat (communism, terrorism, fascism), to make critical or oppositional statements appear unrealistic, unpatriotic, and childish. The unification of the social around shared beliefs and values is inculcated through the technical and ideological unification of mass persuasion technologies of education, media, consumerism, and aesthetics. Such consolidation of the public language has normalized some values while eliminating numerous voices and making obsolete, or at least suspect, the ability to think or speak outside well-defined lines. Social language, and hence social reality, become administered. Kovel writes that 'the phrase "administration of reality" means that every communication takes on a dual quality, being on the one hand a statement about the world and, on the other, an instrument of administration' (1981: 185).

States have always manifested the need to establish symbolic social orderings to enact themselves in the world among people. However, the techniques by which such orderings can assimilate other values and symbolic systems had been greatly refined through the twentieth century.

Mitchell Palmer and the Rise of the American Reality Administration

One of the first instances of this dual use of the administration of reality took place in the early twentieth century: the red scare of 1918–1920 and the 'Palmer raids' on suspected communists and radicals. Even now these events stand as a symbolic moment in American history, and the fact that they are still used as an icon of repression by the progressives and a demonstration of determination by conservatives demonstrates their importance and places them within the trajectory of evolving forms of social control. For example, a few months after 9–11, Pat Buchanan (2001) published an opinion piece titled, 'Let the "Ashcroft raids" begin'. With its numerous historical inaccuracies and logical inconsistencies, Buchanan's piece aimed not at historical awareness but at drawing on the same xenophobic, anti-alien sentiment as fueled the initial raids. Buchanan paints a mythic picture of idealized, homogeneous, white, middle-class America, safely wrapped in the 'Eisenhower–Kennedy era', which was 'one nation and one people. We learned the same history, spoke the same language, listened to the same radio and TV shows, went to the same movies, sang the same songs, honored the same heroes, read the same books' (Buchanan 2001).

Such a distorted and idealized view of society is essential for stripping both past and present of contradictions and complexities so that inequalities, differences and injustices can be replaced by the glittering generalities and 'values' of a social in-group. It is these that can be threatened by outsiders, foreigners, and those advocating an examination of and potential reordering of the social. That Buchanan's vision of America existed only in the imaginations of a few people safely secluded from African-Americans, Hispanics, the poor, the well-educated, etc. illustrates that the historical moment of which he speaks, and the illusion of the culture itself, never existed. Rather they are a rhetorical trope whose function is the mythologizing of a certain view of culture toward the end of symbolic closure. Buchanan writes that 'we are only just beginning to see the dark side of diversity' (Buchanan 2001).

One might reasonably speculate that people such as Buchanan long for a lost sense of *isonomia*, the shared beliefs and ideas that created the conditions for the emergence of the *polis* in ancient Greece. However, he, and others, seek to locate this shared sensibility within the commodified, commercial, and mythic mass culture of the industrialized West. It was never there. The *isonomia* of the Greeks developed within a context of existing differences in power and influence between people and between groups. The *polis* was not a mythic state of harmony but a living process of negotiation, compromise, and disputation between people taking one another as equals. However, the contemporary social order, manifesting the beliefs and values of a limited number of ruling elites, masquerades as the site where an *isonomia* that never existed is presumed to have perished and the site from which it shall rise, Phoenix-like, from the ashes.

As demonstrated in previous chapters, social controls of various types have borrowed from religion, class, science, and other discourses in order to deflect the direction of social change or in some cases to limit it altogether. Such moral panics are especially likely during times of social change or perceived threat and uncertainty. For example, in the second decade of the twentieth century, A. Mitchell Palmer, the Attorney General of the United States, together with various publishers, industrialists, and politicians, sought to eliminate the threat of 'Bolsheviks' in the United States. Under Palmer's instigation, federal, state, and local police and agents arrested thousands of people, beating many and torturing some; ransacked union offices for membership and mailing lists; and eventually deported more than 200 people. The attacks on Marxists and anarchists extended to trade unionists, notably the International Workers of the World (IWW).

While instigated from leadership positions within government, publishing, and industry, the wave of anti-alien and anti-radical sentiment culminating in the Palmer raids fed existing nativist trends and fueled these trends while building upon them. 'From the 1890s on, the antialien and antiradical movements had established a series of precedents for dealing with the marginal groups in society. This groundwork was of immense aid to the proponents of the red scare' (Preston 1963: 7). The branding of the IWW as a Bolshevik organization ignored much of its history and most of its aims, but the 'terrible simplifiers' did not concern themselves with accuracy in Palmer's day and still do not. The image of immigrants, particularly East Europeans, as radicals and communists likewise did not comport well with reality.

Palmer's activities took place during the two years immediately following World War I and drew some of their social legitimacy from the patriotic war fervor that still lingered, from concerns about terrorist bomb attacks (including one against Palmer), from the Russian Revolution (1917), from large numbers of immigrants, and from the moral panic that unionists, anarchists and syndicalists instilled in the industrial elite. While earlier 'slacker raids' had been conducted to round up suspected draft dodgers during the war, these later raids exploited the xenophobic patriotism of the time. Utilizing the Sedition Act and the Alien Act, Palmer and his confederates conducted a series of raids culminating in the great roundup taking place on 2 January 1920 in several cities and towns. Rather than trials, mock hearings were held, sometimes conducted by immigration officials, before those to be deported were loaded onto a ship in New York referred to as the 'Red Ark'. Hearings by immigration officials allowed the government to circumvent court proceedings and thus treat immigrants, as well as naturalized citizens, in extra-legal procedures (Levin 1971: 58).

Palmer and the red scare crowd were deeply skeptical of the ability of the American government's own institutions to survive an ideological challenge. Palmer explained:

> So long as our country remains prosperous and we have abundance of employment for the masses at good pay, the condition is not alarming so far as the likelihood of revolutionary outbreaks is concerned, but given a condition of depression, bread lines, and the pressure of any wide-spread real want, then I think the 'menace' would prove grave indeed. (in Levin 1971: 193)

A similar sentiment underpins the current belief that protection against unspecified enemies requires the suspension of civil liberties and drastic increases in the secret powers of security services. Any institution that might conceivably provide any power to a suspect individual, allowing him or her to speak within the discourses of law or rights, is immediately suspect. Illegal activities in suppressing such persons are thus expressly permissible, and so the long history of wiretaps, buggings, break-ins, and other surveillance activities finds its justification in a suspicion of and contempt for precisely those governmental institutions that are mythically upheld as the defenders of liberty.

A young J. Edgar Hoover considerably aided Palmer's ends with his compilation of cross-indexed files compiled from the Library of Congress, and later from confiscated records, newspaper reports, and reports from civilian informants and organizations about the activities of suspect persons. One's arrest, questioning, occasional beating, and possible deportation depended upon the construction of a subversive identity within these files, sometimes supported with informant denunciations. As a model for the FBI, Hoover's earlier activities established and proved some of the mechanisms necessary for the modern administration of social power through information: a mythic public language built through propaganda and a set of techniques for establishing 'truth' about persons based on disembodied information attained through various forms of surveillance. The attacks on radicalism in the US also provided the testing-ground for the use of information to suppress dissent. Information thus became the new truth and self-apparent justification for government actions.

The major difference between Palmer and Hoover's day and the contemporary situation lies in the extent to which information in general is substituted for and accepted as the real and the extent to which alternative points of view are excluded from the social sphere. Scientific rationality as a concept had already been proven before the twentieth century, and its application to documenting the world of people in the abstract was already accepted in census taking, insurance underwriting, and so on. As a belief system, it fit well with prevailing notions of progress, improvement, and reason. Yet, the application of scientific methods to *defining* social reality was just hitting its stride. Such a consolidation of power around information was facilitated by the linking together of several technologies and people's beliefs about them. Palmer and Hoover had the Library of Congress, index cards, and other paper and pencil technologies little changed from the middle ages with which to compile and cross-reference their lists of subversives. The social climate in which their surveillance was conducted was influenced with the assistance of the telegraph, the telephone, and the increasingly interlinked national news services supplying the papers. Had Hoover and Palmer the same networks of computerized data collection and analysis, the same centralization of mass media, and the same impoverished and polluted public language as exists today, the red scare of 1918–1920 would not have died so quickly, and its effects would have been far more sweeping. The short-lived, immediate threat of the 'reds' could have become an ongoing, dominant theme in American social life to the end of suppressing an ever widening sphere of political thought.

The Totalizing Tendency of Information

As demonstrated in previous chapters, the social order of industrial, capitalist societies came to be represented primarily in and through the production and consumption of particular forms of information. No longer something that people created in the acts of creating things together, industrial information became instead a prescriptive ordering of the social that was imposed by institutions of education, medicine, transport, and so on. This information existed within ongoing discourses of power, hygiene, science, and religion, and increasingly within discourses about information itself; and this last, the creation of theories of information, its transmission and uses, is especially important. The metacriticisms of information, the addressing of info as if it were something substantive, real, and ontologically independent of human consciousness and language, mark a profound shift in how information came to be seen and experienced.

In the minds of many, the establishment of media as a social mechanism that is used expressly to create a mass in place of a public has firmly fixed the reality of information as something real in itself. In other words, there is a tendency in contemporary writing, thought, and perception for information – now separate and separable from the human beings who spoke, wrote, heard, and read language – to appear as ontologically equivalent with the obdurate reality of the world. In this formulation, meaning is no longer seen to be contingent upon circumstances and subjectivity but instead is circulated through words and images. Speakers still speak: Tony Blair and George Bush are recognized as the 'origins' of speeches, phrases, and so on, but they only contribute to the flow of information in a stream which seems inexorable, measureless, and without beginning. Further, an express purpose of official language is the elimination of vernacular, local, hand-crafted language.

This destruction of the vernacular is accomplished in two main ways. First, the vernacular is simply drowned out and so finds no place in public language. The pronouncements of leaders are amplified through news media discussions and analyses, through their repetition in most of the major media, and at times are propagated by propagandists masquerading as intellectuals, experts, journalists, and the like. Second, the vernacular stands in direct opposition to the creation of a well-ordered, carefully managed society that would embody the values of those in power and that would institute the social relations desired by those in power. Local language rejects the totalitarian direction needed to ensure that voters act in predictable ways, that consumers purchase the necessary amounts, that people show up for work, and so on. Local language also resists the imposition of particular kinds of selves and hence of particular kinds of relationships between people. The elimination of the historical and traditional aspects of language ensures that only the official interpretations of the world are heard, and it helps ensure public support for the next war, or the next environmental policy, or the next assault on human rights. In the absence of a language of their own, people need not even consider the problems inherent in the official view of things.

Thus, the structurings of contemporary, industrial societies necessarily tend toward a form of totalitarianism, but this unity of thought can only exist with the destruction of the local and the vernacular and their replacement with a systematized language. In order for the ever more complex and integrated social system to operate, all options and choices (for action and for thought) that lie outside the predicted and expected must be eliminated in the name of efficiency, order, and positive control. These structurings become ever more pervasive and extensive into all aspects of life. De Certeau (1984) observes that these characteristics of contemporary postindustrial societies limit the possibilities of meanings which might introduce unmanageable dimensions of human historical time and remembered place into official language. Totalitarian language attacks 'superstitions: superogatory semantic overlays that insert themselves "over and above" and "in excess"' (1984: 106). Local speech tends to 'compromise the univocity of the system'. He continues that 'stories and legends ... haunt urban space like superfluous or additional inhabitants' (1984: 106). It is these 'unwanted citizens', that is, the words and stories of real people told from within their own experiences and linked to unofficial histories, that are most thoroughly expunged from the official language and so from the public sphere. The words of soldiers in the field in Iraq, for example, are policed and blocked from public view unless they support the official story, while the numbers of dead Iraqi civilians are not even tallied by occupying forces, much less reported.

Information as salvation from the social

Originating in a dialectic form in conversations, that is, in speech between people, language is not an individual's product created *ex nihilo*. The symbolic exists first in the shared space of the social. For most of human existence, language could not be conceived as separate to or separable from the social. To be alone was to be an idiot, *solus ipse*. In order to remove someone from existence, an action beyond simple killing was called for: exile. Even when dead, one lived on so long as one's words and deeds were spoken of and recounted, so long as one's name continued in the conversations and stories of others. However, the advent of distributed data systems, cybernetic and interactive information sources of all sorts, and the overwhelming presence of information and data gives rise to the perception that language and signification exist independent of human beings, as if the machines were talking to themselves, or more appropriately, as if information itself had become a living entity.

One such statement emerges from the writings of John Barlow, a co-founder of EFF, the Electronic Freedom Foundation. In works such as 'The economy of ideas' and 'A declaration of independence of cyberspace', Barlow articulates a view of information as something alive, declaring 'Information is a life form', a statement he credits to Stewart Brand. He writes that this statement recognizes 'both the natural desire of secrets to be told and the fact that they might be capable of possessing something like a "desire" in the first place' (Barlow 1996). In this attribution to information of desire, Barlow is close to a paranoiac identification of self in something external to self; of being, literally, 'outside his mind' (the etymological meaning of paranoia). Such is the position of ascribing to information the characteristics of life. I am not saying that John Barlow or other people who use the metaphor of information as a life are insane. Rather, their argument, taken seriously, raises the phenomenological experience of perceiving the unanticipated yet self-initiated words and images on a screen to the level of an encounter with an ontologically independent other different from the other speaker in a conversation or the author of a letter or book.

Even if the imputation of life to information is taken as something of a metaphor or hyperbole, the positioning of information as equivalent to a living form, even philosophically, changes how people will act toward it. The imposition of information as ontologically separate from people reintroduces numerous opportunities for committing the 'category mistake' discussed later in this chapter. The easiest mistake is holding that the existence of information *per se* is a predicate for the existence or reality of what the information represents or 'means'. The information has no meaning separate from someone's perception of it, but in believing that information corrupts or liberates, one supposes also the notion that information now stands in the same place where previously ideas and thoughts had stood. The failed Cartesian dichotomy of mind and body is replaced with the new false dichotomy of self and information.

If people are more commonly engaged in the consumption of information in the forms of television, radio, the internet, and so on, then their face-to-face talking and participation with other people decline (see Putnam 2000). Thus, the social interactions in which people are implicated are increasingly impersonal, and information comes to stand in the place of other people. However, information can only occupy this position if it is seen as independent of the viewer or reader. Information itself then constitutes the world itself and is no longer simply representation. In his essay 'A world picture', Heidegger wrote that 'When the world becomes picture, what is, in its entirety, is juxtaposed as that for which man is prepared and which, correspondingly, he therefore intends to bring before himself' (1977: 129). One thus makes an 'essential decision' about what is. If some fact, discourse, or construction of the world does not appear within the world picture, it does not exist substantially. Television and the internet validate the 'external' world and limit what is deemed knowable about it. That the new world picture is transient, ephemeral, and protean creates a condition where, try as one might, the real is never attainable, is always receding from grasp. To paraphrase García Lorca, signs slip away like startled fish. And with the signs, reality vanishes as well.

An example of such a private dream taken to the point of absurdity is discussed by Paul Virilio:

> When cosmonauts floating in their interstellar dustbin cry out to the camera that 'the dream is alive', why shouldn't Internauts take themselves for cosmonauts? Why would they not, like overgrown fairytale children, cross the space between the real and the figurative, reaching as far as the interface with a virtual paradise? Why would they not believe that the extra-terrestrial light of the Hale–Bopp comet is the light that lights up an emergency exit from the physical world? [A reference to the Heaven's Gate sect who believed that the comet was a spaceship and who killed themselves to join it.] (2000: 42)

A corollary is that one's experience of information, for example, in viewing multimedia pornographic materials, is somehow simultaneously not real and yet real enough to require intervention from the state and evasion by the individual. Another corollary is that the data collected from people's library use, video rentals, and internet surfing habits constitute sufficient cause for arrest, detention, and questioning.

Accidenting the real

Information, as distinct from knowledge or wisdom, has now achieved a symbolic status such that it exists outside people, no longer dependent on being known; it has its own status of being. This is recognized implicitly in the characteristics which are imputed to it and explicitly in the expectations about its relationship to human life. From Lyotard's battle cry 'Open up the data-banks, set the information free' to the present, information is increasingly discussed as though it were a living entity, on a par with a gnostic demiurge: 'Information wants to be free.' In some senses, information has become the new gnosis, a replacement for divine or transcendent knowledge, and in so doing has moved into a new form of being. Knowledge in the old sense scarcely seems to matter anymore. Information has become autonomous, self-augmenting, indeed self-aware. In some sense the world has changed and the now near instant access to near limitless amounts of digitized words and images can promote a sense that there is another being, a consciousness, in the world, living just beyond the screen, gazing back as one looks into it.

No doubt some part of this apprehension arises from the subjective experience of projection, encountering some part of one's own mind as an external manifestation; and electronic communications, especially in their dominant forms, are especially well suited for being the screens upon which our dreams, fantasies, and fears can be made to dance. Finally freed from the tyranny of normalizing social interactions, a person at a screen can call forth an external object in the form of a phosphor glow accompanied by surround sound which presents not representations but wholly new creations, in ever increasing degrees of power and sophistication. One must consider here that the aim of the trend toward virtual reality is not to reproduce reality, but to replace it with something more wondrous, more powerful, louder, brighter, faster, and finally more gratifying than the real (see Faulkner 1950). As Virilio (1994) noted, the aim of virtual reality is not verisimilitude but the destruction of the real, the 'accidenting of the real'. The real is displaced. Precisely as current surveillance technologies superimpose new identities on the existing and ongoing social identities that people have and can so create new crimes for which people can be suspected, tried, and punished, other virtualizing technologies accident other kinds of selves by creating new conditions in which they will emerge.

This 'accidenting', of course, manifests itself on many levels of culture, not the least significant of which are philosophy and psychology. Psychologically, we are witnessing the rise of technologies of deception, duplicity and surveillance, not only as threats from the outside but as ways of protecting the individual's activities while online or of transforming other areas of the interpersonal world into electronic forms. With this arises a kind of digital antinomianism: whatever one does online is one's own business, private, and so acceptable. Online life arises from one's personal relationship with and implication in information in a singular form that arises at that moment. No matter that tens of thousands of others might be looking at the same picture, reading the same webpage, participating in the same blog or chatroom; the perception that a person is isolated from the physical presence of others in this interaction makes the exchange personal and private. The experience of this private moment makes every intrusion or monitoring immediately an invasion of privacy, an eavesdropping.

Here, too, arise the technologies of surveillance. As people begin to act on multiple perceived realities formed out of the wealth of information to which they have access, increasingly sophisticated forms of surveillance and counter-surveillance appear in order to enable what the military used to call 'confidence building', that is, the assurance that some belief fits with reality. Home detection kits for semen and drug use are available for purchase at drug stores and online. Miniature wireless television cameras, as well as the proliferation of video recording equipment of all kinds, allow people to surreptitiously record the actions of others. Key-logging software may be bought that runs in the background of a computer, allowing one's every click to be recorded. Each of these technologies appeared first in the corporate or military realm, and each has found itself being used in homes. The mindset of surveillance is thus naturalized and necessitated.

The New Mythic Space

The space most commonly under surveillance today is by definition an urban space, that is, the space in which human beings live and communicate with one another. Urban space today is both the physical space of the city and the shared symbolic space of electronically mediated discourse. This is more than a metaphor, for the electronic communications of the current day are the stage, setting, and characters of the drama of contemporary life. As such, electronic media are precisely those which must be governed, and so arises the media's deep implication in the processes of governmentality and power. Gary Marx (1986) observes that:

> The state cannot watch everyone all the time. It is far more efficient to have all eyes riveted on common mass media stimuli offering messages of how to behave. Mass media persuasion is far more subtle and indirect than a truncheon over the head. Though the force involved is psychological rather than physical, it is not necessarily less coercive. Both violence and manipulation seek to counter informed consent and free choice.

Few would question that the media world operates through a manipulation of opinion and desires, through the selective presentation and exclusion of news, and through the stupefaction of public discourse with banality, pointless excesses, sexual titillation and violence.

Guy Debord (1995) noted that modern capitalist countries had developed into consumer cultures which depend for their existence on the integration of language and representation into a unified system which he termed 'the spectacular society'. The spectacular society is 'not a collection of images; rather, it is a social relationship between people that is mediated by images' (1995: 12). This system is tautological and induces separation of people from each other and from their world (1995: 12, 20). It arises in a society 'in which social life is completely taken over by the accumulated products of the economy' (1995: 16). He notes as well that within the spectacular society, nothing exists except as images and spectacle. If it is not on television, it does not exist. In a sense, Debord's spectacular society marks the triumph of form over content. While the tendency of the form of communication to overwhelm the meaning of communication has been noted for some time (for example, Barthes 1972 [1958]; Baudrillard 1983), in Debord's writing this characteristic of contemporary communication is symptomatic of the commodification of all of the social realm. Further, the spectacular society brings about the integration of government with business by alloying political power and economic production within a system that displaces the real world in favor of a manufactured (and often unnecessary) world. The 'spectacle's job is to cause a world that is no longer directly perceptible to be seen via different specialized mediations' (1995: 17). These mediations constitute the social truth, for they are what are acknowledged, spoken about, and deemed worthy of notice.

For an example, American President G.W. Bush apparently relied upon his family's wealth and influence to avoid military service during the Vietnam War, securing instead a leap to the head of the line of perhaps 500 other people seeking alternative service in the Texas Air National Guard (Lardner and Kurtz 2000). Further, G.W. Bush apparently did not finish his last year of service and did not even report to his duty station. He suffered no punishment or even reprimand for this. Such news about the Commander-in-Chief of the United States would, in many circumstances, appear damning. Nonetheless, at the conclusion of the Gulf War, President Bush appeared on the flight deck of an aircraft carrier clad in a full pilot's flightsuit. According to some reports, the carrier was even diverted from its course (and so delayed in its arrival) so as to provide the best possible camera angle with which to shoot the landing plane, that is, an angle which did not show the California coastline in the background (Millbank 2003). The image of the President emerging from a military aircraft to announce victory in the invasion of Iraq appeared throughout the US press and television. However, very few mentions appeared of the discrepancy between his own military record and the spectacle. Instead, the image consumed the historical facts and stories, and in so doing fulfilled the purpose of a social/linguistic myth: 'To transform meaning into form' (Barthes 1972 [1958]: 131).

It is important to note that the extreme spectacular event just described was *not the result* of communication technologies. Technologies did not create either the mythology or the forms within it. Rather, the spectacle reaches full unfolding through the deliberate use of media for political ends, and such an extreme use of contemporary media can only take place as a consequence of the merger of government and industry, a merger that has in recent years achieved unprecedented centralization and consolidation of control and ownership (see McChesney 1997; Bagdikian 2000). However, is there a significant difference between the staged act of public amnesia cited above and the everyday activity of promoting politicians as though they were toothpaste? The boundaries between news and entertainment, politics and puffery, have long been blurred. So long as government and industry – with media being one example – demonstrate a unity of interests and operate together, there is little incentive for mass media to take a different position.

By definition, mass media operate at the level of cultural mythology, and this mythic level weaves together various threads of culture into immediately comprehensible events and forms. Critical language, on the other hand, does not have access to the narratives that comprise the myth. A useful distinction emerges from Roland Barthes who observed that the languages of critique and the languages of power differ greatly in their expression. The language (*parole*) of power creates a myth, a structuring of language and representation, that appears completely natural and depoliticized. The spectacle thus leads to the creation of narratives and episodic views of real life that are complete in themselves and require no interpretation or negotiation. Barthes notes that myth on the right 'is essential; well fed, sleek, expansive, garrulous, it invents itself ceaselessly. It takes hold of everything' (1972 [1958]: 148). The mythic form of power binds together religion, ideology, and desire, making of them the seamless spectacular moment that can only be rebutted by a critique that does not itself exist within the forms of contemporary media.

Debord is insightful when he writes that the spectacular society 'functions as a specious form of the sacred' (1995: 20). While religion has historically been used to serve the functions of power, the new form of spectacular state religion, especially in its American avatar, utilizes the extent of the market of news and information to ensure its closure as a belief system without external referents. That is to say, as nothing socially meaningful exists outside the realm of spectacular presentation in media, everything within the spectacle is immediately true for the believers. Believers are closely aligned with various leaders in the US, Australia, and the UK who no longer feel bound to rational discourse but who, buoyed by the success of the spectacular as a social form, have come to rely on the image and the staged event to create beliefs contrary to all evidence, all history, and any test in reality.

Crises are well suited to the contemporary social world, for they ensure that ever emerging new events destroy people's attempts to create narrative and historical continuities out of the information flow. Hence, the endless state of ongoing wars: the war against drugs, the war against terror, the war against the Taliban, the war against Saddam, and so on, contribute to the simultaneous strengthening of the myths of state and corporate correctness and to the dissolution of a meaningful sense of history within the society. While the usefulness of external threats to the maintenance of a propaganda state has been known at least since A. Mitchell Palmer and Joseph Goebbels, its re-emergence in the early twenty-first century as an official discourse indicates that in the hands of ruthless powers, the mechanisms of the spectacle in creating beliefs and eliminating knowledge are highly effective and generate public support even when there is no logical basis for the beliefs.

The effectiveness of mass news coverage of events in supporting the perspective of power was highlighted by research conducted in 1991 at the end of the first US–Iraq War. This research suggested 'an ongoing process in which support for the war, lower levels of knowledge, and greater media exposure all interact and reproduce each other in dynamic and systematic ways' (Lewis et al. 1991). The research found that watching television coverage did not increase knowledge about the conflict or the region, but instead increased the dissemination of selective misinformation. The researchers noted an important distinction between being ignorant and being selectively misinformed. Further, this misinformation leads generally to the support of the spectacular and mythic forms of public discourse. On the basis of this misinformation 'there is an extremely strong positive relationship between [the] general amount of television viewing and support for the war' (Lewis et al. 1991).

The researchers' conclusion is especially interesting:

> The more people know, in other words, the less likely they were to support the war policy. We are not saying that people against the war are right and those in favor of it are wrong, merely that since our study shows a clear relation between knowledge and opinion, and, since the things people do not know tend to undermine the Administration's moral position, it is plausible to assume that an increase in knowledge could lead to an increase in the opinion more strongly associated with it. (Lewis et al. 1991)

The authors offer various theories of why media coverage would have produced these effects, but they neglect the most logical and telling: the media and the government have achieved a consolidation of the mechanisms of public language, and this centralization allows the mediated world to appear as the real world.

The Creation of New Legal Spaces and Cyber-Identities: Surveillance

The current spate of 'anti-terrorism' laws in the US and the UK bear only a superficial resemblance to the censorship of previous centuries. The aim of the contemporary laws is not to prevent the spread of information but to establish privileged interpretations of information as a new form of social truth which can be used as an instrument for the furtherance of the spectacular society. The rules of truth in connection with the USA PATRIOT Act are remarkably *ad hoc*. The ACLU notes that:

> One of the most significant provisions of the Patriot Act makes it far easier for the authorities to gain access to records of citizens' activities being held by a third party. At a time when computerization is leading to the creation of more and more such records, Section 215 of the Patriot Act allows the FBI to force anyone at all – including doctors, libraries, bookstores, universities, and Internet service providers – to turn over records on their clients or customers. (ACLU n.d.)

Once having these records, analysts for intelligence agencies or other government policing agencies look for matches between data sets that, in their view, constitute evidence of illegal or terrorist planning or activity. Data mining on a vast scale utilizing the same, supposedly liberating, technologies of personal computers and internet access allows intelligence and police agencies the opportunities to sift though large data bases of credit cards, internet access, travel, library records and the like and map profiles of suspects to patterns of reading and purchasing. In this way, the cyber identities of individual persons are transformed into entities with legal reality. The corporeal, historically situated person is displaced through the constructed fiction of the individual in the data base.

In one sense this is nothing new. Insurance companies have historically based their assessments of the insurance risk posed by a person on statistical analysis of selective data of their own choosing. Yet the new acts in America and the United Kingdom create the possibility of the prosecution of persons for the historical traces of their reading, correspondence, and online association: in short, for thought crime. Both the British and US laws have another similarity in having rushed through legislation on the heels of the shock of 9–11. Presented to Congress and passed only 45 days after the 9–11 incident, the USA PATRIOT Act followed the British version which had been previously drafted in connection with IRA attacks in Ireland and England. The British Act was presented to the House of Lords on 12 September 2001. This bill was widely criticized for precisely the same reasons as the US version. The *Guardian* newspaper reported that:

> The bill will allow confidential information about an individual held by any government department or local authority to be disclosed to the police and intelligence services for any criminal investigation – not just an investigation into terrorist offences. (Travis 2001)

These Acts allow their respective governments to gather information and use it to establish the criminality of people with no regard to their lives, histories, or the contexts of their many relationships to other persons. Thus, a *de facto* condition of truth is created in the structuring of information itself, and this condition of truth is used to further political ends.

Each person living in a contemporary, postindustrial society exists both as physical entity and as a disparate set of records left as the traces of that person's movement through the world of computing and communication systems. These traces may include information about purchases, library use, internet surfing histories, medical records, student records, employment histories, insurance histories, credit histories and reports: in short, they contain information about every aspect of life that takes place within the electronic systems of the modern world. These activities are routinely cross-matched for correlations of interest to the searchers. Haggerty and Ericson (2000) describe the convergence of multiple forms of surveillance technologies as 'the surveillant assemblage' which supersedes any particular technology or system. Using the works of Deleuze and Guattari, they theorize an *ad hoc* and unstable collection of entities and processes.[7] Drawing on an analogy to Marx's notion of surplus value, they posit the emergence of 'surplus information that different populations trail behind them' (2000: 616).

The end product of this is the creation of 'data doubles' – cybernetic constructs created specifically for the purpose of fixing identities, actions, motivations, and the like out of the otherwise unmapped and unregulated activities of people's lives. It is these data doubles, these electronic doppelgangers, that are the redefined reality of human existence. While legal and economic identities have shadowed the lives of people since official records and census reports have been kept, the new electronic doubles exist specifically as a predictive and philosophically positive statement with the power to define a person's activities as terroristic. Even the full, official name of the USA PATRIOT Act reveals this intention: Uniting and Strengthening America by Providing Appropriate Tools Required to Intercept and Obstruct Terrorism (USA PATRIOT) Act of 2001.

Gary Marx (1986) notes that the new surveillance technologies have attributes that distinguish them from the technologies that went before. Among these he writes that the new surveillance methods are decentralized and promote self-policing. Further, they bring about a shift from specific suspicions to categorical suspicions, meaning that everyone is a suspect to be examined and probed, and to have an electronic self created and scrutinized. Most dangerous to civil society in his perspective is the creeping encroachment of surveillance *per se* rather than any particular surveillance project. He writes, 'The issue, instead, is whether the system should be there to begin with. Once these systems are institutionalized and taken for granted, even in a democratic society, they can be used for harmful ends.'

When he wrote these words, Gary Marx hypothesized a catastrophe that could turn such surveillance projects into mechanisms for widespread abuse and social control. Such an event had not happened in 1986, but in 2001 the destruction of the World Trade Center complex and the subsequent 'war on terrorism' had created a climate in which the institution of abusive surveillance would be proposed and enacted. In addition to empowering existing agencies to gather intelligence in new ways, legislation, funding, and institutions were provided to create new realities out of the data of people's lives. Among these is a project called Total Information Awareness.

Total Information Awareness as Technicistic Delusion

For the most part, information constitutes the whole of the social and physical world that exists beyond one's immediate experience. Not only is the physical world displaced by information, but the presence of other persons is similarly no longer necessary. The *Oxford English Dictionary*'s documentation of historical uses of the word 'information', and its connotations in various times and settings, demonstrates that a common contemporary meaning of the word emerged only in the twentieth century. Historically, information existed in the context of human speech. In uses dating from the fourteenth century, information was 'the act of informing; formulation or moulding of the mind or character'. It could also appear as 'a fact or circumstance of which one is told'. In earlier use, 'an account, relation narrative'. In every case, information exists only within the context of human beings and implies a human subject who is informed. However, a more modern definition appears in 1937:

Separated from, or without the implication of, reference to a person informed; that which inheres in one or two or more alternative sequences or arrangements, etc. that produces different responses in something, and which is capable of being stored in, transferred by, and communicated to inanimate things.

The logical space of people and the logical space of inanimate things are not the same. The attributes of people's talking, of minds engaged in dialogue, are not the same as the characteristics of a thing. Pöksen writes that the word 'information' has undergone a shift in use from emphasizing a course of action to emphasizing 'a result or kind of object' (1995: 39). As a consequence, concepts such as this 'are not grounded in history ... but rather they are ahistorical manipulations of the world' (1995: 35).

The implications of this modern conception of information lead to a collapse of difference between the natural world and the world of information. For example, there are two ways of making identical information as something exchanged between people and information, as something that makes no reference to people. The first is to transform people into things, and the second is to transform information into something living. So long as the matter is muddled and unresolved, all manner of brain-splitting, illogical and nonsensical statements are possible.

An example of such confused thinking (and syntax) may be found in documents regarding the recently renamed Total Information Awareness project run by the US Department of Defense. Funded for over 27 million dollars, one part of the larger program, called The Human Augmentation of Reasoning through Patterning (HARP) project, shows how far Vannevar Bush's ideas have developed. In the 'description of work' for this project conducted by the Air Force Research Laboratory, Rome Research Site in New York, the authors describe their goals as the development of needed technology in applying 'automation to team processes so that more information can be exploited, more hypotheses created and examined, more models built and populated with evidence'. They continue:

> Specific areas include: (a) cognitive aids that allow humans and machines to think together in real-time about complicated problems, (b) means to overcome the biases and limitation of the human cognitive system, (c) cognitive amplifiers that help teams rapidly and fully comprehend complicated and uncertain situations, and (d) the means to rapidly and seamlessly cut across and complement existing stove-piped hierarchical organizational structures by creating dynamic, adaptable, peer-to-peer collaborative networks. (HARP 2002: 3.1.2)

These statements extend far beyond the usual sort of obfuscation and double-talk of bureaucratic writing and demonstrate the extent to which unexamined technicistic thinking dominates their project.

To begin with, the authors of HARP apparently believe that humans and machines unproblematically 'think together' and that both are in need of cognitive aids. In other words, human thought and machine processing of data are taken as identical: the same verb describes each. In part (b), human thought is reduced to being a limited and biased 'cognitive system'. Furthermore, the limitations of this 'system' can be overcome, leading one to ask, what need can the human race have for philosophy with such noble projects in the works? In part (c), 'cognition' – no longer 'thought' – will be technically amplified for the sake of speed and *full comprehension* of uncertain situations. Logic is apparently not as valued as skills in the data mining of computer records, for how could a situation, given to be uncertain, be fully comprehended?

Such flaws of simple logic and such atrocities committed on the English language might be forgiven but for the rationale that lies behind these statements and is revealed through them. Technology itself will create a special space with its own logic, a space within which things have new characteristics and in which relations between things are created around these new rules. Thus, humans and computers think in similar ways. Human thought is a cognitive system, like machine systems, and so can be mapped, described, detailed and ordered to produce a close fit with processes found in computing. Indeed, such an identification of mind with machine processes is necessary if the activity of the mind is to be judged by machine criteria and rules of proof. By the same token, the aim of the project, sifting large amounts of data to find evidence of forthcoming terrorist activity, creates new kinds of proof out of the new evidence. The relations between things – relations that may exist nowhere in the human world – may now be used as evidence of future wrongdoing. Under current US law, such 'evidence' could provide the basis for a permanent detention without any legal recourse. In other words, no other system of thought, judgment, or values would enter into the decision-making process. The Total Information Awareness program is a *vas hermeticum* within which all manner of miracles may be performed that cannot exist outside such a rarified space.

The Category Mistake in Information Sciences

The interplay between self and other has become instead the interface of mind and screen, and the images and sounds of the screen differ dramatically from the voice and presence of other people. At some level of complexity and quantity, the steady flow of information of all types ceases to be composed of distinguishable individual stories, pictures, video clips, and so on and achieves a unity in people's perception. Rather than being the manufactured product of propagandists, advertisers, psychologists and artists, information appears as the world in itself. Consequently, a new Cartesian dualism has arisen in which information exists separate from the mind. Such a separation reintroduces the 'category mistake' described by Ryle (1984). To accept a representation as the world is to assume that the same rules apply to that representation and to the physical world, that they have the same characteristics and qualities. The physical world and information do not occupy the same logical space. Information can be infinitely reproduced and transmitted while the world cannot. Information is created while the physical world is not. The mistake arises at the instant that the whole world is seen as manufactured or engineered. Only in this sense can the two share the same logical space. No longer a mind–body dualism, this new way of thinking creates a mind–information dualism. This separation of information, first from language and second from the immediate presence of human thought, has several consequences.

The first consequence, as noted in previous chapters, is that information and knowledge have become conflated into a single thing, and the categories that previous eras applied to knowledge (as a concept imbedded in human existence) are now applicable to information. No longer do people know some thing; rather they are informed about or have been exposed to some information spasm from within the range of mass communications and are therefore resonant about some image, phrase or event. For example, information itself now possesses a soteriological function, exhibits a loss of the quality of truth, and additionally is increasingly used as if it may stand in the place of a sentient being, that is, as the other to a human being. Within such a setting, the self that elaborates is no longer a social self but a private one, complete with its own private symbolic system. Words and images do not lead to the conscious formation of shared symbolic activities that are meaningful but instead bypass language and operate on a much more personal and psychological level. Dewey noted that:

> When words do not enter as factors into a shared situation, either overtly or imaginatively, they operate as pure physical stimuli, not as having a meaning or intellectual value. They set activity running in a given groove, but there is no accompanying conscious purpose or meaning. (1985a [1916]: 20)

Meaning and intellectual value cannot arise because the language is presumed to exist or to function outside the realm of the human beings. Disembodied symbols and words can have no meaning for the self.

The quality of truth can no longer be applied to information that is taken as real or that exists within a spectacular society. The mere existence of information is its truth, and petty squabbles about whether it is the whole truth or simply a part of it are misleading. To return to the example cited above: when television and newspapers showed G.W. Bush on the deck of the aircraft carrier dressed as a Navy aviator, the representation was neither true nor false, for representations are never true or false – only the statements made about them may have this property. Criticism of the media event could append various narratives to the image but only by seeing the event as information. However, it appeared not as information but as an event in the world. The eyes of the audience had already been well trained to see the image as a part of 'the show' (see Illich 2001). Any criticism or speculation would have to exist in a new relationship between the image and the media system that produced it, and so the media system could not contain or transmit the critique.

Another consequence is the loss of the physical world and a concomitant loss of the space in which human beings have traditionally met to argue, discuss, barter, and form the bases of a politics of the self within society. The self is now capable of (self) presentation largely isolated from the physical presence of other people. Thus, the range of social activities in which the self is implicated are shortened and the range of ethical and affective attachments are similarly diminished. The human race need not wait until it is superseded by artificial intelligence; the natural world both as a reality and as a testing ground for human realities has already been displaced, broken, and 'accidented' in the creation of people who inhabit virtual worlds, a plight anticipated in 1922 [1965] with the 'pictures in our heads' of Walter Lippmann.

There are those who believe that the truth will set them free in so far as they hold that a part of the liberal, Anglo-European project of a democratic society continues to revolve around the consensus about truth. These people erect websites discussing the news as if it described or accounted for real events in the world. The justification for this belief lies in the historical function and form of journalism. There are those on the other hand who use information primarily as a form of social control. They are unembarrassed by facts and a lack of narrative or historical consistency in their words. While many politicians and their minions have lied throughout recorded time, the legitimation of their lie seldom depended on the absolute mechanical control of the words that would constitute the public discussion. It is not that words reveal the truth, but that they create the social space within which people can contest for the truth of the world, that is they create the space of the public. This works only so long as society and the people within it are reified into objects in relationships that cannot provide human reciprocity or dialogue.

The soteriological function was originally applied to the social products of communication systems as early as the mid nineteenth century. As noted by L. Marx (1964), Carey (1989), Nye (1996), and as demonstrated in previous chapters, the early postal system was seen as heralding a new age of universal understanding and peace. As the telegraphic system developed, contemporary commentators wrote of the dawn of a new era of human understanding. Similar claims were made about the radio. Nascent electronic communications such as the telegraph and radio emerged into a world that still had one foot in the age of speaking and conversation between people. The salvation of the new technologies emerged from the naïve belief that these would amplify conversational functions. Certainly, 'the notion that communication, exchange, motion bring humanity enlightenment and progress, and that isolation and disconnection are obstacles to be overcome on this course' (Schivelbusch 1977: 188) are enduring beliefs of the modern age. Combined with an arrogant belief in their own moral, social, and intellectual superiority to all other nations, such persons might well believe that communications would create the great dialogue that would enable others to be convinced of truth. At best, however, the idea of these technologies provided a distorting mirror.

Belief in the civilizing virtue of communication technologies was less acceptable in the later twentieth century as the myth of progress was tarnished by two world wars and the new threat of near instant global annihilation. Television, for example, was deemed a cultural wasteland within a decade of its appearance in the US. However, with the rise of the internet and the web, the soteriological function returned. The promise of nearly unlimited access to information available to individual persons, combined with access to near instantaneous telecommunications, proved to be a heady combination. Virtual communities would make McLuhan's vision of the global village a reality at last. Freed from the gatekeeping and other limitations of corporate mass media, people would be free to create new communities based around localized inflections of discourse and language that might have little direct correlation to the mainstream or dominant discourses of their society.

The Critical Function: 'Are We at The Global Village Yet?'

The current political scene is online, and it is a modern, or postmodern, updating of the activities which gave rise to the early broadsheets and papers of the eighteenth century. Individual persons or small groups publish their thoughts, news compilations, and articles in blogs (weblogs), webpages, and listservers instead of on paper. However, a fundamental difference between the contemporary and the historical practices is that the current practice uses the existing language and discourses to create oppositional or subversive readings out of the dominant texts of newspapers, television, and so on. This is accomplished in various ways, but one practice of particular popularity is the gathering of diverse sources of information and the establishing of cross-linkages and cross-references. On the one hand, such activities seem very much like the academic practices of anthropology, textual analysis, and sociology as well as bearing some similarities to journalistic practices and intelligence analyses. On the other hand, however, such practices are often expressly political online, and they often seek to establish 'the truth' about current events or governmental actions. Other sites seek to explore contradictions, unanswered questions, and inconsistencies in official discourse. In the wake of 9–11 and the subsequent diminution of civil liberties in the UK and the US, as well as the invasions of Afghanistan and Iraq, information from various sources began to appear on websites offering alternative theories and explanations about contemporary events, particularly about hijackings and the destruction of the World Trade Center complex. Thus, in their development and application of cultural critique, such dissensions from the mainstream narratives show the emergence of a new set of cultural techniques that borrow in spirit, if not in substance, from the observations made 50 years ago by Adorno, Horkheimer, Habermas, Benjamin, and others.[8]

Officially dismissed as 'conspiracy theories' or 'revisionist histories', such alternative interpretations are perhaps the only meaningful responses to news organizations that have close ownership ties with defense contractors and other multinational companies. In the face of governments that hire public relations firms to manufacture public opinion and 'astroturf'[9] support for war,[10] the critical dimension of reflection can only exist outside the mainstream media. The invasion of Iraq highlighted the extent to which news coverage in the United States had become the voice of corporate and government interests. People may spend hours searching for information that is more credible, factual, or simply unavailable through conventional media sources such as newspapers and television. A case in point is the reported surge in hits on news websites in the UK during the 2003 American invasion against Iraq (Croad 2003). The UK journalist Robert Fiske, who reports on the Middle East for *The Independent,* notes that of the roughly 1000 letters he receives each week, almost half now come from the US, a condition that he describes as 'an indictment of the American media' (Fiske 2003).

Certainly, there are numerous possible and necessary criticisms of much of the mainstream media. The traditional gatekeeping and agenda setting functions of media have solidified into a near hegemonic totality in the US. Pro-government and pro-industry biases transform news reporting into a conduit for official pronouncements and propaganda. In a survey of television coverage of the invasion and war, FAIR (Fairness and Accuracy In Reporting) noted that:

> [J]ust 3 per cent of US sources represented or expressed opposition to the war. With more than one in four US citizens opposing the war and much higher rates of opposition in most countries where opinion was polled, none of the networks offered anything resembling proportionate coverage of anti-war voices. The anti-war percentages ranged from 4 per cent at NBC, 3 per cent at CNN, ABC, PBS and Fox, and less than 1 per cent – one out of 205 US sources – at CBS. (Rendall and Broughel 2003)

Other news stories such as the 'rescue' of US Private Jessica Lynch, and the fabrication of evidence for WMDs (Weapons of Mass Destruction) have proven to be less than accurate, and although some writers in the UK mainstream press have raised questions about the veracity of the reporting, little has appeared in the major US media outlets. Furthermore, when such reports have appeared in the US media, they typically appear as 'one-off' reports with no follow-up. A major point of contention has centered around inconsistencies in the official versions of the events of 11 September 2001.

Alternative narratives and histories arise in the face of totalizing information when the official narratives and histories cease to make sense. As argued in Chapter 2, the process of creating a vernacular language (and hence a vernacular history) is a critical one. Just as Socrates sought to establish a critical conscious break with the tribal mindset of Homeric Greece, the contemporary critical function seeks to create a position outside the mythic and outside the timelessly eternal half-truths and children's tales that make up much of the popular understanding of the world. Such activities constitute the resistance to power through the revealing of its invisibility and presence. They constitute saying no to the social demands to be something and assert a desire for a different identity in a different social milieu. In the creation of these counter-histories, such persons become authors, but their authorship differs from the usual understanding of the term. Their work is more critical than original in that it seeks to explore public discourse 'through its structure, its architecture, its intrinsic form, and the play of its internal relationships' (Foucault 1985: 103). Among these relationships are history, narrative consistency, and some reasonable fit with other descriptions of the world. Such authors work with an expectation that language still may function not as a replacement for the world but as an intermediary between the person and the world. As such, ideas such as truthful representation and historical consistency are still valid for them.

In a strange paradox, such critical thought is more socially and politically conservative than the mass of official discourse. The blogs, discussion groups, and archives recapitulate the old liberal space of the public in electronic form, and the ongoing problem of how to articulate such spaces with political and social action is being undertaken by groups such as MoveOn.org who transform the online activities into political actions within government through petitions, entreaties to contact congressional representatives, and so on.

Alternative and critical websites, as well as the motivation for people who visit them, are created in response to the centralization of news organizations and the banal similarity of their reporting. Among the services that these sites provide are the elaboration of news stories into counter-narratives and histories, preventing this moment's news from disappearing into the latest surge of words and images that follow and that erase all that went before from discussion and popular consciousness. Unanswered questions always arise to the critical mind that refuses to simply accept the official narratives. Numerous examples exist of absent or missing history. Labor struggles and the massacres, legal frame-ups, and repression of popular resistance are generally unknown within the popular social histories of the United States, and university students express disbelief or amazement upon hearing of them. This lack of understanding of the history and social structure of one's world is in turn a contributing factor to one's susceptibility to the reductive thinking of stereotypes and prejudices of all kinds. In 1956, C. Wright Mills wrote that:

> Each is trapped by his confining circle; each is cut off from easily identifiable groups. It is for people in such narrow milieux that the mass media can create a pseudo-world beyond, and a pseudo-world within themselves as well. (1956: 321)

The question yet remains as to whether or not alternative news sites, blogs, and other electronic forms of political expression contribute to the loss of a shared and lived social reality even as they create a virtual one.

Pornography, Addiction and Duplicity

One of the clearest places to witness the ascendance of a virtual reality over a physical one is in the realm of sex and sexuality. Sex is the medium of exchange for an increasing number of interactions both with the information world and with other persons. The motivation of sexual desire in advertising, in politics, and in everyday life has tended to compress all other forms of desire into one. The simultaneous social alienation of people from one another, the obscuring of historical social narratives, and the extreme promiscuity of information of all forms have effectively reduced the ways in which people may be together into those forms that articulate well with the overall levels of sexual desire required to maintain the consumer culture. Instead of possibilities as fractal and infinite as perception itself, the range of permissible experiences is overly small, narrowed either to the consumption of commodified culture or to the desire (equally commodified) for the displacement or indeed the temporary dissolution of self in the endless re-enactment of personal trauma (see Ballard 1990). Thus eros, which Augustine said leads people to god, appears as yet another set of signifiers, leading large numbers of people to the porn site catering to the particular taboo which speaks to their personal psychic trauma.

This is not to take a moral stand for or against erotica. However, pornographic use has been greatly facilitated by new technologies including cable television, VCRs, DVDs, and especially the internet. Adult movies also account for 90 per cent of pay-per-view revenue (Horn 2001). One industry executive said that 'the key to pay-per-view's popularity is the promise of anonymity for those who buy it'. 'The technology has helped us tremendously,' he says. 'It's very private now.' The privacy is what allows pornography to be used by persons who wish to fantasize about or observe sexual activities without others knowing, that is, separate from the ongoing social activities that would create meanings. The odium attached to sexual activity, and especially sexual activity outside traditional views of what Pharr (1993: 309) calls heterosexism, points toward the high levels of gendered and ideologically structured social policing that take place around sexual behavior.

Internet addiction is a curious but revealing example of how such management of sexual behavior operates: significations become decontextualized, freed from the moorings of their original positions in discourse. The signifiers walk through other domains until they are recontextualized in new settings. In the case of IAD (internet addictive disorder) the signifiers went from parody to pathology. The only ones who appreciated the humor were those who knew that the original use of the term was as a joke. The psychologist Dr Ivan Goldberg, who coined the term 'internet addictive disorder' (IAD) as a parody of the DSM-IV (APA 1994), said of his runaway appellation: 'It's all bullshit … There's no such thing as Internet addiction' (Brown 1996). However widespread might be the online use that causes distress either to the user or to others, the consumption of pornography is not the major purpose of internet use. Rather, e-mail, instant messaging, and accessing information are most commonly reported as the major activities for people online (see, for example, Telecommunications 2001).

Certainly, there are people who consume pornography to excess, but there are also those who watch television compulsively and engage in other activities to excess, though they do not have 'addictions'. Yet, pornography remains the great demon which must be contained for those who wish to exert controls on the internet. Addiction is a marker of pathology which indicates that the territory to which it is attached is under the control of any number of professionals, government agencies, and NGOs. As a signifier, 'addiction' reinscribes the threat of viewing pornography back into the discourses of drug addiction, as that which can be treated and so contained.

Private sexual behavior is also strongly policed, and the expectation of social disapproval may lead some to hide behavior that is outside the normative expectations. For example, the condemnation of male masturbation is indicated in the common use of pejorative terms such as 'wanker', 'tosser', and 'jerkoff'. While it is one thing to invoke a modicum of discretion toward the general public about one's sexual activities, it is another thing altogether to hide such activities from one's partner or spouse, yet this splitting is an activity that technology readily facilitates.

Let me be perfectly clear on this point. I am not suggesting that technology necessarily creates a culture of duplicity and deception; I am simply saying that the existence of two competing realms of reality creates the conditions and opportunities for a competition to exist between the claims of each world. It is important not to underestimate the role that the real interactions of people play in providing moral and psychological centers to our daily lives. For those persons whose positions and relationships in the world of non-mediated social relations are somewhat tenuous and contingent, the virtual holds out the promise of transgressing with minimal risk of detection or consequence.

One product available, History Kill, describes the following scenario on its webpage:

> Here you are surfing the web at work ... You have 3 web browser windows open that absolutely have nothing to do with work ... then suddenly ... Your BOSS walks in (or anyone else you don't want to see your screen) ... you instantly press the CTRL-SPACEBAR keys and all web browser windows hide immediately! ... Then when they leave you simply ... press the CTRL-SPACEBAR again and all your web browser windows will unhide!
> HistoryKill just saved your job!
> (http://www.historykill.com/bosskey.html)

Ignoring for a moment the fact that all accessed URLs as well as e-mail are available from the workplace server, let us consider the activity described in a social context: a person at work is sufficiently alienated from his employment that he decides to go websurfing. Note that in the scenario described, the surfer has three browser windows open simultaneously. This is not a simple task of looking up the price of shoes or checking on a sports score but a lengthy search for something which would have serious social consequences if the nature of it were known. Modern work is inherently alienating, and workers are sufficiently filled with anomie that this modernized form of 'slacking off' comes as no great surprise. While embarrassing to be caught wasting time, unless excessive, this is generally not a reason for being fired. It is not the pictures *per se* on the browser which cause damage or embarrassment, rather it is the reintroduction of the activity of this particular search back into the social. What is interesting here is the application of a technology, in this case software, to maintain the duplicitous self in a fiction with another person. Technology holds the interpersonal social at bay, protecting the digitally mediated social and its activities from scrutiny and discussion.

The duplicitous nature of this first example extends even further. Most employers have access to the URL records of their employees and can easily determine how long a person has been online and precisely which sites have been visited. Indeed, some recent dismissals of US academics and others in business have been proven in precisely this way. Dow Chemical dismissed 24 employees and disciplined 235 others for viewing or exchanging sexual or violent material (Shankland 2000), and according to a study conducted by the American Management Association over 42 per cent of firms surveyed routinely monitor the internet activities of all employees and over 32 per cent examine employee e-mail (AMA 2001). Some firms are even developing software using 'fuzzy logic' to analyze URL histories and determine automatically which sites are non-work related. According to Jason Dingley, a software developer in South Australia who was writing such a program, these are primarily pornographic sites. The ad copy in this example completely neglects to mention this means of tracking usage, suggesting that either this is not a concern to which they wish to alert the potential purchaser, as their product can do nothing about it, or the real duplicity is being perpetrated against someone who doesn't have access to URL records, such as a partner or spouse.

Deceiving a partner is condoned and tacitly supported in the advertising for a similar product. On this company's site, the advertising copy is even more explicit:

> You have just visited some compromising Web sites. You are aware of the fact that your Web browser has stored text and images from those sites in a special folder for quick viewing later (Internet Explorer's Temporary Internet Files or Netscape Navigator's cache). To hide your tracks, you use the Web browser's option to delete any temporary Internet files (or the cache) stored on your computer. Do you think you got rid of those compromising files? Think again! They are still on disk! Disk tools like Norton Utilities can easily recover those deleted files! You'd better start thinking: How am I going to explain to my boss (or worse: my wife) why I visited those sites? (http://165.121.190.90/page10.html)

This particular program is designed to 'scrub' data off the hard drive by repeatedly overwriting the deleted file areas on the drive, making any kind of recovery impossible.

Again, one finds the normalizing of deceit: 'How am I going to explain to my boss (or worse: my wife) why I visited those sites?' Placing this question in context, it is plain that this person is deeply implicated in relationships of deceit and mistrust. He (the masculine is explicitly given, overdetermining the gender of the audience) must cover up his surfing habits not from a casual observer but from someone who suspects deceit and is specifically looking for evidence of it, and in this example, the worst case is his wife. So even if one is deceiving his spouse and even if she is computer savvy enough to scan his hard drive cache directories for recently deleted files, his activity is still kept secret.

Originally this technology was developed for use by government agencies and some businesses having a perceived need permanently to remove data from a magnetic storage system such as a hard drive in such a way that the deleted material could never be recovered, reconstructed, or even inferred from magnetic traces left on the drive. Most importantly, the idea of History Kill and similar products, used in this way to deceive persons with whom one is supposedly emotionally close, suggests that the act of deceit itself is negated if the evidence is removed: no physical trace means no reality. The past, as that which actually happened, can be eliminated or altered by altering the information about that history. History itself becomes information.

The surfer caught by his wife would have to confront himself, his activities, and his deception at the same time. Thrust in this way back into the social, he would immediately be positioned within a variety of discourses. There is a freedom to be had in visiting porn sites, from interacting with other men in the exchange of pornography and information about it; it creates a boys' own world of adolescent masturbatory fantasy which, unfortunately for our surfer, conflicts with the activities, values, social situations, and relationships in which he is otherwise implicated. Further, it is precisely this highly sexualized climate which has led many women to file sexual harassment suits when presented with screen images, e-mails, and the like at the workplace and which has driven some to seek divorce or separation from their mates. However, the compelling need for secrecy does not derive necessarily from a need to ward off lawsuits. The surfer is not protecting himself against law so much as against exposure itself and the concomitant re-introduction of the social to this private world of internet activity. The secret self must be protected; rather as an alcoholic will deny and hide his or her drinking from significant others, so the deceptive websurfer must deny and hide his surfing habits. Because of the reprobation attached to pornography, and to some extent to masturbation, the need for secrecy arises even without an internet addictive disorder.

The world of digital information accessible over the internet or cable television is the social world recreated on terms of one's own choosing. Whatever appears on the screen is there because either one has stumbled upon it (a scandal in the original sense of the word) or else one has chosen to put it there. Much of the surfing which people would have protected, such as viewing pornographic materials, challenges the taboos which outline areas of profound psychic threat and risk of engulfment. Yet, it is not pornography *per se* that is the risk. The 'addiction' arises from the taboo. At each moment where the individual would escape into the alternative, taboo, virtual universe, a system of controls has emerged to check this trajectory of escape, and a concomitant set of escape devices has emerged to overcome the controls technologically. What elaborates is an unnecessarily complex game of cat and mouse which hides the larger issue. However, the game maintains the taboo, illuminating it clearly for all who follow.

As I noted from Dewey above, language does not exist in isolation. Even reading involves an interior dialogue. With much online material though, the dialogue is replaced by the process of 'interfacing' with the screen. Already established as a shameful and therefore necessarily private activity, the act of viewing pornography eliminates the social realm. What transpires is not meaningful in the usual sense of the word. Rather, it links direct gratification of desire, often through masturbation, with the projection of one's own psychic material into a space that is not quite imagination. The object of pornography does not transcend its given moment in time. It is fixed forever in the relationship with the viewer and for this reason is a fitting receptacle for various fantasies, expressed as libidinous, to be had free of the restraints of the real world. To imagine oneself free of worldly restraint creates not an escape from the content of the real so much as an escape from the form of the real, that is, its unpredictability and independence (see Sass 1992: 296–7). In this, the contemporary uses of pornography reconstruct at the level of the individual the social fixation with control, fixity, and objectification. It is a surveillance not of the self but of the world in which the self exists: filled with commodified, disembodied desire and alienating in its appearance. In this context, the virtuality of pornography is neither celebratory nor liberating but rather retraces an existing linkage between the individual person and the social domain of disembodied images.

The Digital Antinomian World

Contemporary forms of surveillance create hidden places, lacunae in the social world, that minimize or hide the position of the observing subject. In state surveillance, what is hidden is the subjectivity of the agents of the state. The social evil of covert state surveillance is revealed in the tendency of such systems to hide their own activities, ends, and purposes behind walls of 'national security' and state secrets. In pornography, the hidden is the subjective self enjoying its pleasures separate from other social contexts. The covert 'evil' of pornography is revealed in the using of it in separation from other social contexts. Here arises the digital antinomianism of the information age. Whatever one does in the domain of pure information is defensible because it is by definition divorced from connections with other discourses except those of one's own choosing. There is a collapse of the distinctions between the social and personal world of the individual as well as a collapse of the distinctions between the surveillance assemblage, other political institutions, and the public.

During the early days of the printed book, standard editions and identical texts helped to create a society of letters, of people who knew the same texts and who contemplated and discussed them (Eisenstein 1974). However, the works these people read were not the world, but were closer to conversations. Early readers, such as Montaigne, did not believe that the book mediated between themselves and the world. Rather, 'the object that books mediate for Montaigne is his isolated self' (Sherman 1996: 73). The book and the library allowed the self to meet itself in the act of reading and reflection. In the contemporary setting, reflection is eliminated by both the immediacy and the din of yet more unsolicited information.

State surveillance, whether surreptitious or overt, takes place in domains that are separable from other discourses. Power, at both the individual and the social levels, exists in the information world as a disconnection from historical, social narratives, histories, and especially from dialogue. In the place of dialogue is either the monologic drone of information or the solipsistic projection of one's desires into some image or text. That the projection of self into information focuses upon power is not surprising, especially in the case of the contemporary state. The modern state, despite politicians' protestations of deep religious convictions, exists without reference to anything except its ability to extend itself into the world and to take the place of god. The guiding philosophies of the state are now mechanistic expressions of capital and militarism; they provide no clear manifestations of their doctrine but rather obscure their *telos* behind secrecy, expediency, efficiency and the other virtues of modern life. This is not the absent or hidden god who fails to answer prayers, the *deus absconditas* who presents no evidence of himself. Rather, the transcendent order for the values of the modern state derive from the unknown god.

The digital antinomianism bears similarities to gnostic antinomianism. For example, information becomes real not through traditional systems of justifying truth but either through one's experience of it or through one's own *ad hoc* definitions. As the experience of information is secret, or at least private, there need not be any external validations or checks on this experience; reality testing is suspended because one knows on the one hand that this experience is only of information and on the other hand that it can be split off from other social domains. Similarly, the social 'archetypes', to use Eliade's term, no longer exist. All validation, reality, templates for thought, action, and self-identity exist only in the world of information. '"More and more information" should be understood as *"less and less absent information"* ' (Dupuy 1980: 16). There is no place to hide, no respite from the constant yammering of media and from the psychic invasion of one's engineered desire. Such private spaces as people can carve out for themselves for meditation, self-reflection, and intimate dialogue either have disappeared or are under assault from society itself. The sort of self-reflection in texts mentioned by Montaigne requires new feats of imaginative power and genuine creativity.

The writer Philip K. Dick, in his last trilogy of novels (and in some of his late interviews), put forward the idea of information as a living entity, a kind of contemporary gnostic Sophia which was alive as an entity and could be transmitted into people's minds. In the first novel of the trilogy *Valis*, Dick describes the lived confusion which results from the inability to attribute knowledge in a character's mind to information as a source. The protagonist is Horselover Fat, whose name is a cryptonym for Philip Dick. This character is torn by confusion, madness, grief, and is 'infected' with a living information.

Freed finally of all epistemological constraints, information itself becomes a character in Dick's novel and is free to move about through time and place, infecting people as they are exposed to it. Explicitly gnostic, Dick employs the writings of Edward Hussey, Will Durant, and Hans Jonas, and excerpts from the Nag Hammadi gnostic texts as well as various world mythologies, to recreate the myth of humanity fallen into ignorance, madness, and matter. The counterpoise and the salvation arise in the form of information and living knowledge. Dick writes:

> 'Living information?' His eyes fixed themselves in intent scrutiny of Fat.
> 'Living information,' he echoed. And then he said, 'The Logos.'
> Fat trembled.
> 'Yes,' Dr. Stone said. 'The Logos would be living information, capable of replicating.'
> 'Replicating not through information,' Fat said, 'in information, but *as* information.'
> (1981: 60)

In this story, which is to some extent autobiographical of Dick's own experience, Fat comes to know things without knowing whence the knowledge came. He and his friends encounter others who also have experienced this *logos*, the prime end of which is the same as the gnosis of the second century Christians: the liberation from confusion and delusion, which are synonymous with sin. In the book, the narrator ends up sitting before the TV screen, waiting for the next sign, the next message from god via the Hagia Sophia. With this image, Dick has neatly captured the world view of people who believe on some level that information can free them from the world in which they are implicated, that is, the world of accepted language and representation.

Conclusion

The characters in Philip K. Dick's novel finally understand the source of the information coming from the sky: it is the transmissions of alien civilizations. Behind the hidden messages of the television and the direct visions that they receive, the characters postulate a hypothetical other. In 'real life' the other that lies behind the information is the hidden truth, the lacunae in which reside both the hidden purpose of the information and the 'truth' about the world. The truth to which Dick's characters aspire, which would free them from the fascist state in which they live, is the communion with the alien civilizations. Similarly, the ancient gnostics believed that the physical world was created by the demiurge. The divine, namely god, lay beyond the world, separate from it, and one's knowledge of the divine was obstructed by the world. Only through a knowledge of the existence of the divine and of one's state of fallenness could one start on the path to freedom. It was this inner knowledge of the true state of the universe and of one's place in it that allowed the antinomian freedom to act outside merely moral or physical laws.

In the current situation, living in a world of information, some believe they possess the inner knowledge that the virtual world is the real, that consciousness and the world meet in unity within information. For such people, the physical, shared world into which they have fallen is less real than the information world. To escape from the fallenness into mere information, one requires a belief in something beyond and behind it. However, as information itself is the primary other of the world, information itself must provide the 'true' knowledge, that is, it conveys the truth about itself. This knowledge can be either the truth of one's desires or the truth of a higher good or some other belief. Access to the right information, or rather to the right form of information, reveals the truth and provides salvation from ignorance. Various deities, such as national security, power, the loss of self, and the state, provide their own versions of salvation, that is, that which will be achieved through correct knowledge. And as one is in pursuit of 'god' or 'the truth', armed with correct knowledge, all other orderings of the world, other explanations, and other values may be ignored with impunity.

A major part of the anthropomorphizing of the internet and of information in general derives from the philosophical move of positing the domain of information as in some way being equivalent with or even superior to the world. To hold the representation or even the processes of perceiving representation as the world itself transforms both the person and the world. Perhaps the amount of information and its complexity appear to the individual as something which has not been called forth: could one person be responsible for bringing what appears to the screen, that is, for bringing into being the multivarious world that appears? Must one not stand in awe of the new nature? Yet this construction proves ultimately solipsistic. If the world in which people live is the world that has been created for them through the assemblage of techniques, then an examination of the ordering of this world will reveal nothing about the 'real' world and a great deal about the world of information and technique.

The cosmologically ordered universe – that some could take to be the manifestation of and extension of the divine – has disappeared almost completely from contemporary society. The last vestiges are manifested in the fundamentalisms that continue to resurrect this or that version of a deity whose existence is demonstrably manifested only textually. Nowhere else in the orderings of the social world is there a correlation between the transcendent and the physical, despite numerous attempts by creationists in the United States to posit their textual version of the world against the scientific one. But the world is of a whole, and material science (alloyed with capital) is the ordering philosophy. If creationism could derive a way to produce physics or chemistry or engineering from its principles, then it might compete, but failing that task it fails to show its relevance in a world built upon these ideas.

The information society sets a new challenge regarding the ordering of the world and the subsequent derivation of values consistent with it. If it stands increasingly in the place of the real and must be treated as if it were the world, then this engineered electronic world must either reveal its order or allow people to acknowledge that the world of information admits of Descartes' evil deceiver. In the latter case, the information world is deliberately tricking people into believing that it reflects ontological truths about itself and about the universe, truths that it cannot present. Much of the history of Western civilization is, as Voegelin observed, the search for an order of the universe that is reflected in everyday life as well as in the philosophies of state and the structure of society. With the loss of the physical world, such a search is untenable, although the ancient forms continue to lurk about like orphaned ghosts.

Within six years of Nietzsche's declaration of the death of god in *The Gay Science* (1883), Andrew Carnegie, together with many theologians of the late nineteenth century, revealed the religion that had both killed the Christian god and would supersede it: the Gospel of Wealth through manufacturing. This new religion fit much more closely with the emerging world and its societies. Fusing characteristics of capital, the machine, consumption, production, and the alienated individuals who would inhabit that world, the new god was much more palatable than the old, and in the hands of advertisers, public relations consultants, propagandists, and ministers of all sorts, the new god would influence the shape and form of the emerging virtual world, but it could never be revealed through the virtual world.

Despite such attempts to structure its meaning, the world as information has no inherent hierarchy, no hidden order around which to model the social or to elaborate philosophy and law. The attempts to treat it as though it were the physical world, as in intellectual property and copyright law, for example, ignore the transient and evolving nature of the information world itself (see Lessig 2001). Information is ordered by the systems that create it, but our use of it is capable of occurring separate from the dominant orderings of the social. In the absence of a hierarchy of being, one is set free in a moral and semantic universe of his or her own design. Hans Jonas put it nicely:

> A universe without an intrinsic hierarchy of being ... leaves values ontologically unsupported, and the self is thrown back entirely upon itself in its quest for meaning and value. Meaning is no longer found but is 'conferred'. Values are no longer beheld in the vision of objective reality, but are posited as feats of valuation. As functions of the will, ends are solely my own creation. Will replaces vision; temporality of the act ousts the eternity of 'the good in itself'. (2001 [1958]: 323)

As a student of both Bultmann and Heidegger, Jonas was deeply concerned with negotiating the philosophical space arising when a world picture is presented in place of the world.

In state surveillance, the antinomian appears in the attempt to shape reality through the shaping of information and its interpretation. This is cosmic engineering. In the consumption of pornographic materials, in the emergence of digital selves from data bases, and in myriad other ways, the antinomian manifests itself in the closed world of desire projected into the image and the data. Throughout, the manufactured, second-order characteristics of the created society are obscured and hidden in the mythic ordering that everywhere replaces nature with culture (see Barthes 1972 [1958]). Such is the new gnosis of living in a manufactured world of information.

Scientia est potentia. Knowledge is power. This was the slogan of the Information Awareness Office run by DARPA in the US. The original logo of this organization depicted a flaming eye poised above a pyramid, casting its light on a globe of the world. This image is revealing, though it has since been discarded and replaced with corporate stylings and bureaucratic word salads. Antinomianism is characterized as a state of belief in which the norms of the non-spiritual world are not binding to one who is of the spirit, that is, to one who has the true belief or correct knowledge. Digital antinomianism is a state of belief in which the values and mores at variance with one's own are not binding on one who has access to the 'right' information. The antinomianism characteristic of one part of the experience of information arises from the rejection of the real, the rejection of the lifeworld of people and of the signifying processes of making meaning and identity in that world. Filled with the certainty of true knowledge, one can reject all normative values in favor of the higher good. He or she who obeys outside laws and norms has 'abdicated the authority of his self' (Jonas 2001 [1958]: 273). Living beyond mere subjectivism, the new gnostic has a metaphysical, psychological, and philosophical interest in 'repudiating allegiance to all objective norms and thus a motive for their outright violation' (2001 [1958]: 273). The new gnostics have little reason to invest in the creation of normative ideals that all could share, such as governed the *polis* of ancient Greece; they have no sense of 'the *nomoi* and *ēthea* of all' (see Chapter 2).

Information in its present avatar presents us with two distinct ways of beholding it. We may see it as a resource, that which we can call forth in a particular form to a particular end; or we may see it as a substitute for the world, a representation of it as a 'world picture'. The end is the same: a totalizing view of information. The *distanciation* of consciousness from the world through a highly mediated language and the fragmentation of the self necessitated by the divisions of labor and various refinements of desire have together positioned us in a precarious place. The great danger lies in believing that the world so brought before oneself, either as a resource or as a mistaken statement of value about the world, is the world in its totality. Such a belief presumes that the represented world operates in the same sphere of ontology as the considerably older, obdurate world.

We have accepted digital traces and their transformation as a semblance of the old physical universe, and we have invested totems of the new with such symbolic power that they seem to stand before us to demand their birthright. To deny them is to reassert the primacy of the physical, to return to the real, and to accept the communal activity of making meaning and knowledge in conversation with other people. Our task is to reassert the moral and philosophical necessity to find ourselves in self-reflection and dialogue, to create ourselves in the engagement with texts as if ideas, words, and symbols were still the bridges that consciousness builds to consciousness across the gulf of being. The mutual recognition of human consciousness as a primary perception and the claiming of our existence through the ongoing creation of language remain our first acts as moral and social beings as well as our best tests of reality.

Notes

1 Numerous important points of fact surrounding the events of 11 September 2001 continue to be unresolved. An examination of these points lies outside the scope of the present work, but many websites and books have explored the subject. For example, see
http://www.buzzflash.com/perspectives/911bush.html;
http://emperors-clothes.com/indict/911page.htm#1;
http://www.questionsquestions.net/;
http://www.whatreallyhappened.com/911_navbar.htm;
http://www.fromthewilderness.com/free/ww3/02_11_02_lucy.html.

2 People still negotiate media messages whenever the information they receive is too incongruous with their local knowledge to be integrated. Whenever possible, people tend to compare what they are told with what they believe to be true based on their experience (see Krug 1993). Of course, the opposite may happen as well. On the basis of news about the world, people may alter their beliefs about and relationships with others, in the same manner as Muslims and people of Middle Eastern appearance have been scapegoated in the US and UK following the 9–11 events. Negotiation works both ways.

3 In medieval education, the various skills for manipulating language were developed into art forms, grouped together as the *trivium*, and constituting one part of education. The trivium consisted of dialectics, rhetoric, and grammar. The trivium teaches how to orient relationships to others through language. The second area of education was the *quadrivium*, consisting of arithmetic, astronomy, geometry, and music. These are the second-order epistemologies for describing the nature of the physical universe. Traditionally, the practices from the trivium and the quadrivium have been referred to as arts, something made and therefore a technology, and together these constitute what the Romans would call the *ars liberalis*, the liberal arts.

4 Certainly people were excluded from the *agora* on the bases of gender, franchise, and so on, as those outside the linguistic community were also denied participation. The social model only worked within a limited and more or less well-defined sphere.

5 This same technique for selling music continues in an institutional form today with the preliminary publicizing of music on radio and television. The difference is that the sixteenth or seventeenth century purchaser would have to perform the music, while today music is more of a commodity to be consumed by electronic reproduction. If today purchasers perform music, it is more likely to be in a minimalist way, singing along or miming the playing of instruments.

6 I am indebted to Dr Mimi Marinucci for this observation.

7 Their description of the growth of the surveillant assemblage is remarkably close to the words of Jacques Ellul in describing the growth of technology in general. Haggerty and Ericson write that 'surveillance is driven by the desire to bring systems together, to combine practices and technologies and integrate them into a larger whole' (2000: 610).

8 It is perhaps partly for this reason that the conservative right in the US has recently begun a new propaganda campaign aimed at the 'Frankfurt School'. As is typical in such diatribe, the actual historical meanings or writings typically ascribed to this 'school' (for example, that it is 'Bolshevik') are never stated or engaged. Rather, it stands as a kind of bugbear threatening the mythic structure of America, the maintenance of which is the apparent goal of such persons. In this sense, the vilification of Horkheimer, Adorno, et al., is the replacement for the failed attempt to make 'liberal humanism' the great enemy of the mythic American past. William Lind of the Free Congress Foundation and Pat Buchanan are among the leaders of this attack.

9   Astroturf is used here to mean the manufactured 'public opinion' that masquerades as grassroots interest. See, for example, Beder (1998).
10   I refer here to the Kuwaiti hiring of Hill and Knowlton to build public support for the US counter-invasion of Kuwait. See, for example, Stauber and Rampton (1995).

References

ACLU (n.d.) Surveillance under the USA Patriot Act. Accessed from http://www.aclu.org/SafeandFree/SafeandFree.cfm?ID=12263&c=206 on 13 June 2003.

Adams, H. (1961 [1918]) *The Education of Henry Adams*. Boston: Houghton-Mifflin.

Adorno, T. (1991) *The Culture Industry*, ed. J.M. Bernstein. New York: Routledge.

Alland, A. (1993) *Jacob A. Riis: Photographer and Citizen*. New York: Aperture.

AMA (2001) *Workplace Testing: Monitoring and Surveillance. Summary of Key Findings*. American Management Association.

APA (1994) *Diagnostic and Statistical Manual of Mental Disorders*, 4th edn (DSM-IV). Washington, DC: American Psychiatric Association.

Arendt, H. (1958) *The Human Condition*. Chicago: University of Chicago Press.

Arnold, M. (1969 [1869]) *Culture and Anarchy*. London: Cambridge University Press.

Augé, M. (1995) *Non-Places: Introduction to an Anthropology of Supermodernity*, trans. John Howe. New York: Verso.

Austin, F. (2000) Letter writing in a Cornish community in the 1790s. In D. Barton and N. Hall (eds) *Letter Writing as Social Practice*. Philadelphia: Benjamins. pp. 43–61.

Bagdikian, B. (2000) *The Media Monopoly*, 6th edn. New York: Beacon.

Ballard, J.G. (1990) *The Atrocity Exhibition*. San Francisco: Re/Search.

Barlow, J. (1996). A declaration of independence of cyberspace. Accessed from www.eff.org/Misc/Publications/John_Perry_Barlow/barlow_0296.declaration on 2 January 2003.

Barnhurst, K. and Nerone, J. (2001) *The Form of News: a History*. New York: Guilford.

Barthes, R. (1970) *Writing Degree Zero*, trans. A. Lavers and C. Smith. Boston: Beacon.

Barthes, R. (1972 [1958]) *Mythologies*, trans. Annette Lavers. New York: Hill and Wang.

Baudrillard, J. (1981) *For a Critique of the Political Economy of the Sign*. St Louis, MO: Telos.

Baudrillard, J. (1983) *Simulations*. New York: Semiotext(e).

Baudrillard, J. (1990) *Fatal Strategies*. New York: Semiotext(e).

Bazerman, C. (2000) Letters and the social grounding of differentiated genres. In D. Barton and N. Hall (eds) *Letter Writing as Social Practice*. Philadelphia: Benjamins. pp. 15–29.

Beder, S. (1998) Public relations' role in manufacturing artificial grass roots coalitions. *Public Relations Quarterly* 43 (2): 21–3.

Bell, G. (1849) *Day and Night in the Wynds of Edinburgh*. Edinburgh: Johnstone and Hunter.

Benhabib, S. (1992) *Situating the Self: Gender, Community and Postmodernism in Contemporary Ethics*. Cambridge: Polity.

Benjamin, W. (1969) *Illuminations*, ed. Hanna Arendt, trans. Harry Zohn. New York: Schocken.

Benveniste, E. (1973) *Indo-European Language and Society*. Miami: University of Miami Press.

Bernard, J. (2001) London publishing 1640–1660: crisis, continuity and innovation. In E. Greenspan and J. Rose (eds) *Book History*. University Park, PA: Pennsylvania State University Press. pp. 1–16.

Blumer, H. (1933) *Movies and Conduct*. New York: Macmillan.

Blumer, H (1969) *Symbolic Interactionism: Perspective and Method*. Englewood Cliffs, NJ: Prentice Hall.

Boorman, S. (1986) Early music printing: working for a specialized market. In G. Tyson and S. Wagonheim (eds) *Print and Culture in the Renaissance: Essays on the Advent of Printing in Europe*. Newark, NJ: University of Delaware Press. pp. 222–45.

Bourdieu, P. (1977) *Outline of a Theory of Practice*. Cambridge: Cambridge University Press.

Bourdieu, P. (1990) *Photography: a Middle-Brow Art*, trans. Shaun Whiteside. Cambridge: Polity.

Bourdieu, P. (1991) *The Structural Transformation of the Public Sphere*, trans. Thomas Burger. Cambridge, MA: The MIT Press.

Briggs, A. and Burke, P. (2002) *A Social History of the Media: from Gutenberg to the Internet*. Cambridge: Polity.

Brown, J. (1996) BS Detector: 'Internet Addiction' meme gets media high. Accessed from www.wired.com/news/culture/0,1284,844,00.html on 3 December 1999.

Buchanan, P. (2001) Let the 'Ashcroft raids' begin. Accessed from http://www.townhall.com/columnists/patbuchanan/printpb20011112.shtml on 11 October 2003.

Buckland, G. (1974) *Reality Recorded: Early Documentary Photography*. London: David and Charles.

Burke, C. (1994) *Information and Secrecy: Vannevar Bush, Ultra, and the Other Memex*. Metuchen, NJ: Scarecrow.

Bush, V. (1945) As we may think. *The Atlantic Monthly*. July. Accessed from http://www.isg.sfu.ca/~duchier/misc/vbush/vbush-all.shtml on 14 January 2002.

Bush, V. (1949) *Modern Arms and Free Men: a Discussion of the Role of Science in Preserving Democracy*. New York: Simon and Schuster.

Carey, J.W. (1989) *Communication as Culture*. New York: Unwin.

Carruthers, M. (1990) *The Book of Memory: a Study of Memory in Medieval Culture*. Cambridge: Cambridge University Press.

Chartier, R. (1989) The practical impact of writing. In *A History of Private Life. Vol. III: Passions of the Renaissance*, trans. Arthur Goldhammer. Cambridge, MA: Belknap. pp. 111–59.

Chartier, R. (1995) *Forms and Meanings: Texts, Performances, and Audiences from Codex to Computer*. Philadelphia: University of Pennsylvania Press.

Chartier, R., Boureau, R. and Dauphin, C. (1997) *Correspondence: Models of Letter Writing from the Middle Ages to the Nineteenth Century*, trans. Christopher Woodall. Princeton, NJ: Princeton University Press.

Clanchy, M.T. (1979) *From Memory to Written Record*. Cambridge, MA: Harvard University Press.

Clarke, A.C. (1945) Extraterrestrial relays: can rocket stations give world-wide radio coverage? *Wireless World* October: 305–8.

Clarke, M.L. (1971) *Higher Education in the Ancient World*. London: Routledge and Kegan Paul.

Croad, E. (2003) US public turns to Europe for news. *Dot Journalism*. Accessed from http://www.journalism.co.uk/news/story576.html on 12 June 2003.

Daunton, M.J. (1985) *Royal Mail: the Post Office since 1840.* London: Athlone.

Daval, J. (1982) *Photography: History of an Art.* London: Macmillan.

Debord, G. (1990) *Comments on the Society of the Spectacle,* trans. Malcom Imrie. New York: Verso.

Debord, G. (1995) *The Society of the Spectacle,* trans. by Donald Nicholson-Smith. New York: Zone Books.

De Certeau, M. (1984) *The Practice of Everyday Life.* Berkeley, CA: University of California Press.

Deleuze, G. (1992) Postscript on the societies of control. *October,* 3–7.

Deleuze, G. and Guattari, F. (1987) *A Thousand Plateaus: Capitalism and Schizophrenia.* Minneapolis: University of Minnesota Press.

Denzin, N.K. (1989) *Interpretive Interactionism.* Newbury Park, CA: Sage.

Denzin, N.K. (1991) *Images of Postmodern Society.* Newbury Park, CA: Sage.

Denzin, N.K. (1992) *Symbolic Interactionism and Cultural Studies.* Oxford: Blackwell.

Denzin, N.K. (1995) *The Cinematic Society: the Voyeur's Gaze.* London: Sage.

Derrida, J. (1972) *Dissemination.* Chicago: University of Chicago Press.

Derrida, J. (1976) *Of Grammatology.* Baltimore: Johns Hopkins University Press.

Devereux, G. (1980) *Basic Problems of Ethnopsychiatry,* trans. Basia Miller Gulati and George Devereux. Chicago: University of Chicago Press.

Dewey, J. (1985a [1916]) *Democracy and Education.* Carbondale, IL: Southern Illinois University Press.

Dewey, J. (1985b [1927]) *The Public and Its Problems.* Athens, OH: Swallow.

Dick, P.K. (1981) *Valis.* New York: Vintage.

Dick, P.K. (1995) *The Shifting Realities of Phillip K. Dick,* ed. L. Sutin. New York: Vintage.

Dierks, K. (2000) The familiar letter and social refinement in America, 1750–1800. In D. Barton and N. Hall (eds) *Letter Writing as Social Practice.* Philadelphia, PA: John Benjamins Publishing Company. pp. 31–42.

Ditz, T.L. (1999) Formative ventures: eighteenth century commercial letters and the articulation of experience. In R. Earle (ed.) *Epistolary Selves: Letters and Letter Writers, 1600–1945.* Aldershot: Ashgate. pp. 59–78.

Dumouchel, P. (1992) A morphogenetic hypothesis. In F.J. Varela and J.-P. Dupuy (eds) *Understanding Origins: Contemporary Views on the Origin of Life, Mind, and Society.* London: Kluwer.

Dupuy, P. (1980) Myths of the informational society. In K. Woodward (ed.) *The Myths of Information.* Madison, WI: Coda.

Edwards, P. (1996) *The Closed World: Computers and the Politics of Discourse in Cold War America.* Cambridge, MA: The MIT Press.

Egan, T. (2000) Technology sent Wall Street into market for pornography. *The New York Times* 23 October

Eisenhower, D.D. (1961) 'Farewell radio and television address to the American people', accessed from http://www.eisenhower.utexas.edu/farewell.htm, on 12 Jan 2004.

Eisenstein, E. (1974) The advent of printing and the Protestant revolt: a new approach to Western Christendom. In R.M. Kingdon (ed.) *Transition and Revolution: Problems and Issues of European Renaissance and Reformation History.* Madison, WI: University of Wisconsin Press. pp. 235–70.

Eisenstein, E. (1979) *The Printing Press as an Agent of Change: Communications and Cultural Transformations in Early Modern Europe,* 2 vols. New York: Cambridge University Press.

Eisenstein, E. (1984) *The Printing Revolution in Early Modern Europe*. Cambridge: Cambridge University Press.

Eliade, M. (1954) *The Myth of the Eternal Return: or Cosmos and History*, trans. Willard Trask. Princeton, NJ: Princeton University Press.

Ellul, J. (1966) *The Technological Society*, trans. J. Wilkinson. New York: Vintage.

Ellul, J. (1980) *The Technological System*. New York: Continuum.

Engelsing, R. (1973) *Analphabetentum und Lektüre; zur Sozialgeschichte des Lesens in Deutschland zwischen feudaler und industrieller Gesellschaft*. Stuttgart: Metzler.

Exon, J., Senator (1995) Remarks on the Communication Decency Act. Congressional Record 9 June 1995 (Senate), pp. S8087–92. Accessed from http://www.epic.org/cda/exon_remarks.html.

Faulkner, W. (1950) Nobel Prize acceptance speech. Accessed from www.nobel.se/literature/laureates/1949/faulkner-speech.html on 12 July 2004.

Febvre, L. and Martin, H.-J. (1976) *The Coming of the Book: the Impact of Printing 1450–1800*, trans. David Gerard. London: NLB.

Fiske, J. (1989) *Understanding Popular Culture*. New York: Routledge.

Fiske, R. (2001) The wickedness and awesome cruelty of a crushed and humiliated people. *The Independent* 12 September.

Fiske, R. (2003) Covering the Middle East: an interview with Robert Fiske. Accessed from http://www.zmag.org/content/showarticle.cfm?SectionID=36&ItemID=3699 on 12 June 2003.

Foisil, M. (1989) The literature of intimacy. In *A History of Private Life. Vol. III: Passions of the Renaissance*, trans. Arthur Goldhammer. Cambridge, MA: Belknap. pp. 327–61.

Foucault, M. (1970) *The Order of Things: an Archeology of the Human Sciences*. London: Routledge.

Foucault, M. (1980) *Power/Knowledge: Selected Interviews and Other Writings, 1972–1977*, ed. Colin Gordon. New York: Pantheon.

Foucault, M. (1984) What is an author? In P. Rabinow (ed.) *The Foucault Reader*. New York: Pantheon. pp. 101–20.

Foucault, M. (1988) Technologies of the self. In L. Martin, H. Gutman and P. Hutton (eds) *Technologies of the Self*. Amherst, MA: University of Massachusetts Press.

Geddes, P. (1968 [1915]) *Cities in Evolution: an Introduction to the Town Planning Movement and to the Study of Civics*. London: Benn.

Gernshein, H. and Gernshein, A. (1956) *L.J.M. Daguerre: the History of His Diorama and the Daguerreotype*. London: Escher and Warburg.

Giddens, A. (1972) *Émile Durkheim: Selected Writings*. London: Cambridge University Press.

Giddens, A. (1991) *Modernity and Self-Identity: Self and Society in the Late Modern Age*. Stanford, CA: Stanford University Press.

Giedion, S. (1970) *Mechanization Takes Command: a Contribution to Anonymous History*. New York: Oxford University Press.

Gilmore, W.J. (1989) *Reading Becomes a Necessity of Life: Material and Cultural Life in Rural New England, 1780–1835*. Knoxville, TN: The University of Tennessee Press.

Girvetz, Harry K. (1966) *The Evolution of Liberalism*. New York: Collier.

Gottlieb, B. (1993) *The Family in the Western World: from the Black Death to the Industrial Age*. New York: Oxford University Press.

Graham, I. (1999) Blinded by smoke: the hidden agenda of the net censorship bill 1999. Accessed from http://libertus.net/liberty/blnded.html on 2 July 2004.

Habermas, J. (1991) *The Structural Transformation of the Public Sphere*, trans. Thomas Burger. Cambridge, MA: MIT Press.

Haggerty, K.D. and Ericson, R.V. (2000) The surveillant assemblage. *British Journal of Sociology* 51 (4): 605–22.

Halévy, E. (1955) *The Growth of Philosophic Radicalism*, trans. Mary Morris. Boston: Beacon.

Hall, D.D. (1996) *Cultures of Print: Essays in the History of the Book*. Amherst, MA: University of Massachusetts Press.

Hall, N. (2000) The materiality of letter writing. In D. Barton and N. Hall (eds) *Letter Writing as Social Practice*. Philadelphia: Benjamins. pp. 83–108.

Hall, S. (1980) Encoding/decoding. In Michael Gurevitch et al. (eds) *Culture, Media, Language*. New York: Methuen.

Haraway, D.J. (1991) *Simians, Cyborgs, and Women: the Reinvention of Nature*. New York: Routledge.

Harker, M.P. (1988) *Henry Peach Robinson: Master of Photographic Art 1830–1901*. Oxford: Blackwell.

HARP (2002) Human Augmentation of Reasoning through Patterning. Statement of Work. Air Force Research Laboratory, Rome Research Site, Rome, New York. Accessed from Electronic Privacy Information Center at http://www.epic.org/foia_docs/tia_contractors/harp_sow.pdf on 22 August 2003.

Harris, W.V. (1989) *Ancient Literacy*. Cambridge, MA: Harvard University Press.

Havelock, E.A. (1963) *Preface to Plato*. Oxford: Blackwell.

Havelock, E.A. (1976) *Origins of Western Literacy*. Toronto: Ontario Institute for Studies in Education.

Havelock, E.A. (1982) *The Literate Revolution in Greece and Its Cultural Consequences*. Cambridge, MA: Harvard University Press.

Havelock, E.A. (1986) *The Muse Learns to Write*. New Haven, CT: Yale University Press.

Hebdige, D. (1979) *Subcultures: the Meaning of Style*. New York: Methuen.

Heidegger, M. (1977) *The Question Concerning Technology and Other Essays*, trans. William Lovitt. New York: Harper and Row.

Hillman, J. (1989) 'Terrorism', in J. Hillman *A Blue Fire*. Edited by Thomas More. New York: Harper and Row, pp. 185–7.

Hoggart, R. (1957) *Uses of Literacy*. New York: Penguin Books.

Home, S. (1991) *The Assault on Culture: Utopian Currents from Lettrisme to Class War*. Stirling: AK Press.

Horn, D. (2001) Home is where the porn is. *The Cincinnati Enquirer* 13 May. Accessed from http://www.enquirer.com/editions/2001/05/13/loc_home_is_where_porn.html on 12 January 2002.

Houston, R.A. (1988) *Literacy in Early Modern Europe: Culture and Education 1500–1800*. New York: Longman.

Hudson, N. (1994) *Writing and European Thought, 1600–1830*. Cambridge: Cambridge University Press.

Hughes, R. (1991) *The Shock of the New*. London: Thames and Hudson.

Husserl, E. (1962 [1931]) *Ideas: General Introduction to Pure Phenomenology*, trans. W.R. Boyce Gibson. New York: Collier.

Hussey, E. (1972) *The Presocratics*. Indianapolis: Hacket.

Illich, I. (1973) *Tools for Conviviality*. New York: Harper Colophon.

Illich, I. (1985) *H_2O and the Waters of Forgetfulness*. Berkeley, CA: Heyday.

Illich, I. (1992) *In the Mirror of the Past: Lectures and Addresses, 1978–1990*. London: Boyars.

Illich, I. (1993) *In the Vineyard of the Text: a Commentary to Hugh's Didascalion*. Chicago: University of Chicago Press.

Illich, I. (2001) Guarding the eye in the age of the show. Accessed from http://homepage.mac.com/tinapple/illich/2001_guarding_the_eye.PDF on 12 July 2004.

Illich, I. and Sanders, B. (1988) *ABC: the Alphabetization of the Popular Mind*. New York: Vintage.

Innis, H.A. (1950) *Empire and Communications*. Oxford: Clarendon.

Innis, H.A. (1951) *The Bias of Communication*. Toronto: University of Toronto Press.

Jammes, A. and Janis, E.P. (1983) *The Art of the French Calotype*. Princeton, NJ: Princeton University Press.

Jansen, S.C. (1988) *Censorship: the Knot that Binds Power and Knowledge*. New York: Oxford University Press.

John, R.R. (1995) *Spreading the News: the American Postal System from Franklin to Morse*. Cambridge, MA: Harvard University Press.

Johns, A. (1998) *The Nature of the Book*. Chicago: University of Chicago Press.

Jonas, H. (2001 [1958]) *The Gnostic Religion: the Message of an Alien God and the Beginnings of Christianity*. Boston: Beacon.

Kaster, R.A. (1988) *Guardians of Language: the Grammarian and Society in Late Antiquity*. Berkeley, CA: University of California Press.

Kern, S. (1983) *The Culture of Time and Space, 1880–1915*. Cambridge: Harvard University Press.

Kernan, A. (1987) *Samuel Johnson and the Impact of Print*. Princeton, NJ: Princeton University Press.

Kitchen, P. (1975) *A Most Unsettling Person: an Introduction to the Life and Ideas of Patrick Geddes*. London: Gollancz.

Klein, N. (2002) *No Logo*. New York: Picador.

Korzybski, A. (1980 [1933]) *Science and Sanity*. Lakeville, CT: The International Non-Aristotelian Library Publishing Company.

Kovel, J. (1981) *The Age of Desire: Case Histories of a Radical Psychoanalyst*. New York: Pantheon.

Kraus, K. (1984) In these great times. In Harry Zohn (ed.) *XXX*. Manchester: Carcanet Press Limited.

Kroker, A. (1984) *Technology and the Canadian Mind*. New York: St Martin's.

Krug, G.J. (1993a) The day the earth stood still: rumor and society in the Arkansas earthquake. *Critical Studies in Mass Communication* 10 (3): 273–85.

Krug, G.J. (1993b) Visual ethnographies and the postmodern self: reflections on aesthetics and meta-text. *Studies in Symbolic Interactionism 14*. Greenwich, CT: JAI. pp. 63–73.

Krug, G.J. (2001) At the feet of the master: three stages in the appropriation of Okinawan karate into Anglo-American culture. *Cultural Studies: Critical Methodologies* 1 (4): 395–410.

Kuhn, T. (1970) *The Structure of Scientific Revolutions*, 2nd edn. Chicago: University of Chicago Press.

Lardner, G. and Kurtz, H. (2000) Democrats: Bush let guard down. *The Washington Post* 3 November: A22.

Lassam, R. (1979) *Fox Talbot: Photographer*. Tisbury: Compton.

Lerner, D. (1958) *The Passing of Traditional Society*. New York: Free.

Le Saux, F. (1966) Listening to the manuscript: Editing Lazamon's *Brut*. In Pilch, H. (ed.) *Orality and Literacy in Early Middle English*. Tubingen: Gunter Narr Verlag. pp. 11–20.

Lessig, L. (2001) *The Future of Ideas*. New York: Random House.

Levin, M.B. (1971) *Political Hysteria in America: the Democratic Capacity for Repression*. New York: Basic.

Levinson, P. (1997) *The Soft Edge: a Natural History and Future of the Information Revolution*. London: Routledge.

Levy, P. (1998) *Becoming Virtual: Reality in the Digital Age*, trans. Robert Bononno. New York: Plenum.

Lewis, J., Jhally, S. and Morgan, M. (1991) The Gulf War: a study of the media, public opinion and public knowledge. The Center for the Study of Communication, Department of Communication, University of Massachusetts–Amherst. Accessed from http://www-unix.oit.umass.edu/~commdept/resources/gulfwar.rpt on 10 August 2003.

Lippmann, W. (1965 [1922]) *Public Opinion*. New York: The Free Press.

Lord, A. (1960) *The Singer of Tales*. Cambridge, MA: Harvard University Press.

Luhman, N. (2000) *The Reality of the Mass Media*, trans. Kathleen Cross. Stanford, CA: Stanford University Press.

Magnusson, M. (2000) *Scotland: the Story of a Nation*. London: Harper Collins.

Manville, P.B. (1990) *The Origins of Citizenship in Ancient Athens*. Princeton, NJ: Princeton University Press.

Marx, G.T. (1986) The iron fist and the velvet glove: totalitarian potentials within democratic structures. In J.E. Short Jr (ed.) *The Social Fabric: Dimensions and Issues*. Beverly Hills, CA: Sage.

Marx, L. (1964) *The Machine in the Garden*. New York: Oxford University Press.

Mattelart, A. (1996) *The Invention of Communication*, trans. Simon Emanuel. Minneapolis: University of Minnesota Press.

McChesney, R. (1997) *Telecommunications, Mass Media and Democracy*. New York: Oxford University Press.

McGuigan, J. (1996) *Culture and the Public Sphere*. New York: Routledge.

McKeon, M. (1987) *The Origins of the English Novel 1600–1800*. Baltimore: Johns Hopkins University Press.

McKitterick, R. (1989) *The Carolingians and the Written Word*. Cambridge: Cambridge University Press.

McLuhan, M. (1964) *Understanding Media: the Extensions of Man*. New York: McGraw-Hill.

Mead, G.H. (1962 [1934]) *Mind, Self and Society*. Chicago: University of Chicago Press.

Meier, C. (1990) *The Greek Discovery of Politics*, trans. David McLintock. Cambridge, MA: Harvard University Press.

Meller, H. (1990) *Patrick Geddes: Social Evolutionist and City Planner*. London: Routledge.

Merleau-Ponty, M. (1962) *Phenomenology of Perception*, trans. Colin Smity. London: Routledge and Kegan Paul.

Mill, J.S. (1987 [1859]) *On Liberty*. New York: Viking Penguin.

Millbank, D. (2003) Explanation for Bush's carrier landing altered. *The Washington Post* 7 November: A20.

Mills, C.W. (1956) *The Power Elite*. New York: Oxford University Press.

Montaigne, M. (1952) *The Essays*, ed. W. Carew Hazlitt, trans. Charles Cotton. Chicago: William Benton.

Moore, R.L. (2003) *Touchdown Jesus: the Mixing of Sacred and Secular in American History*. Louisville, KY: Westminster John Knox.

Morris, G. (1996) Public enemy: Warner Brothers in the pre-code era. *Bright Lights Film Journal*. Accessed from http://www.brightlightsfilm.com/17/04b_warner. html.

Mowery, D.C. (1997) The Bush Report after fifty years: blueprint or relic? In C.E. Barfield (ed.) *Science for the Twenty-first Century: The Bush Report Revisited*. Washington, DC: AEI Press. pp. 24–41.

Mumford, L. (1952) *Art and Technics*. London: Oxford University Press.

Mumford, L. (1963 [1934]) *Technics and Civilization*. New York: Harcourt Brace.

Mumford, L. (1964) *The Pentagon of Power: Volume Two of the Myth of the Machine*. New York: Harcourt, Brace, Jovanovich.

Munsterberg, H. (1916) *The Photoplay: a Psychological Study*. New York: Appleton.

Nie, N.H. and Erbing, L. (2000) Internet and society: a preliminary report. Stanford Institute for the Quantitative Study of Society. Accessed from http://www.stanford. edu/group/siqss/Press_Release/press_release.html on 12 September 2002.

Niskanen, W. (1997) R&D and economic growth: cautionary thoughts. In C.E. Barfield (ed.) *Science for the Twenty-first Century: the Bush Report Revisited*. Washington, DC: AEI. pp. 81–94.

Noble, D. (1984) *Forces of Production: Social History of Industrial Production*. Oxford: Oxford University Press.

Noble, D. (1993) *Progress without People: in Defense of Luddism*. Chicago: Kerr.

Nye, D. (1996) *The Technological Sublime*. Cambridge, MA: MIT Press.

Nye, D.E. (1997) *Narratives and Spaces: Technology and the Construction of American Culture*. New York: Columbia University Press.

O'Donnell, J.J. (1998) *Avatars of the Word: from Papyrus to Cyberspace*. Cambridge, MA: Harvard University Press.

Olson, D.R. (1994) *The World on Paper: the Conceptual and Cognitive Implications of Writing and Reading*. Cambridge: Cambridge University Press.

Ortega y Gasset, J. (1966) *Mission of the University*, trans. Howard L. Nostrand. New York: W.W. Norton and Company, Inc.

Ostrander, G.M. (1970) *American Civilization in the First Machine Age: 1890–1940*. New York: Harper and Row.

Ovenden, R. (1997) *John Thomson (1837–1921): Photographer*. Edinburgh: National Library of Scotland.

Parry, A. (ed.) (1971) *The Making of Homeric Verse: the Collected Papers of Millman Parry*. Oxford: Clarendon.

Pharr, S. (1993) Homophobia: a weapon of sexism. In A. Jagger and P. Rothenberg (eds) *Feminist Frameworks*. New York: McGraw-Hill.

Pöksen, U. (1995) *Plastic Words: the Tyranny of a Modular Language*, trans. Jutta Mason and David Cayley. University Park, PA: Pennsylvania State University Press.

Polanyi, K. (1957) *The Great Transformation*. Boston: Beacon.

Poster, M. (1995) Cyberdemocracy: internet and the public sphere. Accessed from http://www.hnet.uci.edu/mposter/writings/democ.html.

Preston, W.J. (1963) *Aliens and Dissenters: Federal Suppression of Radicals, 1903–1933*. Cambridge: Harvard University Press.

Pryce, H. (1998) *Literacy in Medieval Celtic Societies*. Cambridge: Cambridge University Press.

Putnam, R.D. (2000) *Bowling Alone: the Collapse and Revival of American Community*. New York: Simon and Schuster.

Raven, J., Small, H. and Tadmor, N. (eds) (1996) *The Practice and Representation of Reading in England*. Cambridge: Cambridge University Press.

Ray, R.B. (1985) *A Certain Tendency of the Hollywood Cinema, 1930–1980*. Princeton, NJ: Princeton University Press.

Rendall, S. and Broughel, T. (2003) Amplifying officials, squelching dissent. *Extra Online* May/June 2003. Accessed from http://www.fair.org/extra/0305/ warstudy.html on 19 June 2003.

Report on Regulation of Computer On-Line Services Part 2 (1995) Senate Select Committee on Community Standards Relevant to the Supply of Services Utilizing Electronic Technologies. Accessed from http://www.aph.gov.au/senate/committee/ comstand_ctte/online2/index.htm.

Rheingold, H. (1993) *Virtual Communities*. New York: Addison Wesley.

Rheingold, H. (1996) Democracy is about communication. Accessed from http://www.well.com/user/hlr/texts/democracy.html on 2 July 2004.

Ricoeur, P. (1981) The hermeneutical function of distanciation. In John Thompson (ed.) *Paul Ricoeur: Hermeneutics and the Human Sciences*. Cambridge: Cambridge University Press.

Rilke, R.M. (1977) *Ausgewählte Gedichte*. Frankfurt am Main: Suhrkamp.

Robinson, H. (1948) *The British Post Office: a History*. Princeton, NJ: Princeton University Press.

Rossi, P. (2000) *Logic and the Art of Memory: the Quest for a Universal Language*, trans. Stephen Clucas. London: Athlone.

Rouse, R.H. and Rouse, M.A. (1986) Bibliography before print. In P. Ganz (ed.) *The Role of the Book in Medieval Culture: Proceedings of the Oxford International Symposium*. Turnhout: Brepols. pp. 133–53.

Ryle, G. (1984) *The Concept of Mind*. Chicago: University of Chicago Press.

Saenger, P. (1997) *Space Between Words: the Origins of Silent Reading*. Palo Alto, CA: Stanford University Press.

Sass, L.A. (1992) *Madness and Modernism: Insanity in the Light of Modern Art, Literature, and Thought*. Cambridge, MA: Harvard University Press.

Saul, J.R. (1992) *Voltaire's Bastards: the Dictatorship of Reason in the West*. New York: Penguin.

Schaff, L.J. (1996) *Records of the Dawn of Photography: Talbot's Notebooks P and Q*. Cambridge: Cambridge University Press.

Scherpe, K. (1987) Dramatization and de-dramatization of 'the end': the apocalyptic consciousness of modernity and post-modernity. *Cultural Critique* 5 (Winter 1986–1987): 95–129.

Schramm, W. (1964) *Mass Media and National Development*. Stanford, CA: Stanford University Press.

Schivelbusch, W. (1977) *The Railway Journey*. Berkeley, CA: University of California Press.

Shankland, S. (2000) Dow Chemical fires 24 in email controversy. CNET News.com. Accessed from http://news.cnet.com/news/0-1007-200-2787458. html.

Shapin, S. (1994) *A Social History of Truth: Civility and Science in Seventeenth-Century England*. Chicago: University of Chicago Press.

Sherman, W.H. (1996) The place of reading in the English Renaissance: John Dee revisited. In J. Raven, H. Small and N. Tadmor (eds) *The Practice and Representation of Reading in England*. Cambridge: Cambridge University Press. pp. 62–76.

Shotter, J. (1993) *Cultural Politics and Everyday Life*. Buckingham: Open University Press.

Stallybrass, P. and White, A. (1984) *The Politics and Poetics of Transgression*. Ithaca, NY: Cornell University Press.

Stanley, M. (1978) *The Technological Conscience: Survival and Dignity in an Age of Expertise*. Chicago: University of Chicago Press.

Stauber, J. and Rampton, S. (1995) How PR sold the war in the Persian Gulf. Accessed from http://www.prwatch.org/books/tsigfy10.html on 10 January 2003.

Tadmore, N. (1996) 'In the even my wife read to me': women, reading and household life in the eighteenth century. In J. Raven, H. Small and N. Tadmor (eds) *The Practice and Representation of Reading in England*. Cambridge: Cambridge University Press. pp. 162–76.

Teeter, D.L., Le Duc, D.R, and Nelson, H.L. (1989) *Law of Mass Communications*, 6th edn. Westbury, NY: Foundation Press.

Telecommunications (2001) *Telecommunications: Characteristics and Choices of Internet Users*. GAO 01–345.Washington, DC: Government Accounting Office.

Thomas, R. (1992) *Literacy and Orality in Ancient Greece*. Cambridge: Cambridge University Press.

Thomson, R.M. (1986) The Norman Conquest and English libraries. In P. Ganz (ed.) *The Role of the Book in Medieval Culture: Proceedings of the Oxford International Symposium*. Turnhout: Brepols. pp. 27–40.

Travis, A. (2000) Cock-up and cover-up. The *Guardian* 13 September. Accessed from http://www.guardian.co.uk/Archive/Article/0,4273,4062942,00.html.

Travis, A. (2001) Anti-terror bill damned for catch-all powers. The *Guardian* 14 November. Accessed from http://www.guardian.co.uk/guardianpolitics/story/0,3605,593051,00.html on 22 January 2002.

Turkle, S. (1995) *Life on the Screen: Identity in the Age of the Internet*. New York: Simon and Schuster.

Turkle, S. (1998) Drag net. *The Utne Reader* September–October: 51–5.

Turner, B.S. (1990) The interdisciplinary curriculum: from social medicine to postmodernism. *Sociology of Health and Illness* 12 (1): 1–23.

Van Ham, P. (2001) The rise of the brand state. *Foreign Affairs* 80 (5): 2–6.

Veblen, T. (1978 [1904]) *The Theory of Business Enterprise*. New Brunswick, NJ: Transaction.

Virilio, P. (1986) *Speed and Politics*. New York: Semiotext(e).

Virilio, P. (1989) *War and Cinema: the Logistics of Perception*. New York: Verso.

Virilio, P. (1991) *The Aesthetic of Disappearance*. New York: Semiotext(e).

Virilio, P. (1994) Cyberwar, god and television. Interview with Paul Virilio by L. Wilson. *CTHEORY Electronic Journal* 21 October.

Virilio, P. (1997) *Open Sky*, trans. Julie Rose. London: Verso.

Virilio, P. (2000) *The Information Bomb*, trans. Chris Turner. London: Verso.

Voegelin, E. (1987) *Order and History. Volume Five: in Search of Order*. Baton Rouge, LA: Louisiana State University Press.

Voegelin, E. (1989) *Modernity Without Restraint*. The Collected Works of Eric Voegelin, vol. 5. Columbia, MO: University of Missouri Press.

Walker, A. (1976 [1866]) Wealth and the division of labor. In *The Science of Wealth: A Manual of Political Economy*, Boston 1866. Reprinted in *The Annals of America. Vol. 10. 1866–1883. Reconstruction and Industrialization*. Chicago: Encyclopeadia Britannica. pp. 66–73.

Ward, J. and Stevenson, S. (1986) *Printed Light: the Scientific Art of William Henry Fox Talbot and David Octavius Hill with Robert Adamson*. Edinburgh: Scottish National Portrait Gallery.

Watt, I. (2000 [1957]) *The Rise of the Novel*. London: Pimlico.

Weiner, N. (1954) *The Human Uses of Human Beings*. New York: Avon.

Whyman, S. (1999) *Sociability and Power in Late-Stuart England: the Cultural World of the Verneys, 1660–1720*. Oxford: Oxford University Press.

Wilkerson, K.E. (1994) From hero to citizen: persuasion in early Greece. In Edward Schiappa (ed.) *Landmark Essays on Classical Greek Rhetoric*, vol. 3. Davis, CA: Hermagoras Press. pp. 17–34.

Williams, J.H. (1999) *The Significance of the Printed Word in Early America: Colonists' Thoughts on the Role of the Press*. Westport, CT: Greenwood.

Williams, R. (1983) *Keywords*. New York: Oxford University Press.

Winner, L. (1985) Do artifacts have politics? In D. MacKenzie and J. Wajcmon (eds) *The Social Shaping of Technology*. Buckingham: Open University Press.

Wyman, L.C. (1952) *The Sandpaintings of the Kayenta Navaho*. Albuquerque, NM: University of New Mexico Press.

Wyman, L.C. (1983) *Southwest Indian Drypainting*. Albuquerque, NM: University of New Mexico Press.

Zachary, G.P. (1997) *Endless Frontier, Vannevar Bush: Engineer of the American Century*. New York: The Free Press.

Zirker, M.R. Jr (1966) Richardson's correspondence: the personal letter as private experience. In H. Anderson, P.B. Daghalian and I. Ehrenpreis, I. (eds) *The Familiar Letter in the Eighteenth Century*. Lawrence, KA: University of Kansas Press. pp. 71–91.

Index